Project CRISS[SM]

A research-based, staff development program

CReating
Independence *through*
Student-owned
Strategies

THIRD EDITION

Carol M. Santa, Ph.D.
Lynn T. Havens
Bonnie J. Valdes

KENDALL/HUNT PUBLISHING COMPANY
4050 Westmark Drive   Dubuque, Iowa 52002

Project CRISS^{SM} authors pictured from left to right: Lynn Havens, Carol Santa, Bonnie Valdes

If you have any questions, concerns, or a request for staff development, please contact:

Project CRISS^{SM}
40 Second Street East, Suite 249
Kalispell, Montana 59901
(406) 758-6440

Email: *info@projectcriss.com*
Web site: *http://www.projectcriss.com*

CONTENTS

Chapter 6   Organizing for Learning: Two-Column Notes, Frames, and Story Plans   116

Chapter 7   Informal Writing to Learn: Learning Logs   154

Chapter 8   Formal Writing to Learn: Writing Reports and Essays   174

PREFACE

Introduction. We designed Project CRISS^SM, **CR**eating **I**ndependence through **S**tudent-owned **S**trategies, to help our students learn more effectively throughout the curriculum. Our project focuses on teaching students how to learn through reading, writing, talking, and listening. Students learn to apply CRISS^SM principles and philosophy in all subject areas.

Project History. Originally, Project CRISS^SM was designed for high school students. It arose from our concern about students' inabilities to learn from reading assignments. At that time, we assigned reading selections only to find our students gained little information on their own. Our solution to their lack of learning was to review the material in class; little time remained to expand upon textual information. Student passivity became the rule. The more teachers assigned and reviewed, the more passive our students became. Teachers began to avoid reading assignments as a mode of instruction. It became easier to lecture about the information.

We began a collaborative effort. Initially supported by an ESEA Title IV-C innovative grant, teachers of science, social studies, English, and mathematics worked together to develop practical approaches designed to help our students learn. We met in teams, read professional literature, and then designed teacher-researcher studies to examine strategies in our classrooms. Through this process, we gathered instructional ideas that made a difference to our students. We wrote our ideas down so that other teachers could try them out in their classrooms, and we began doing workshops for teachers in other districts.

What began as a local experiment has now become a national project. In 1985, Project CRISS^SM became validated as an exemplary high school program by the National Diffusion Network (NDN). The NDN, part of the U.S. Office of Educational Research and Improvement, provided validated projects with initial grant support for dissemination. In 2002, Project CRISS^SM became a private corporation. As we write this third edition of our manual, CRISS^SM is being used by hundreds of thousands of teachers representing nearly every state of the United States, three Canadian provinces, Egypt, and Norway.

Project CRISS^SM has changed and broadened. It is no longer a project just for high school content teachers. Teachers from all content areas and from all grade levels have incorporated CRISS^SM as part of their day-to-day teaching. In fact, in 1993, Project CRISS^SM was validated as a new project in the National Diffusion Network for grades 4–12. To gain this validation, we conducted a research study in adoption sites in Virginia and Florida. We examined effects using experimental and control groups in elementary (grade 4), middle school (grades 6–8), and high school (grade 10) classrooms. In each case, students who learned CRISS^SM strategies as part of classroom instruction performed significantly better on reading and studying evaluations than did students in control classrooms without a CRISS^{SM} focus.

Over the years, we have continued to expand the project and to collect data using experimental and control comparisons. The effects are consistent. (See the research section available on our web page for the latest data collections: www. projectcriss.com)

Implementation.   The CRISS^{SM} program begins with a two- or three-day workshop during which participants experience the philosophy and instructional strategies through a series of CRISS^{SM} Strategic Learning Plans. We provide processing and reflection time so teachers can adapt CRISS^{SM} to their own teaching situations.

Successful implementation occurs when teachers and administrators work together to share, extend ideas, and problem solve. The initial workshop must be supported by follow-up sessions in which participants have opportunities to talk about how they are implementing the project. Our strongest adoptions occur in schools and districts where several participants become Certified District Trainers responsible for continuing to disseminate and support the project within their own districts. For more information on Project implementation see our web site www.projectcriss.com.

Manual.   This manual is used as part of a CRISS^{SM} workshop. It is not designed as a stand-alone book, but as support for teachers and administrators who participate in a two- or three-day workshop. Although we organize the workshop around a set of CRISS^{SM} Strategic Learning Plans—an integration of principles and strategies, each chapter of the manual covers a specific topic or a specific type of strategy, e.g., discussion strategies. The following is a quick overview of each chapter.

- Chapter 1 presents the theory and philosophy which form the core of Project CRISS^{SM}
- Chapter 2 provides an overview of research about text structure and many ideas for helping teachers identify the author's craft and design. It also includes several rubrics for evaluating text.
- Chapter 3 focuses on understanding patterns and structure. Here, we show students specific strategies to identify and use the author's craft and to structure information from their reading.
- Chapter 4 presents an overview of research and a variety of strategies for encouraging student discussion. This chapter contains a host of ideas for facilitating talk about learning.
- Chapters 5 and 6 take the reader step by step through a variety of practical approaches for teaching comprehension. These pages include activities for before, during, and after reading.
- Chapters 7 and 8 describe how writing plays a major role in every aspect of Project CRISS^{SM}. Writing is inseparable from learning.
- Vocabulary is the topic of Chapter 9. After a brief overview of research, this chapter presents a variety of strategies for helping students internalize new concepts.
- Chapter 10 provides an overview of ways to assess the effectiveness of Project CRISS^{SM}. We describe ways to assess project implementation, to evaluate the impact of CRISS^{SM} on classroom instruction, and to examine effects on student performance.
- Chapter 11 presents an overview of the various teacher and student research projects which not only led to the development of Project CRISS^{SM}, but continue to sustain it.

▶ This manual closes with Chapter 12, which contains example lessons that demonstrate how CRISS[SM] strategies fit within an overall CRISS[SM] Strategic Learning Plan.

Project CRISS[SM] is designed to help teachers and their students become better learners and writers. Many of the ideas we offer, you will already know—good teachers make these same discoveries on their own. Moreover, our ideas are borrowed from many places. They come from teachers, students, and professional articles. This manual represents a rich collection. Use what you feel makes the most sense for you.

ACKNOWLEDGMENTS

Revising this Project CRISS[SM] training manual has truly been a labor of love as we so strongly believe in the principles elaborated upon in this book. This work is a collaborative effort. The three of us spent countless hours head-to-head and phone-to-phone debating and reviewing the components of the previous edition along with the exciting new strategies developed since its publication. This final product arose not only from our collaboration, but depended heavily on the experience and knowledge shared with us by hundreds of educators across the country—especially by our CRISS[SM] trainers. Although we cannot mention everyone, we would like to thank and recognize our Master Trainers, without whose support we would not have this program. They are: Judy Bramlett, Peggy Clark, Cheryl Conn, Maureen Danner, Maureen Dombrowski, Kit Granat, Evelyn Maycumber, Jeff Means, Donald Meints, and Elmer Whitcraft. In addition, we want to acknowledge the help, support, and tireless energy of the Project CRISS[SM] office staff, Dorothy Huff, Stacy Liebig, and Christina Sjoquist.

During the early editing stages of this project we relied heavily on the expertise of Fiona McKinnon, who has a wonderful way with words. Later on, we turned to our publisher and the able hands of Tamra Keller. We thank these ladies for their dauntless efforts in keeping us organized and "parallel!"

CReating
Independence *through*
Student-owned
Strategies

1

CRISS℠ Principles and Philosophy

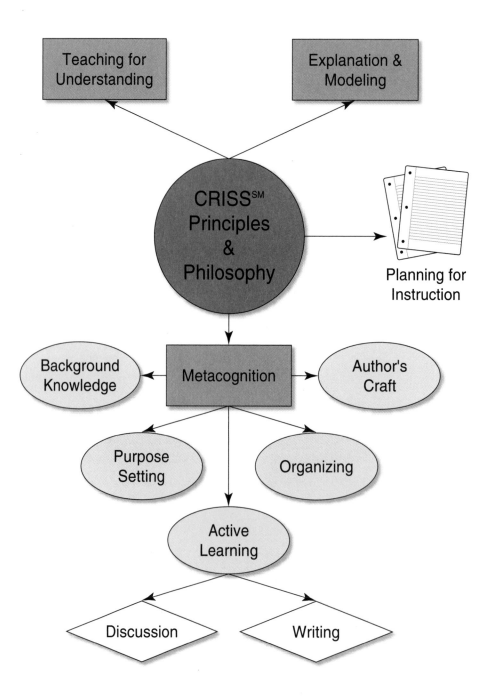

We teach based on who we are and what we believe. Our personal philosophies about how children learn make us the kind of teachers we are. Usually, we don't take the time to think about how our personal theories permeate every aspect of our teaching. Yet, taking time is important because our own personalities, our own instructional theories, and our understanding of what is important in our own particular content define how we teach.

Project CRISS^{SM} has helped us uncover what we believe about teaching and has helped us continually modify our philosophies based on what we now know about how students learn. When we know where we stand philosophically and take time to examine our own practices, we become even better at what we do.

Project CRISS^{SM} emerged because our students did not have sufficient knowledge about how to learn and, consequently, remained dependent upon us to do the learning for them. Our students weren't leaving our classrooms with the skills needed for life-long learning. We began to examine our own teaching. Perhaps the problem rested more with us than with the students. Maybe our teaching models were wrong. At the time, the most prevalent teaching model in our high school was the lecture-read the chapter-answer the chapter questions-take a multiple choice test paradigm. Teachers taught like they were taught. This flat, boring methodology degraded our own vitality and curiosity. Even more important, it was degrading to our students! Such a passive teacher-directed paradigm also conflicted with common sense and with our growing knowledge of theoretical principles about how students read, write, study, and learn.

As developers of Project CRISS^{SM}, we became teacher scholars. We began to read professional research, conduct our own classroom research, and present at conferences. We also started teacher support groups in our schools where we took time to talk with other colleagues about our discoveries. We became learning communities of knowledge seekers and questioners, unwilling to be stagnant in our professional lives. As scholars, we puzzled about the progress of our students, asked hard questions, and kept up to date on research. Our CRISS^{SM} community of teacher learners continues to nourish our scholarly life.

We have evolved a philosophy of teaching and learning that guides our practice and forms the basis of our self-evaluations. This philosophy is based on classroom practice, professional reading, and our own classroom research; it represents a merging of work from cognitive psychology, social learning theory, and neurological research about how our brain learns. Our philosophical stance remains fluid as we modify it based on new ideas learned from our students, from our colleagues, and from our own research. Articulating and rearticulating our belief system was and still is vital to the development of Project CRISS^{SM}. Our theoretical framework provides us with a way to think about how a particular lesson may or may not reflect what we now know about teaching and learning.

The power of CRISS^{SM} rests upon its underlying instructional philosophy; without this context for all our teaching, CRISS^{SM} would simply be a collection of individual, discrete strategies. We plan and evaluate our lessons based on this framework. Does a particular lesson reflect what we know about how students read, learn, and remember information? Have we helped our students internalize their own theories about learning? The framework integrates the strategies presented into a coherent whole. Therefore, we begin this book with an overview of what we believe about teaching and learning and show how we use these principles to analyze a sample lesson. We then close this chapter with an overview of the CRISS^{SM} Strategic Learning Plan which teachers have found helpful for integrating CRISS^{SM} principles and strategies into their day-to-day teaching.

CRISS^{SM} philosophy includes the following overlapping principles:

1. * Project CRISS^{SM} Principles and Philosophy
     2. **Metacognition:** Good readers are metacognitive. They are goal-directed, and they know how to attack print to create meaning.
          3. **Background Knowledge.** Background knowledge is a powerful determinant of reading comprehension.
          3. **Purpose Setting.** Effective readers have purposes in mind as they read.
          3. **Active Learning.** Good readers are actively involved in making sense from their reading.
               4. **Discussion.** Students need many opportunities to talk with one another about what they are learning.
               4. **Writing.** Students need many opportunities to write about what they are learning.
          3. **Organization.** Good readers know a variety of ways to transform and organize information for learning.
          3. **Author's Craft.** Good readers and writers have an intuitive understanding of the author's craft.
     2. **Explanation and Modeling.** Students learn to become strategic when teachers teach these processes directly through explanation and modeling.
     2. **Teaching for Understanding.** Students come to truly understand by focusing on thought-demanding content.

*For an explanation of our numbering system, see page 38, Power Thinking.

Let's take a moment to see how the CRISS^{SM} principles and philosophy might play out in a lesson. To provide a context, let's step inside a social studies classroom to view a high school teacher and her students at work.

▶ Sample CRISS^{SM} Lesson

Carmen, a history/English teacher, asks her students to read the first stanza of *The Star-Spangled Banner.*

> O! Say can you see, by the dawn's early light.
> What so proudly we hail'd at the twilight's last gleaming?
> Whose broad stripes and bright stars thro' the perilous fight,
> O'er the ramparts we watched were so gallantly streaming?
> And the rockets' red glare, the bombs bursting in air
> Gave proof thro' the night that our flag was still there.
> O! Say, does the Star-Spangled Banner yet wave
> O'er the land of the free and the home of the brave?

Carmen decides not to tell the students her own ideas about the song first. She wants her students to feel comfortable developing their own interpretations. She uses a CRISS^{SM} strategy called "Free Response."

Carmen begins by reading the first stanza of the song aloud. She asks her students how many times they have they heard and sung this song? Then she says, "Read the stanza through several times. Write down any thoughts, questions, and personal stories the song triggers. Anything you write down will be correct. Don't give up. Remember, there are no wrong answers. As you write, think about the strategies you use as a reader to create meaning for yourself."

Her students begin to read and write. Carmen models by writing her own journal entry. Let's focus on one student. Derrick reads the poem several times and begins to write in his journal.

Who wrote this song?
What was going on when the song was written?
What does "ramparts" mean?
Why were bombs bursting in air?
Was a war going on at the time the composer wrote this song?
I wonder why there is a question mark at the end of the last line.
Does the composer think freedom is in jeopardy?
This song makes me think about maintaining America's freedom today.

After about ten minutes, Carmen asks her students to discuss their ideas with a partner. Derrick talks with Matt. They share comments and ask each other questions. Together they begin to make meaning. When conversations begin to run their course, Carmen asks each student to write about what the song means. "What is your personal response to the song?" Derrick writes the following in his journal:

This song reminds me of what happens in the time of war. Rockets are glaring and bombs are bursting in air. I keep thinking about the World Trade Center and 9-11. Afterwards there were American flags everywhere. The flag means honor, freedom. I guess you can't take it for granted—have to work for freedom. I will never forget seeing firemen carrying the American flag in front of the huge fire!

Then, they talk as a whole group. Carmen shares her journal entry with the class and asks volunteers to share theirs. Each student offers his or her own interpretation. Together, they build a variety of meanings.

Carmen then asks her students to write a process entry about the strategies they used to derive meaning from the song, "What did you do to make meaning from this song?"

Derrick writes:

I read through the stanza once but I didn't understand very much. I had heard this song many times and I guess I just never thought about what the words meant. I had lots of questions. Then I went back and reread. I thought about what each phrase might mean. It helped talking with Matt. He had some different ideas. We both talked about where we were on 9-ll and about all the flags we saw. Both of us thought the song was about war and how the flag stood for freedom.

Derrick is an example of an active, self-regulated reader who energetically attacked the problem of making sense from his reading. After the first reading, he knew that he did not understand. He created meaning by bringing his own life to the words of the author. Through his conversation with Matt, he began to think through and elaborate on his ideas.

Next Carmen asks, "What did I do as a teacher to help you read and interpret this song? How did I help you use your own background knowledge? What did I do to help you become more actively involved in the lesson? I could have read the song to you, asked you questions about it, and then given my own interpretation. Instead, I did something quite different. I want to know what you think."

Students talk while Carmen summarizes their comments on an overhead transparency.

1. I liked it when you told us that everything we wrote or talked about was right. That made me feel OK about writing about my own ideas. We each had different ideas about the song.

2. I got more out of the song when you made us write about what we were thinking. I wouldn't have come up with the same ideas if you had told us the real meaning—your meaning first.
3. It helped to talk about our ideas with someone else.
4. Talking about the song and writing questions has made me really curious. I want to know when and why *The Star-Spangled Banner* was written.

Finally, Carmen leads a short discussion about why process conferences like these are critical to their ultimate success as students. They discuss why talking and writing about learning help them become more aware of strategies that work. Carmen explains why the **how** of learning is just as important as **what** they learn in her classroom.

With this sample lesson in mind, let's take an in-depth look at CRISS[SM] principles and philosophy to see how this lesson reflects these principles.

◗ Metacognition

The concept of metacognition and strategic learning is the foundation of Project CRISS[SM]. In fact, the central goal of this project is the development of expert, strategic readers. Students who achieve well in school have heightened metacognition and a repertoire of self-regulatory behaviors. They know when they have understood, and they know how to employ a variety of strategies to attain meaning (Paris, Wasik & Turner, 1991; Michenbaum & Biemiller, 1998).

In our example, Derrick is an expert reader. Refer again to his response to the question about what he did to gain meaning. He was aware of his thinking. He tried to understand the meaning of single words. He thought about his own background as he read the song several times and organized his ideas.

Good readers like Derrick are in control as they energetically attack the problem of making sense from their reading. They sort through the author's meaning to fit with their own background experiences and knowledge. Mature readers set learning goals, know how to use a variety of strategies to meet those goals, and can revise their plans to reach their goals effectively. They know how to reread, to self-question, and to organize information. They constantly assess their own learning progress. Do I understand this point? Do I need to reread? Should I write this idea down? Is the author making this clear, or do I need additional information?

Contrast this profile with the research about the poor reader (Duke and Pearson, 2002). Poor readers are not in control. They don't understand the need for setting goals and have no flexible plans for comprehending. Often they do not know whether they have understood a selection; they may read through a selection once without knowing their comprehension has failed. If they know they have failed, they may not know why. They lack flexibility and deliberate plans for correcting comprehension. Poor readers respond with helplessness. Whereas good readers attack the problems, poor readers shut down and give up.

The conceptualization of the good reader as a goal-directed, active strategist and the poor reader as lacking in control has far-reaching consequences and sets the stage for the strategic instruction offered in this project. CRISS[SM] strategies help students understand how to set their own goals for learning and, through teacher modeling and guidance, students learn a variety of comprehension strategies for narrative and content text.

In fact, everything in this chapter is really about metacognition. For example, students need to become more aware of the link between background knowledge and their own comprehension. They need to understand why they have to do more than simply read an assignment. They need to preview, organize, talk, and write about what they are reading. They must act on the information in order to find their own meaning. Every aspect of CRISS^{SM} theory is directed toward making students more strategic and aware of what to do to be successful learners.

Background Knowledge

Integrating new information with prior knowledge lies at the heart of metacognition and comprehension. The richer our background, the richer is our comprehension. The more we bring to a reading situation, the more we can take away. This conclusion is not only documented by multitudes of research studies (Pearson and Fielding, 1991, Pressley, 2000), but by neurological research—particularly that on selective attention (Jensen,1998). We are far more likely to attend to information when we have some previous knowledge or mental priming about the topic. We have trouble paying attention to something we know nothing about; and without focusing, we cannot record information in memory. Work from brain physiology also helps to explain the link between background knowledge and learning. The brain is a meaning-maker requiring the building of networks of neural connections (Jensen, 1998). Teachers cannot impose meaning on students; students have to create it for themselves in order to build rich, interconnecting neural fields. Brains need time to build these personal connections with incoming information.

Carmen began her lesson by asking students to read, write, and then talk about their personal reactions to the song. She created a safe and active classroom environment wherein students felt comfortable exploring their own thoughts and feelings. She offered several opportunities for her students to bring their own knowledge to the reading. Readers must have opportunities such as these to interpret text based on their own backgrounds.

In the beginning, Derrick struggled to find a personal link with the song. He reread each line to construct meaning. He thought about the significance of individual words, and began putting together his thoughts, incorporating his own background knowledge.

Carmen's students had opportunities throughout her lesson to make meaning—to build physiological connections by integrating their own backgrounds with the lesson's content. They examined through writing and talking how issues of background knowledge influenced their learning.

Project CRISS^{SM} teachers put emphasis on background knowledge. Before beginning a lesson, we think about the role of prior knowledge and ways to get students' attention. If our goal is for students to generate personal meanings, as in the song example, we might not talk much about background knowledge before students read. Instead, we allow students to bring their own thoughts and experiences to bear on the piece. In this example, Carmen waited until later in the lesson to have her students share their background knowledge and to provide her own factual information about *The Star-Spangled Banner.* She wanted her students to concentrate on their own interpretations before expanding their ideas with historical details.

Knowing what a student knows about a topic also helps teachers deal with misconceptions. Frequently students have incorrect background knowledge that can become a powerful impediment to learning. Eliciting students' prior knowledge about a topic helps bring to light misunderstandings, simplistic knowledge, or flawed interpretations. Once brought to light, we can help students repair misconceptions with accurate information.

Purpose Setting

Reading for specific purposes positively influences comprehension (Narvaez, 2002). Orienting students to read or listen for specific information in text influences what one recalls (Pickard & Anderson, 1977; Anderson & Pickert, 1978).

The way a student deals with *The Star-Spangled Banner* will be quite different if the purpose is to

1. memorize the words to prepare for a concert (choir).
2. recreate the images being described (art class).
3. rewrite a verse of *The Star-Spangled Banner* to describe it as the flag planted by the New York City Firefighters in the rubble of the Trade Center Buildings (language arts).
4. relate the song to the events in history when it was written (social studies), or, as was in Carmen's case, analyze the kinds of learning processes they use when confronted with sometimes confusing information.

Recall that Carmen did not set a specific content purpose, but asked her students to generate personal stories the song triggered. There were no wrong answers. She wanted them to think about the strategies they use as a reader to create meaning for themselves. To be fair to our students, we need to make sure they are clearly aware of their purpose for reading, viewing, or listening.

Students with metacognitive skills assess their learning in order to know when they are comprehending. This assessment relies on the setting of a comprehension goal. Frequently, we have to be direct with purpose setting: "After reading this selection, you should be able to . . . After viewing the video, you should be able to identify . . ., and you should be able to evaluate the best process for . . ."

Therefore, we keep certain questions about background knowledge and purpose setting in mind as we teach, such as:

▶ How can I help students figure out what they know or don't know about a topic?
▶ How can I help students assess the accuracy of their background knowledge?
▶ How can I help them use this knowledge to guide their own comprehension?
▶ What knowledge do my students need before they read? Or what misconceptions need to be changed before students read?
▶ What do I want students to focus on during this assignment?
▶ How can I help them read and listen selectively, focusing on portions of text and content most relevant to their goals? And even more important. . .
▶ How can I help students understand why background knowledge and setting purposes are so critical to their learning?

In sum, it is not enough for *us* to understand why background knowledge and purpose setting are so powerful. Ultimately, theoretical principles must become a part of our *students'* understanding of how reading and learning works. We cannot keep these important principles to ourselves.

Active Learning

In order to learn, we must be actively involved. Neural connections are made when we act on incoming information and do something with it. Research in cognitive psychology provides documentation of this activity principle. Learning happens when students actively process information through writing, talking, and transforming by using a variety of organizing strategies (Duke & Pearson, 2002, Keene & Zimmerman, 1997). Just reading or listening isn't enough.

Think about how students were actively engaged throughout Carmen's lesson. Her students read, reread, wrote down ideas, read again, and then discussed their thoughts. They wrote again. Every aspect of her lesson invigorated students to action. Everyone participated.

Carmen could have taken the "all-knowing—all-powerful" teacher stance with the song by introducing it with her own critical interpretation. While she talked, her students could have passively listened. She could have acted like so many of her own previous English teachers who couldn't get off stage. But Carmen understands this attitude strips students of self-confidence, creates passivity, and is simply ineffective. Few students feel they can compete with the wisdom of the English teacher.

In the process conference concluding her lesson, Carmen and her students discussed what they did to gain understanding. "What did you do in this lesson to grapple with meaning? What active strategies did you use? What did I do as a teacher to help you become more actively engaged? Why did I have you do more than just read the song? How did writing and talking about the song help you understand it?" Again, questions such as these help students begin to internalize theory about how they learn. This lesson is as important as the content involved.

CRISS[SM] strategies take the notion of the active learner to heart. Whenever we teach, we think about ways to engage students in applying and thinking about their own strategy use. Conceptualizing the student as an active strategist has led to changes in our approaches to teaching. We aren't on stage very much, giving our lectures or asking countless questions. Instead, we assist our students to become engaged in their learning; in the process, they learn content more effectively. Strategies involving instructional conversations and writing provide the cornerstone for successful, engaged learning.

Discussion.   Learning is an active, constructive process and a social, interpersonal process. Work in brain research highlights the importance of students interacting with one another. Students create meaning by transforming information and by building their own connections. Discussion is essential to these constructive processes (Muth and Alverman, 1999). We live in a social world and learn by interacting with others (Goldenberg, 1994; Wilkinson & Stillman, 2000). By pooling our understandings and talking about what we think we know, we develop deeper understandings. Teachers who use one-sided lecture methods as their primary mode of teaching not only discount key principles drawn from cognitive and social psychology, but violate important principles of our brain. Discussion is critical as we are biologically wired for communicating with one another (Jensen, 1998).

Refer once more to our sample lesson and note how Carmen made sure her students had opportunities to talk to one another about their ideas. Notice how discussion enriched individual comprehension.

Conversations among communities of learners is an important part of Project CRISS[SM]. Discussion revolves around the students, not the teacher. This is not the sort of conversation in which the teacher remains the authority figure with students reciting answers to teacher-directed questions. Instead, with CRISS[SM] strategies, students learn to take responsibility for creating their own meaning and for leading their own discussions. They learn why discussion is so critical to the development of new, deeper conceptual understandings (Wilkinson et. al., 2000). CRISS[SM] strategies create an environment for collaboration in which students invest in their own learning by expressing and exchanging ideas.

Writing.   Writing is integral to all learning (Santa & Alvermann, 1991; Blanchowicz & Ogle, 2001). If we can explain concepts in writing to ourselves and to others, we can claim knowledge as our own. Writing helps each of us make personal sense out of our reading. We cannot write about something we do not understand. Writing forces us to make choices about meaning. It lets us know what we know.

Writing forces organization. As we write, we begin to see clusters of information and hierarchies of ideas. Writing also encourages active involvement in learning. It is impossible to remain passive as a writer.

Writing also gives students personal processing time, allowing neural connections to solidify. After each new learning experience the brain needs time for learning to imprint (Jensen, 1998). Writing is vital to this process.

Our sample lesson demonstrates the power of writing to help us understand and learn. Through writing, Derrick grappled with meaning. Writing helped him connect his own knowledge to the song, and through writing he analyzed his learning processes.

Because writing is such a powerful vehicle for learning and thinking, it is integrated into every component of Project CRISS^SM—before, during, and after a reading or learning experience.

Organization

The past thirty years of research in cognitive psychology, as well as more recent research about brain physiology, has demonstrated that learning and memory depend on transforming information (Jensen, 1998). Our short term memories have limitations. The average adult can remember from five to nine discrete units of new information at once. However, our ability to remember increases dramatically when we transform information by clustering discrete bits into categories, by developing hierarchical relationships, and by converting information into charts or pictures. The more organized, the better remembered.

In our example, Derrick organized information informally by supplying structure to his learning through writing. Then, after discussing his ideas with Matt, he again wrote about them.

Through Project CRISS^SM, students learn about their need to organize information for understanding and for retention. They learn flexible ways for processing, including power thinking, selective underlining, two-column notes, and concept mapping. They learn multiple ways to be strategic, metacognitive readers and learners.

Author's Craft

Strong research supports this idea that knowledge of expository and narrative text structures plays an important role in comprehension (Goldman & Rakestraw, 2000). When students know how authors structure their writing, they can more readily understand and remember what they read. Good readers and writers know how text structure aids comprehension. Good readers know about poetic forms, as well as the structure of a word problem in mathematics.

In our example, Carmen did not direct her students to analyze the author's craft because earlier in the year she had completed a unit on poetry. During this study, her students looked at the many structures and features poets use. When she began her lesson on *The Star-Spangled Banner,* she knew her students had a comfortable knowledge of poetry and the poet's craft.

CRISS^{SM} strategies help students become aware of the author's craft. Students learn ways to get "inside an author's head" to determine an author's style of presentation. They can use this knowledge as a basis for a variety of studying and writing strategies.

Each one of the principles described so far in this chapter describes the expert, strategic reader. Background knowledge, purpose setting, active reading, organizing information for learning, and understanding the author's craft merge as overlapping ingredients in the development of metacognitive learners. How can we as teachers facilitate this process of development?

▶ Explanation and Modeling

Students learn to think strategically when teachers and other experts in our classrooms demonstrate processes through explanation and modeling as part of content instruction. Many students, particularly those struggling in school, do not know how to learn; they think reading and rereading are sufficient. In our example, Carmen modeled her own free-response as she demonstrated her initial struggle to attach meaning to the song.

Duffy and his colleagues learned from their research that teacher modeling and guided practice leads to pronounced effects (2002). It even improves student performance on standardized reading tests of comprehension when incorporated over weeks and months of instruction.

When introducing a new strategy, teachers take the stage. They show, tell, model, demonstrate, and explain not only the content, but the process of active reading. As the student learns, there is a gradual release of responsibility from teacher to student. This process of transactional strategy instruction takes a long time.

Transactional strategy instruction includes two steps. The first step involves an explanation of what the strategy is and why students should use it to improve their learning. If students do not know why they are performing an activity, they rarely repeat the behavior on their own (Baumann, l988; Duffy, 2002). The second step is a demonstration and discussion of the strategy procedures. During this step, the teacher models or asks students to show how they do a particular task. The teacher discusses, demonstrates, and thinks-aloud during this modeling stage. After students have had several opportunities to watch their teacher and other students demonstrate a strategy, they have opportunities to practice with guidance and feedback. Throughout, the teacher encourages students to talk about strategies they find personally effective. The teacher needs to think constantly about ways to help students become metacognitive.

This manual is filled with examples of teacher modeling and ideas for helping students reflect on the effectiveness of particular strategies. When teachers and students share how they are learning, students are more likely to internalize these processes. They become more aware of how learning and comprehending take place. We can think of our teaching role as a continuum, which is reflected in the way strategies are presented in this book. Strategy presentations follow a consistent instructional sequence:

1. Introduction, modeling, and reflection.
2. Support and extensions.

Teaching for Understanding

An overriding premise for all of our work deals with teaching for understanding. Students need time to grapple with new learning and to develop insights about the material. As we think back on Carmen's teaching and Derrick's response to the song, we realize that Carmen had prepared the learning environment for Derrick to build meaning and gain understanding.

Our conception of teaching for understanding goes beyond knowing the information in a piece. It is a matter of being able to do a variety of thought-demanding activities with a topic such as explaining, finding examples, producing evidence, generalizing, and representing the topic in a new way. CRISS^{SM} strategies are designed to help students build understanding. We want our students to carry out a variety of learning activities that not only help them gain knowledge of a topic, but advance that knowledge.

Finally, teaching for understanding also rests on the assumption we are teaching content that really matters. Decisions must be made about what content to teach. Teachers feel tremendous pressure to cover content, to get through the textbook. Grant Wiggins and Jay McTighe (1998) cite a body of evidence indicating that students only skim the surface of understanding as they cover topics in a curriculum. Our curriculum is far too scattered. Merely introducing ideas and concepts is insufficient. Instead, we must insist on teaching content that is substantial, meaningful, and worthwhile.

Implementing CRISS^{SM} strategies can never make up for insipid, superficial content. Teaching students how to learn must occur in conjunction with the central and organizing ideas that you want students to remember and understand after they leave your classroom. Once you have identified the big ideas in a curricular unit, CRISS^{SM} strategies become a means for engaging students in learning what is substantial and meaningful.

Planning for Instruction

To summarize, CRISS^{SM} provides a philosophical framework for planning instruction. When planning and evaluating lessons, use CRISS^{SM} as a tool to assess your teaching and as a way for your students to examine their learning.

Start with Content.   Does it really merit study? Is the content significant? Ask yourself, am I stressing the big ideas—the central organizing ideas of a content domain rather than superficial information? Does the content relate to state and local curriculum guidelines?

Set Clear Goals and Objectives.   Are my goals understandable and reachable by all students? Do I have a variety of resources for the students to use that will enable them to reach the content and learning goals? Will students be able to use these goals to monitor their comprehension? How will they know they have successfully reached these goals?

Plan How to Assess the Students.   Have I included a variety of evaluation tools (performance assessments, objective tests, writing prompts)? Are my tools actually assessing the goals and objectives I set? Am I assessing throughout the lesson? How can I make my assessments a learning experience for my students?

Develop a CRISS^{SM} Strategic Learning Plan.   What background knowledge will my students need before starting this lesson? What strategies will my students use to learn the information and reach the intended goals? Where are they with this strategy knowledge? Do I need to introduce the strategies and model them? How will I make sure my students are actively involved in their learning? How can I help them be metacognitive? Have I included a variety of individual, paired, and group activities?

When developing a CRISS^{SM} Strategic Learning Plan, we encourage teachers to think in terms of this general four-step plan:

1. First, we want to prepare our students before the learning "experience" (reading, watching a video, going on a field trip, doing a lab, listening to a speaker). Usually, this includes bringing out the students' background knowledge and directing them to the purpose for learning.

2. Next, we want our students to be actively involved with the content as they are reading, listening, viewing, or doing. For example, marginal notetaking while reading or journaling while listening can help a student pay attention. These metacognition tools also help students identify if they are "getting it." If not, they can reread or ask questions or work with any of the other metacognition strategies they have learned.

3. After students have read, we want them to organize information so it can be practiced and reviewed for in-depth understanding. CRISS^{SM} provides a large variety of organizing tools and formats which students can apply to transform this newly acquired information.

4. Finally, we want our students to use, adapt, evaluate, and apply the information they have learned. This can be done through writing or a variety of other practical applications.

This plan serves as a guide to lesson planning. Most teachers will adapt it to meet their needs and the needs of their students. In Chapter 10, we provide several different formats of our CRISS^{SM} Strategic Learning Plan. In Chapter 12, we present examples of two entire CRISS^{SM} Strategic Learning Plans. (The lessons we share in this chapter are part of our semester class for grade 6–9 students, *CRISS^{SM} for Students, It's a Brain Thing~Learning How to Learn!*)

Self-Evaluate Your Plan.   Did the assessments adequately measure the desired objectives? What could I do to improve this Learning Plan? Did my Learning Plan move students toward increased independence?

Evaluate Your Plan with Your Students.   Ask your students the following questions: How did you organize the information? Did you assess your learning progress? What strategies worked best for you and why? Did you evaluate your understanding throughout this lesson? What could you do next time to improve your understanding? How can you apply what you have learned to your own life?

With this overview of the principles and philosophy underlying the strategy instruction in Project CRISS^{SM}, we now move to the strategies that operationalize this theory. Choose the strategies that make the most sense for you. You aren't going to use them all. As you turn the pages of this book, think about how these ideas can be adapted to your own teaching plans. Adapt strategies to fit your various domains, whether you are using a science lab in biology, a hands-on activity in mathematics, a field trip for social studies, or a short story in language arts. Take what we offer. Shape it. Mold it. Then, turn strategy knowledge over to your students. Give them control so they leave your classroom with knowledge and power over their own learning.

Research Conclusion	Reference
Good readers monitor their understanding and know how to employ a variety of strategies to attain meaning.	Duke & Pearson, 2002
Integrating new information with prior knowledge lies at the heart of metacognition and comprehension.	Pressley, 2002
Effective learners have clear purposes or goals in mind as they read.	Narvaez, 2002
Learning requires active involvement.	Duke & Pearson, 2002
Learning from reading and listening depends upon transforming information.	Jensen, 1998
Good readers know how author's structure their writing.	Goldman & Rakestraw, 2000
Teacher modeling and guided practice lead to pronounced effects in the improvement of reading comprehension and on standardized test performance.	Duffy, 2002

Identifying the Author's Craft and Design

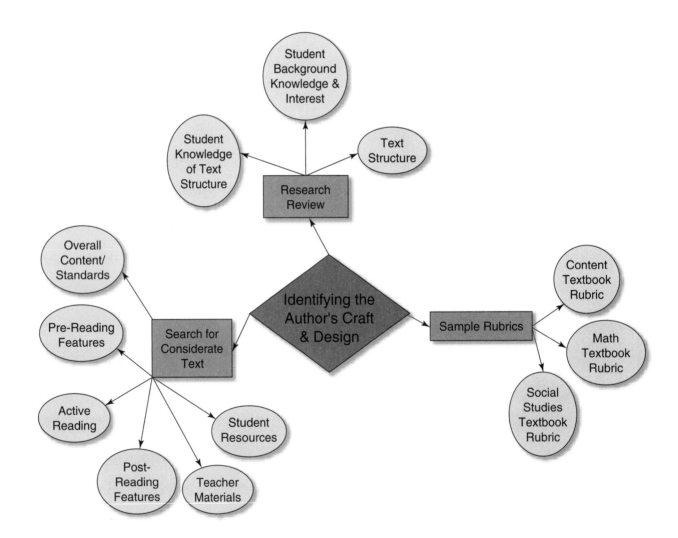

Instructional approaches and students' strategic behaviors are bound to text whether it is fiction, non-fiction, or electronic hypertext. Before assigning a selection, we need to understand the strengths and weaknesses of the reading material. What makes a particular text easier or harder to read? Are there features we should keep in mind?

As with other chapters in this book, we begin by reviewing relevant research and then move to practical applications. In this case, we use research principles to develop a tool for evaluating written materials that can be adapted to practically any text application.

Before moving to this discussion of research, we want to address the issue of using simplistic systems such as readability formulas, lexiles, or the Degrees of Reading Power assessments for evaluating the appropriateness of text. Although these measures are somewhat helpful in matching student abilities with text, they can be misleading. Most of these readability determinations use some kind of formula, such as the average length of words and sentences within a text. According to these systems, simple vocabulary and short sentences reduce the reading level of texts. With these criteria in mind, authors have reduced the reading levels of their texts by replacing key vocabulary terms with shorter, simpler words and by reducing sentence length, which often results in short, choppy sentences with less elaboration of content. As you will see from this review of research, neither of these revisions necessarily makes text more appropriate for student learning. Other factors, however, do play a role in text readability.

▶ Research Review

What factors make some texts more difficult to read than others? A vast amount of research related to this question exists. To make our task manageable, we have limited our review to non-fiction, which follows three different lines of research. The first set of studies examines the relationship of text structure and comprehension; the second focuses on reader factors such as the relationship between the reader's background knowledge or interest and text comprehension; and the third set addresses the importance of making readers more aware of text structure or, more specifically, the author's craft and comprehension.

Text Structure and Text Comprehensibility

The structure of text is critical to comprehension; well-structured texts are easier for students to understand than poorly written materials. This topic has been studied extensively, and several conclusions emerge that have important implications for reading materials used in schools (Goldman & Rakestraw, 2000):

Presentation of Main Ideas.   Readers more readily comprehend the main ideas when they are located at the beginning of paragraphs (Bauman 1986; Taylor, 1984). To show this, Bauman rewrote science passages from four popular textbooks. In these revisions, he presented general topics in the titles and subheadings and made sure that main ideas were explicit in paragraphs. Fifth-grade students read either the original passages or the revisions, then were tested on the key ideas in the selection. Students who read the rewritten passages did better than those who read the original.

Typographical Features.   Ideas marked by typographical features such as italics, bold print, and signal words and phrases are processed longer and recalled better than unmarked information. In addition, information highlighted through typographical mechanisms such as special fonts or underlining tend to be remembered better than material not explicitly emphasized (Lorch, 1989).

Internal Features.   Written clues within the text that help the reader understand structure, guide the development of main ideas, and influence recall of information. For example, readers tend to organize and remember the emphasized information better when authors lead them with signal words indicating main ideas (*the most important point here*), with phrases indicating sequencing (*first, second, third*), or with statements relating disparate parts of text (*as discussed earlier*). Thus, making the structure of the text more salient improves comprehension and retention.

Clarity and Elaboration of Content.   A more subtle but critical aspect of readability is the adequacy of explanations. Students tend to find tersely-written explanations of key concepts more difficult to understand than elaborated explanations (Harp & Mayer, 1997).

One study (reported by Bill Holiday, 1991) seems particularly applicable. Hermann (1984) examined the effects of inadequate explanations on students' learning. She presented eighth-grade students with two versions of an explanation of how the heart works. The original version, published in a popular junior-high text, was tersely written. The revised version was designed to provide students with a clearer explanation of the same topic. It contains more detail, including an explanation of how various parts of the heart relate. Text passages below show the original and revised explanations:

Original Version:

A human heart is a cone-shaped muscular organ about the size of a large fist. The heart is located in the center of the chest behind the breastbone and between the lungs. A human heart contains four chambers—right atrium (AY tree uhm), left atrium, right ventricle (VEN trih kuhl), and left ventricle. Right and left refer to the body's right and left sides. A wall separates the chambers on the right from the chambers on the left.

Revised Version:

The heart is the part of the circulatory system that pumps blood throughout the body. The heart is located in the center of the chest behind the breastbone and between the lungs. The human heart is suited for pumping because it is a hollow, cone-shaped muscular organ about the size of a large fist. Being hollow, the heart can easily fill up with blood. Once filled, the heart muscle provides the power necessary for pumping the blood through the body.

A human heart contains four hollow chambers made for receiving and sending blood. The right atrium (AY tree uhm) and right ventricle (VEN tru kuhl) receive and send blood to the lungs, while the left atrium and left ventricle receive and send blood to the rest of the body. (Note that right and left refer to your body's right-hand and left-hand sides.) The right and left sides of the heart are separated by a wall of muscle. This wall keeps blood going to the lungs separate from the blood going to the body (Hermann, 1984).

As predicted, students learned more about the heart from the revised version. These eighth graders benefitted from an elaborated explanation. The quality of explanations is a critical feature of content materials.

In summary, many studies indicate that text structure does influence the reader's ability to comprehend text. Clear presentation of main ideas, the presence of typographical and internal features, and clarity and elaboration of content all influence how well a text functions as a learning tool. While each of these factors requires consideration when selecting texts for reading assignments, other features should also be examined.

Student Background Knowledge, Interest, and Text Comprehensibility

The preceding conclusions about text structure provide important insights about text, but fail to take the reader into consideration. Another set of literature shows how reader factors interact with text structure to influence comprehension. The following conclusions briefly summarize this research.

Background Knowledge and Text Structure. The more background knowledge a reader has about a topic, the less important text structure is to the reader's comprehension. Readers with significant background knowledge do not need highly-structured text to aid comprehension because they can readily supply the structure themselves. In contrast, when the same reader has little conceptual understanding of content, explicit text structure becomes much more helpful. Reading materials with clearly stated main ideas and with embedded structural cues help the less knowledgeable reader with comprehension and retention of the material (Goldman & Rakestraw, 2000).

Background Knowledge and Interest. Interest also plays a key role in text comprehensibility. While there is a vast amount of research in this area, two conclusions are important to keep in mind. First, readers become more engaged in text and comprehend a selection better when they find the material interesting. Second, background knowledge affects a reader's interest. According to Kintsch's research (1980), interest in a topic tends to be low when a reader has little or no relevant background knowledge.

This conclusion makes sense. If you don't know anything about a topic, it is difficult to be interested in it. Interest, as well as subsequent comprehension, increases with some knowledge about the topic. However, Kintsch also talks about the point of diminishing return. Too much knowledge doesn't help. If the reader already knows the content of a selection, his or her interest diminishes. Therefore, a student's interest and background knowledge influence the potential impact of text structure.

"Seductive" Details and the Comprehension of Important and Unimportant Information. An intriguing research finding is that readers often pay attention and remember information they find interesting irrespective of its importance. In response to admonitions to make expository materials more interesting, authors often embellish content with personalized anecdotes and highly interesting, but non-essential, details. This kind of information has aptly been called *seductive* details.

Researchers have found that including too many seductive details within text can actually backfire and distract students, drawing their attention away from more important content. For example, Garner, Gillingham and White (1989) conclude that inserting an unexpected seductive detail in a paragraph actually reduces the number of main ideas readers recall. Wade and Adams (1990) found similar results.

Nevertheless, the whole issue has to do with whether interesting details and anecdotes expand a reader's understanding of essential information or whether they, instead, seduce the reader away from more important content. Interest interacts with importance. When writers entice readers with interesting details that expand essential information in the text, readers respond with better comprehension and memory for the information. In fact, making important information interesting seems key to making text more comprehensible (Wade, Buxton & Kelly, 1999).

Other Factors Influencing Reader Interest.

An inviting writing style can also enhance interest. Material may be interesting not because of *what* is said, but because of *how* it is said. For example, writers can increase interest by using active rather than passive verbs, by including examples that make the writing less abstract, and by using vivid and unusual words.

Beck, McKeown and Worthy (1995) note that voice, the quality that helps a reader view text as communication between an author and reader, had a positive effect on recall. Beck et al. (1995) compared four versions of the same text: the original textbook passage, a voiced version (with natural, expressive language), a coherent version (with well-structured main idea development), and a version that was both voiced and coherent. The combined voiced and coherent version produced the highest recall for important issue questions.

In other empirical studies, imagery and concreteness positively related to interest and comprehensibility (Wade et al., 1999). When readers can visualize information, they tend to find the text more interesting and remember it better.

In summary, this research clearly documents how reader factors interact with text. A reader's background knowledge and interest influence comprehension. Certain text features such as adequacy of explanations, whether interesting details support or detract from important information, and the author's writing style influence the interaction between the reader and the text. We must keep these conclusions in mind when selecting reading materials for our students.

Student Knowledge of Text Structure and Text Comprehensibility

The third line of research indicates that students' knowledge of text structure plays an important role in comprehension (Goldman & Rakestraw, 2000). If students know how authors structure their writing, they can more readily understand and remember what they read. They learn more from expository material than students who are not aware of structure (Slater & Graves, 1988).

Thus, it is important to teach students about structure (Richgels, McGee & Slaton, 1988). Many students pay no attention to how authors structure their writing, remaining oblivious to introductory paragraphs, the placement of main ideas, and the presence of bold face print and topical headings, unless they receive explicit instruction. Taylor and her colleagues (Taylor & Beach, 1984) found that teaching students to use headings, subheadings, and signals that indicate main points in paragraphs, helped comprehension and retention.

Finally, readers taught to write and edit different types of expository text, improve their comprehension of content (Laflamme, 1997). There is a symbiotic relationship between reading and writing. When students begin to read like writers, both their reading comprehension and their writing improves.

This overview of research leaves us with several insights. First, as teachers we must seek well-written texts for our classrooms. Our students deserve considerate materials. We should be sensitive to differences between well- and poorly-written materials and choose selections carefully. Second, we must also consider the interaction of text factors with student factors. Considerate text becomes even more important when our students have little background knowledge about a topic or when they aren't particularly interested in the content. Third, we can help our students become more aware of how authors write, so they can use the author's style of presentation as a comprehension tool. We want our students to understand why they should get "inside the author's head" and see the author's plan of presentation.

In the next portion of this chapter, we use information gained from research and from our own teaching to discuss in more detail the qualities of well-written text in conjunction with a rubric (see Blacklines 1a–d) useful for analyzing whether a text is considerate.

The Search for Considerate Text

In order to select considerate text for our students, we have to move beyond the "splash" of beautiful pictures, bold face print, and fancy graphics to analyze the author's style of presentation. Take an editorial stance and carefully examine the author's strengths and weaknesses.

While reading through this section, you may want to glance at the Content Text Assessment Rubric located at the end of this chapter. This rubric incorporates the principles from the research just described and serves to summarize the discussion that follows.

The following summary relates to various non-fiction classroom materials—from traditional classroom texts, to non-fiction trade books, to hypertext found on the Internet, to ancillaries and support materials. We have divided our rubric into the following areas; you may pick and choose the areas you wish to evaluate, or use the complete rubric.

OVERALL CONTENT AND CORRELATION WITH STANDARDS

PRE-READING FEATURES

Background knowledge
Purpose setting

ACTIVE READING

Main ideas
Support for main ideas
Organization of information
Vocabulary development
Students' engagement

POST-READING FEATURES

Metacognition

TEACHER'S GUIDE AND OTHER RESOURCES

ANCILLARY MATERIALS FOR STUDENTS

Overall Content and Correlation with Standards

Begin your examination by first evaluating the content. Is the content appropriate to your own and your district's instructional goals? Is it worthy of teaching? Does it focus on essential information and the big ideas critical for students to know? Does the content fit your district or state curriculum? Is the content gender-fair and representative of multiple cultures?

Pre-Reading Features

Background Knowledge.   If the material is a book, choose a chapter and assess its "before reading" features. Note whether it contains an introduction that provides an overview of the key concepts in the chapter. In this overview, does the author remind students of background knowledge needed to understand the upcoming selection? Does the introduction help students recall information previously learned about this subject? Does the introduction help students relate their own life experiences to the chapter topic? These features will help students integrate the new information with what they already know.

Setting Purposes.   Note whether the selection begins with an introduction or a list of objectives, statements, or questions that indicate what students will learn in the chapter. These will provide an initial guide for the students, helping them determine the most important ideas. Next, read the material following the introduction. Has the author developed topics indicated in the introduction and/or objectives? Are these ideas presented clearly? Check the headings and subheadings. Do they reflect the main idea(s) of the section they label? Can headings be changed into clear and focused purpose-setting questions? If students are unable to determine what information is critical, taking notes will be difficult.

Active Reading

Identify the Main Ideas.   Evaluate whether the author has organized information around bold-faced topics and subtopics. Do titles of each section indicate the section's main idea? Note whether main ideas are stated in a single sentence, and if they are obvious and easy for students to understand. As noted in the Research Review, explicitly stated main ideas at the beginning of paragraphs typically lead to improved comprehension.

Support for and Reinforcement of the Main Idea.   A common and well-deserved complaint about most content materials is that they lack adequate explanations. Choose several key concepts and examine the explanations. Are the concepts explained thoroughly? Are they explained using vocabulary and examples students will understand?

Too often authors "list" concepts without really explaining them. We call this the "mentioning" problem. One concept after another is mentioned without a full explanation. So, take some time to examine how the author develops concepts. Keep in mind several key variables:

- Does the author link new concepts to something familiar in the students' background?
- Is explanatory information relevant to the concept? Inclusion of irrelevant information and *seductive* details confuses readers.

- Does the author include clear examples of the concept, and will these examples be more familiar to the students than the concept being explained?
- Is the concept explained through everyday phenomena and tied to known information?
- Does the author simply mention issues and concepts without sufficient elaboration and explanation?
- Do charts, pictures, and other graphics help explain concepts?

Organization of Information. The organization of classroom materials should be apparent to the reader. Is the organization consistent across chapters? Considerate authors practice their craft conscientiously and follow the same organizational style throughout the text.

The text should be arranged logically so students can easily take notes. It should also include signal words to show how ideas within a section are related to one another, as well as written clues to guide the reader in understanding the interrelationships of ideas. Keep the following questions in mind as you read through sections of the material:

- Does the author use explicit signals to indicate sequencing of ideas? (first, second, third)
- Does the author use emphasis words to indicate important concepts? (most important, key idea)
- Does the author use explicit signals to indicate comparisons? (but, nevertheless, on the other hand, at the same time, similarly)
- Does the author use explicit signals for illustration? (for example, such as)
- Does the author use internal cues to help the reader understand the interrelationships of ideas? (as mentioned previously, this idea is similar to)
- Does the author use explicit signals for conclusions? (therefore, as a result)
- Does the author present main ideas consistently?

Vocabulary Development. Content texts usually have a tremendous vocabulary load. For example, some high-school chemistry texts contain an estimated 3,000 words unfamiliar to high school students. The number of words presented in most science books far exceeds the number of words taught in most foreign language classes (Holliday, 1991).

Sometimes content materials contain unnecessary vocabulary. Watch out for jargon. Authors often label important concepts and phenomena that probably do not need technical labels. Bill Holliday (1991) notes that technical vocabulary becomes jargon when words are: (1) difficult for most students to learn, (2) used only by experts, (3) used only for academic testing purposes, or (4) introduced too soon in a student's schooling.

With this in mind, examine the technical vocabulary in your reading assignments. Is the vocabulary unnecessarily technical for the concepts being explained? Critical terms should be highlighted and explained within the context of the material. Students will understand and remember terms better if the author includes pictures or other graphics, examples, non-examples, analogies, and essential components.

Author's Writing/Students' Engagement. Perhaps the most important aspect of text is whether students will want to read it. Is the text written in a boring, bland style, or will students find it interesting to read? Sentence structure, verbs, and voice are a few of the features that affect the style and, therefore, interest. Check for sentence variety and complexity. Note whether the writing sounds natural and fluent. Does the writing glide along with effective phrasing, one sentence flowing effortlessly into the next? Do sentences vary in structure and length, adding interest to the text? Be wary of writers who use consistently long and complex sentences. Good writers choose the simplest, most direct way to communicate. They also vary sentences, so they don't always start in the same way or follow the same subject-verb-direct object format.

Simpler sentence patterns also contain active rather than passive verbs. Note the strong, active voice in the following sentence: "Jargon and passive voice create sentence complexity." The same idea written in passive voice is weak and indirect: "Sentence complexity is usually caused by excessive use of jargon and the passive voice." Passive voice produces cluttered writing and automatically lengthens sentences.

Read through several paragraphs of the text and notice the verbs. Verbs add color to a sentence. They make writing more vibrant. Does the piece contain an abundance of *is* and *are* verbs? Does the author tend to spruce-up imprecise verbs with extraneous adverbs? The sentence "He *walked slowly* along the path" improves when the author uses an active verb to convey the same message: "He *plodded* along the path."

Finally, does the author use imagery and concrete examples so students can visualize information? Can the reader *see* what the author is talking about?

Randomly choose excerpts from your reading materials and examine sentence structure. Are sentences of varied lengths? Are the sentences in active voice? Are verbs specific, or are they imprecise and bland?

Post-Reading Features

Metacognition. A considerate text provides aids to help students monitor their comprehension. Skim through a portion of the assignment. Does the author help students know whether they have understood? Are self-checking questions incorporated into the body of the selection? Do these questions tap higher-order thinking, or do they tap recall of discrete details? Does the author provide opportunities for students to test their knowledge by applying it to new situations, labs, investigations, or hands-on activities? Does the summary provide a good overview of the key ideas in the selection or chapter? Do end-of-chapter questions cover important rather than trivial information, so students can self-review essential content? Do these study questions reflect the objectives specified at the beginning of the selection? How well do text questions match content standards required in your curriculum?

Teacher's Guide and Other Resources

Does the teacher's guide, as well as ancillary materials, include suggested activities for engaging students in learning content? Are there suggestions for helping students organize information? Are there ideas for including cooperative learning activities that focus on student-led discussions, reflection, and problem solving? Do suggested activities lead to in-depth understanding of content and turn ownership for learning back to the students? Or, are they just "fun" activities without any real academic focus?

Be particularly wary of workbooks, blackline masters, skill sheets, and tests accompanying text materials. Are these materials helpful in expanding knowledge of content, or do they distract students with busy work? Do they guide students into creating their own notes and representations, or are they just fill-in-the-blank worksheets?

Ancillary Materials for Students

Finally, does the text or program include additional high quality resources that meet the varying instructional needs of your students (e.g., multi-leveled libraries related to textbook topics, primary resource documents, CDs, videos, Internet resources, and DVDs)? Do these resources expand knowledge of content by focusing on essential ideas? Remember, audio and visual resources need to be evaluated in much the same way as written resources.

▶ Content Text Assessment Rubric

If you haven't done so already, turn to the Content Text Assessment Rubric (Blacklines 1a–d). Use information from this rubric as is or use it to create evaluation instruments more specific to your own content area and district needs. For example, think about how you might modify our rubric to fit the features of a mathematics or science text.

1a Blackline

Name: _____ Date: _____

Content Text Assessment Rubric
for Teaching & Learning

Name of text: _____

Author(s): _____ Class: _____

Copyright: _____ Publisher: _____ Grades: _____

3 = Excellent
2 = Fair
1 = Poor

Section A

Content/Standards	Evidence/Comments	Points (1–3)
The content of this text reflects the essential concepts in your course.		
The content flows in a logical progression appropriate for this topic—from simple to complex, chronological, topical, etc.		
The content, including illustrations and examples, appropriately presents ethnic and gender diversity.		
The content addresses both local and state standards.		

Total points for section A = _____

Section B

Pre-Reading Features: Background Knowledge	Evidence/Comments	Points (1–3)
The chapter introduction helps students relate their own life experiences and previously learned information to the topic.		
The author builds on the students' prior knowledge within the chapter subsections.		

Subtotal _____

Pre-Reading Features: Purpose Setting	Evidence/Comments	Points (1–3)
The chapter begins with a list of objectives, statements, or questions indicating what students will learn.		
Section headings are specific enough that students can convert them to focus questions which direct their reading.		

Subtotal _____
Total points for Section B _____

© Kendall/Hunt Publishing Company   CRISS™ Manual 275 ◀

Name: _____   Date: _____

Content Text Assessment Rubric
(continued)

Section C

Active Reading Features: *Main ideas*	Evidence/Comments	Points (1–3)
Titles of sections within the chapter indicate the main idea of each section.		
The main idea of each paragraph is clearly stated and easy to locate.		

Subtotal _____

Active Reading Features: *Support for Main Ideas*	Evidence/Comments	Points (1–3)
Main idea explanations are thorough.		
Charts, pictures, and other graphics support the main ideas and are appropriately located.		
Interesting details are included to expand on the essential information in the text and to engage students.		

Subtotal _____

Active Reading Features: *Organization of Information*	Evidence/Comments	Points (1–3)
The text is organized logically, so students can easily take notes.		
Signal words are provided to indicate how ideas in the section are related to one another.		
The presentation of main ideas and details is consistent in each chapter.		

Subtotal _____

Name: _____   Date: _____

Content Text Assessment Rubric
(continued)

Section C

Active Reading Features: *Vocabulary Development*	Evidence/Comments	Points (1–3)
Important words/concepts are highlighted in the text (bold, italics, color).		
Important words/concepts are clearly defined or explained within the reading.		
Concrete examples or analogies are included to clarify abstract ideas.		
The author provides more than just a definition (e.g., pictures, examples, analogies, counter examples)		
The number of highlighted vocabulary terms is appropriate for the concepts being explained. (Avoid too much jargon!)		

Subtotal _____

Active Reading Features *Author's Writing/Students' Engagement*	Evidence/Comments	Points (1–3)
The author's style engages students—sentence structure is varied and not overly complex, verbs are mostly in the active voice.		
The author uses imagery and concrete examples to help students visualize information.		

Subtotal _____
Total points for Section C _____

Section D

Post-Reading Features: *Megacognition*	Evidence/Comments	Points (1–3)
The author provides quality questions within and at the end of each chapter. They correlate to the chapter objectives, help students check their understanding as they read, encourage higher order thinking, and promote class or small group discussions.		
The summary accurately reflects the main ideas and key supporting information within the chapter.		

Total points for Section D _____

Name: _____   Date: _____

Content Text Assessment Rubric
(continued)

Section E

Teacher's Guide and other Resources	Evidence/Comments	Points (1–3)
The teacher's guide includes activities for helping students to organize information, to lead their own discussions, and to work in cooperative groups.		

Total points for Section E _____

Section F

Ancillary Materials* for Students	Evidence/Comments	Points
Ancillary materials expand knowledge of content by focusing on essential ideas.		
Ancillary materials meet the varying individual needs of students.		

*Workbooks, blackline masters, skill sheets, CDs, videos, DVDs, multi-level libraries, and primary resource documents

Total points for Section F _____

Total Points Section A =
Total Points Section B =
Total Points Section C =
Total Points Section D =
Total Points Section E =
Total Points Section F =

Total Points for Text
(Possible 84)   [ ]

Additional Comments:

Reviewed by: _____   Date: _____

Notice how social studies teachers in one high school changed the information from this Content Text Assessment Rubric to develop a Textbook Adoption Rubric, which they used for evaluating a number of social studies texts. This streamlined version contains most of the key features found in the original, but was far better suited to their specific needs.

Social Studies Textbook Adoption Rubric

Text Title: _American Social Studies_

Publisher: _Santa Publishers_

Grade Level(s): _8_ Pages/Chapter(s) Reviewed: _Early Exploration (21–55)_

3 = Excellent
2 = Fair
1 = Poor

Curriculum Demands/ Text Structure/ Skills and Strategies	Evidences/Comments	Points
The content aligns with curriculum standards.	Yes. Early Exploration 1000–1600	3
The content is covered in depth.	Yes.	3
Information flows logically (i.e., from simple to complex, chronological, topical, etc.)	Yes. Time line at beginning of chapter to preview events that will be discussed.	3
The chapter begins with objectives, statements, or questions indicating what students will learn.	Yes. Main ideas are stated and the purposes for reading the information are clearly identified at the beginning of the chapter- "Section Theme."	3
The main ideas are clearly presented with adequate supportive details to make the material easy for students to understand.	Main ideas are clearly outlined-Title in large red print, main ideas in blue, supportive details in green. Easy to form a power outline from this text.	3
The charts, pictures, and other graphics are adequate and appropriately placed close to the text they illustrate.	Pictures of historical events w/ thorough explanations/maps with geography skills/ keys for important information presented/direct quotes set off with bold quotation marks/activities for analyzing visuals provided.	3
Key vocabulary words/concepts are identified and clearly explained within the text.	Key terms are identified at the beginning of the chapter. Vocabulary terms are in blue print within the text and defined within the sentences in which they are found.	3
High-order thinking questions correlate to the chapter's objectives, and include writing and reflection for understanding and application.	Definitely! Section assessments include higher order thinking questions: Compare and Contrast, analyzing information, drawing conclusions, applications to the real world.	3

(continued)

Curriculum Demands/ Text Structure/ Skills and Strategies	Evidences/Comments	Points
Cooperative group activities have been included for discussion and problem solving.	*Think-Pair-Share and cooperative discussion group activities have been included.*	3
There are quality multi-level, multi-genre resources and ancillaries to enhance the core text.	*Literature Libraries, Primary Source Documents, CD-Rom*	3

Possible Points = **30**   *Total Points = 30*

Additional Comments:

Textbook Reviewer's Name: _____

School: _____

Number of classes you teach in which this textbook would be used: _____

Date Submitted: _____

Project CRISS[SM] staff worked with teachers in a high school mathematics department in Illinois to develop the following supplement to our rubric. The teachers were in the final stages of their textbook adoption and wanted to assess the practice problems included with their geometry textbook selections. They needed to make sure the problems fit with the state geometry standards and the ACT standards. We created the following rubric based on those standards and other concerns voiced by the geometry teachers.

Geometry Text Adoption Supplement - Practice Problems

3 = Excellent
2 = Fair
1 = Poor

Standards/Criteria	Evidence/Comments	Points (1–3)
1. There are a sufficient number of problems.		
2. Students are asked to create problems as well as solve them.		
3. The author allows for more than one way to solve a problem.		
4. There are open-ended problems—those with several correct answers.		
5. The problems are practical and "real world."		
6. The problems involve hands-on applications to real situations.		
7. The problems use information learned in other math classes, e.g., algebra.		
8. The problems use information learned in non-math classes.		
9. The problems provide for the use of appropriate, up-to-date technology.		
10. The problems correlate to the ACT standards and the following state goals: Goal 7 (7.A.3a, 7.A.4a, 7.A.4b, 7.C.3b, 7.C.4a, 7.C.4c, 7.C.5b) and Goal 9 (9.A.5, 9.B.3, 9.B.4, 9.B.5, 9.D.3, 9.D.4, 9.D.5)		

TOTAL POINTS (30 Possible) =

Ask students to help with the evaluation, so they, too, can become experts of text structure. Talk about the results and begin to think about how to use the information. For example, if your choice for materials provides little help in bringing out prior knowledge, work with your students to develop ways they can do it for themselves—perhaps skimming headings and looking at pictures, then writing a journal entry about what they already know.

▶ Summary

The research on text structure provides valuable insights for examining classroom materials. It also helped us, as CRISS[SM] authors, become more conscious of our writing in this text. In fact, let's step back for a moment and take a brief look at this book.

In writing this book, we have kept you in mind. We have tried to be considerate authors by making each chapter's design consistent. We begin each chapter by providing a graphic that shows an overview of the whole chapter. Next, we provide an introduction that presents the key topics. Then, we summarize the relevant research that addresses these topics wherever such a bank of research exists. From here, we move to a step-by-step presentation of the instructional strategies that reflect some of this research as well as our own expertise as teachers and teacher researchers. We have inserted topical headings reflecting each section's content; and we conclude each chapter with a few summary statements. Finally, to help our research-minded readers, we have synthesized the key research components for each chapter (where appropriate) into a chart found after the last page of the chapter. (See page 31 for the "Research Base" of this chapter.) We have worked to avoid jargon and to keep our sentence structure relatively simple. As fellow teachers, we respect how busy you are and want this manual to be a friend.

Research Conclusion	Reference
Well-structured texts are easier for students to understand than poorly written materials.	Goldman & Rakestraw, 2000
The more background knowledge a reader has about a topic, the less important text structure is to the reader's comprehension.	Goldman & Rakestsraw, 2000
Interesting details, even when unimportant to the overall content of the materials, influence one's comprehension.	Wade, Buxton, & Kelly, 1999
If readers know how authors structure their writing, they can more readily understand and remember what they read.	Goldman & Rakestraw, 2000
An inviting writing style enhances interest and comprehension.	Beck, McKeown and Worthy, 1995

CHAPTER

3

Understanding Patterns and Structure

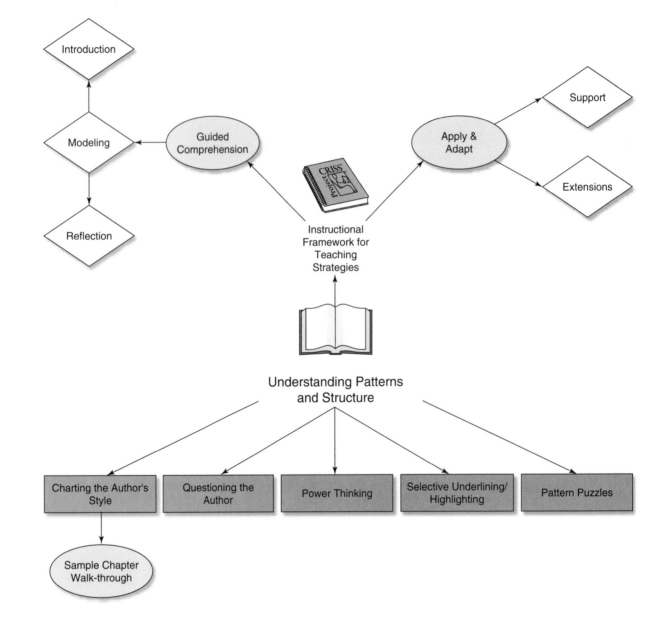

The next several chapters describe the comprehension instruction offered in Project CRISS^SM. For convenience, we have packaged our discussions into discrete chapters, but the ideas across chapters intermingle. Our teaching always involves multiple strategies within the context of the CRISS^SM overall learning plan.

We begin with strategies for helping students understand patterns and structure in text. It makes sense to start by describing ways to help students become acquainted with the various texts they meet in school. In the previous chapter, we provided an overview of research describing how the author's craft and design affects comprehension. Now we examine ways to apply some of these principles to practice. To comprehend, readers take the message from the written page, then react to it and impose their own organization.

◗ CRISS^SM Instructional Framework

Before beginning this discussion, let's digress momentarily, out of consideration to you, our reader, and describe how we present strategies in this manual. Making the structure of this text explicit will, hopefully, make your job of reading it easier. We consistently divide strategy presentations into two sequential events: Guided Comprehension—Introduction, Modeling, and Reflection; Apply and Adapt—Support and Extensions.

Introduction, Modeling, and Reflection

The teacher begins by telling students what the strategy is and why it is important. Psychologists call this step "declarative knowledge." The next step is "procedural knowledge," where the teacher models and talks about when and how to do the strategy. The third step is "reflection," where students engage in discussions about how the instructional strategies helped them apply CRISS^SM philosophy and principles to their own learning. This metacognitive component weaves throughout all of our teaching.

Support and Extensions

The teacher guides students as they apply the strategy to a selection. Once students understand how to do the strategy, they usually practice in collaborative groups until they are comfortable applying it on their own.

◗ Patterns and Structure Strategies

Charting the Author's Style

We need to help our students take a writer's stance with their reading assignments. When students know the author's "style of writing," they gain control over their reading. This fits precisely with the research presented in Chapter 2: readers who understand how authors structure their writing more readily understand and remember what they read (Goldman & Rakestraw, 2000).

Introduction, Modeling, and Reflection

1. Select a reading assignment. Try to find one that is well-written. You may wish to use the social studies chapter "The Two Sides," located at the end of this chapter, for your initial modeling. Photocopy the selection so students can practice underlining and making marginal notes while you model.

2. Begin with a teacher explanation similar to the following:

   Teacher Explanation: Authors want their readers to understand their content. Most try to make it easier for their readers by writing clearly. In order to learn from a book, a nonfiction article, or a chapter from a textbook, the first thing to understand is what the author does to help us learn. We are going to be reading detectives, or editors, and figure out the author's plan. What is the author's style of main idea development? All good nonfiction authors have one. Once we know how the author presents information, we can read the assignment with better comprehension. So let's read the introduction and the first several sections together and try to figure it out.

3. Teacher think-alouds: Make transparencies of the selections you are modeling. Begin by doing a quick "walk-through" of the chapter, thinking aloud as you proceed.

   Turn to the text example from *The American Republic to 1877* (Glencoe/McGraw Hill, 2003), found at the end of this chapter (Exhibit 1) . Teacher think-alouds for this selection might progress as follows:

Chapter Walk-Through: Sample Think-Alouds

*Before reading this chapter, I am going to take a moment and skim it to see if I can figure out how it is organized. Before starting, I will quickly read the "Guide to Reading Section." The authors have listed the main idea. This seems like the "big idea" of the chapter. Paying attention to this will help me set a purpose for my reading. I also notice a section on key terms. It looks like these key terms are presented in the same order that they appear in the chapter. For example, the first key term is **border state** and it is circled in the first section. Paying attention to these key terms will probably help me untangle what is important and will guide my reading.*

As I skim the first page, I notice that it begins with "An American Story," a first-hand account of a real person who lived during this time. The author is probably doing this so I get a better feel of what life was like. I am wondering if every chapter in this book starts with a story like this? Yes, as I leaf through the chapters in this book, every chapter does have this feature.

Now, let's see how main topics are organized within the text. Again, the overall organization helps me. For example, I notice that the main topical headings in the chapters are printed larger. The first main topic, "Choosing Sides," is in larger print than the subtopics contained in this section, "Remaining with the Union" and "Secession from the South." This organization should help me to figure out what is important.

At the end of each section, I notice a Reading Check. It looks like these questions will help me understand important concepts. There are also assessments at the end of each section and at the end of the chapter. It would probably be smart to read through these questions before I read the chapter. These questions probably focus on what is important for me to pay attention to as I read, and I could think about how I might answer them once I have completed the reading. In other words, I can start to sift for important information.

As I continue my "walk-through" of the chapter, I also notice the pictures and diagrams. For example, on the second page, there is a inset called "History through Art." Again, as I leaf through rest of the chapter, I see other cross-curriculum connections. I also note on the next page a graph, "Comparing Resources." It looks like this figure will help me in reading the second section of this chapter, "Comparing North and South." Looking at the figures and reading the cross curriculum connections before I read should help me build background knowledge.

Now that I have completed my quick walk-through, let's take a closer look at the writer's craft.

Let's read this first section, "Choosing Sides." It looks like the main point here is the struggle for border states. The author spends the first several paragraphs giving some background information on the border states. It looks like the key point of this section occurs in the third paragraph. "Losing the Border states would seriously damage the North." I like the way the author sets me up first with an explanation. Otherwise, this main idea wouldn't make much sense. The rest of the section elaborates on this main point. As I reread this first section, it looks like the author usually begins each paragraph with a main point and then expands upon this point in the rest of the paragraph. I think the author does a good job of setting up the overall main idea of the section with the chapter subheading. Using the subheadings and circled vocabulary will be helpful for organizing the chapter information into notes or charts. Let me skim the rest of the chapter to see if the author writes in a consistent way. Yes, the style seems consistent. I should have no trouble taking notes on important information. This author has a considerate style of writing.

---

4. As you talk aloud, summarize text features that describe the author's style. *What does the author do to help me learn?*
    - ▶ The author indicates main ideas with section headings and bold print.
    - ▶ Main ideas tend to be in the first sentences of paragraphs.
    - ▶ Pictures and charts help clarify concepts.
    - ▶ Main topics are presented in the "Guide to Reading" at the beginning of the chapter and in questions at the end of each section. Main idea questions are also located in the end-of-chapter questions.
    - ▶ The author explains new concepts with clear examples.
    - ▶ Important vocabulary is circled.
5. Photocopy several pages of your text or other classroom materials. Pair students. Have them read the selection together and write down in the margins their think-alouds about the author's plan.
6. Ask students to skim through other chapters in their text. Would this plan be consistent for all chapters?

7. Talk about how the authors' clues could be used for determining how to organize the chapter for learning. Should we organize it with two-column notes, content frames, or a concept map? (See Chapters 5 and 6). In the example selection on page 47, "The Two Sides," notice in the "Guide to Reading" how the authors give hints about how students might transform the information into a chart.

8. Follow the same progression with other materials used in class–those less friendly texts. What does this author do to hinder your learning? What makes this text more difficult?

9. Lead a process conference. "How do you think that being aware of the author's style will help you be a better reader? How did this strategy help you? How might you use this process on your own?"

Support and Extensions

- Divide students into groups. Have each group take a chapter from the text. Ask the recorder from each group to write down what the author does to help or hinder learning.
- Talk about the qualities of well-written text as described in Chapter 2. Give students portions of the Content Text Assessment Rubric for Teaching and Learning found in Chapter 2 of this book. Working in small groups, students can evaluate their text to decide whether it is considerate.
- If your text is problematic, have students take on the role of an editor. Ask them to write a letter to the publisher of the book, giving the author suggestions for revisions. Send the letter.
- Have your students take on the role of a textbook adoption committee and write an evaluation of the chapter. The following questions can guide this written evaluation:

Is the content appropriate?
Does the introduction tell you what you are going to learn?
Does the author follow through by developing the ideas?
Does the summary focus on essential ideas covered in the chapter?

Examine paragraphs in the body of the chapter.

Are main ideas developed directly in the paragraphs?
Is the author consistent in the way main ideas are developed?

How are new concepts presented?

Are they noted in bold print?
How well are ideas explained?

Review the chapter's pictures and graphs.

Are there enough? Do they illustrate the ideas in the chapter? Are visuals placed appropriately on the page? Does the author direct your attention to the visuals?

- Have students read the introduction, bold print topics, and conclusion. From this information alone, have them predict and outline the probable text information. Then, have them read the selection and revise their outlines.
- Have students "map" the organization of the chapter. (Notice the sample map of this chapter on page 32.)
- If students identify problems with a text, have them work in teams to establish a procedure for overcoming the difficulties. (They may decide to use other materials, work with the librarian to discover other sources of information, or ask their teacher for help.)

Questioning the Author (QtA)

Think about most discussions that happen in the classroom. Students read; this is followed by the teacher questioning them about what they have read. Frequently, such interactions shut students down because the teacher's role is that of an interrogator, testing students rather than assisting them in interacting with the information in the text to make sense of it. Only a few students take the risk of participating. To compound the situation, most students come unprepared to these interrogations because they bypass difficult text assignments or, at best, skim them to answer chapter questions. Most give up, feeling incompetent and incapable of learning the information. What can we do to challenge students to build understanding of text ideas and not shut down when confronted by challenging, inconsiderate text?

Questioning the Author (Beck, McKeown, Hamilton & Kucan, 1997) takes into account that authors are people like us: they might not always be adept at communicating clearly. It places the onus on the author, not the student. Sometimes problems with comprehension may not be the reader's fault, but the author's inabilities to explain his or her ideas well. Questioning the Author (QtA) assists readers in taking on an active, constructivist approach to comprehension as a spirited group of learners interact with the information in a text to make sense of it.

Queries are the key ingredients of Questioning the Author. Queries differ from typical questions in that they occur during rather than after reading, and are designed to assist students in constructing meaning. Queries change the role of the teacher from an interrogator to a facilitator of discussion. Student-to-student interactions increase as learners grapple with an author's text, as they work together during reading to make sense of it. Queries always deal with what the author says or means.

Isabelle Beck (Beck et al., 1997) loosely divides queries into three types: Initiating Queries, Follow-up-Queries, and Narrative Queries. The following queries are also reprinted on Blackline 2.

Sample Queries

Initiating Queries
What is the author trying to say here?
What is the author's message?
What is the author talking about?
What does the author expect you to know?

Follow-up Queries
What does the author mean here?
Did the author explain this clearly?
Does this make sense with what the author told us before?
How does this connect with what the author has told us before?
Does the author tell us why?
Why do you think the author tells us this now?

Narrative Queries
How do things look for the character now?
Given what the author has already told us about this character, what is this character thinking now?
How does the author let us know that something has changed?

Before introducing students to QtA, take a segment of text and determine the major understandings that students are to construct. Then, identify the stumbling blocks students might encounter, such as lack of elaboration or density of information, that can impede comprehension. Identify places to stop and initiate discussion through QtA to clarify ideas.

For example, the excerpt "Water and Diffusion," found in Exhibit 2, comes from a high school biology text, Biology, The Dynamics of Life (2004), pages 152–153. Notice how the sample queries guide students in comprehending the text.

Introduction, Modeling, and Reflection

The instructional sequence described here is based on Beck, et al.,1997 and Buehl 2001.

1. Select a text or other written materials used in your class. Talk about authorship. Identify names and read any biographical information available in the text. "Who are these authors? Are they university professors? Do you think they are familiar with what students your age might know about this topic?"
2. Take a selection of text. Ask questions similar to these: "Has the author presented his or her ideas clearly? Where in the text is the author having difficulty communicating? What has the author done to help us understand his or her message?"
3. Continue through the text. Pause. "What is the author trying to say? What does the author expect you to know already? Why do you think the author tells us this now? What additional information could the author have given us to help you understand this?"
4. Throughout, talk about how QtA helps one really get inside the author's head to figure out the information the writer wants us to take away from the assignment. Discuss how good readers internalize these self-questioning procedures as a way to monitor their own comprehension. Include in your conversations encouraging remarks about not being helpless or frustrated when reading. Explain that in most situations it is not our fault when we have difficulty understanding. Authors often have trouble communicating their message. "Don't feel defeated by an author. Instead figure out what the author is trying to do. He or she may not be very good at getting information across, but don't give up. Rise up to the challenge. It can be very satisfying to tackle difficult text, to grapple with meaning. This struggle defines what good readers do."
5. Ask your students how QtA helped them understand the selections. Do they want to create new queries for the authors?

Support and Extensions

- Post a chart of queries in the classroom and/or give students copies. Ask students to take sections of text and put astericks by difficult and confusing content. Decide on queries that work for each section, and use them to facilitate a class discussion.
- Pair students, and ask them to pose queries to one another.

Strategy

Learning

Power Thinking

Power Thinking helps students differentiate between main ideas and details (Miller, 1985; Sparks, 1982). The process is easy for students to use because main ideas and details are simply assigned numbers. Main ideas are Power 1 ideas, while details are either Power 2, 3, or 4 ideas. Students can use Powers as an organizational tool for reading, writing, and studying.

Introduction, Modeling, and Reflection

1. Begin instruction by providing students with the following information.

   Power 1. Main idea
      Power 2. Detail or support for a Power 1
         Power 3. Detail or support for a Power 2 (and so forth)

2. Start working with Power Thinking by using individual words. Later, students can incorporate sentences or phrases. Show your students examples such as the following.

   Power 1. Animals
      Power 2. Dog
         Power 3. Collie
         Power 3. German Shepherd
      Power: 2. Cat
         Power 3. Siamese
         Power 3. Calico

   Note: Ideas or words having the same Power numbers must have a similar relationship to the Power above. For example, "bear" could be another Power 2 but "grizzly bear" would be too specific for a Power 2. If "bear" were the Power 2, then "grizzly" could be Power 3.

3. Pick a Power 1 idea on a familiar topic such as sports, food, or TV shows. Have your students give you Power 2, 3, and 4 examples. For instance:

   Teacher: Power 1 is sports. What will Power 2 be?
   Student: Football
   Teacher: Great, now give me another Power 2.
   Student: Basketball
   Teacher: Right, now give me Power 3 examples that will fit under basketball.
   Student: Hoop, court, and basketball

   As students give you these ideas, write them on the board or overhead:

   1. sports
      2. football
      2. basketball
         3. hoop
         3. court
         3. basketball

   Note: you can also write this in a graphic format. The example on page 40 was done using Inspiration® software. One handy feature of this software is that students can convert Power maps to Power notes with one click.

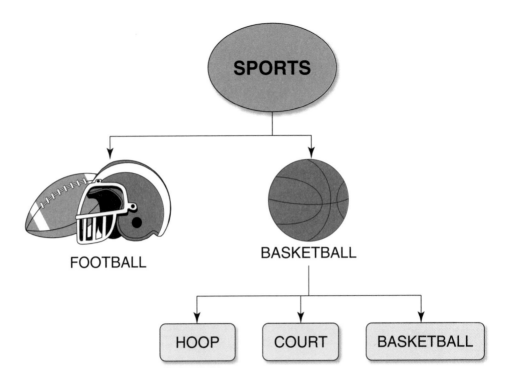

FOOTBALL

BASKETBALL

HOOP   COURT   BASKETBALL

4. Ask students to think about how they might use Power structures to transform information more effectively. For example, how could they use Power structures as part of note-taking, selective underlining, concept mapping, and writing summaries?

Support and Extensions

Apply and Adapt

● Write two Power structures on the board.

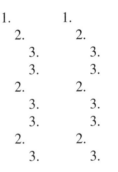

```
1.          1.
  2.          2.
    3.          3.
    3.          3.
  2.          2.
    3.          3.
    3.          3.
  2.          2.
    3.          3.
```

Provide the Power 1 topics such as "TV shows" and "movies." Divide the class into teams and have them race to the board to fill in the different items in order from top to bottom. Ask students to check the winning team's work to make sure they really won. When students are comfortable with the Power structure, choose Power 1 topics from your content area. This can be used for review or to bring out background knowledge.

● Write Power 1, 2, and 3 words on separate 3″ × 5″ cards for several topics. Mix them up and distribute one card to each student. Have students shift their positions to sort themselves out, first into category groups and then into Power structures within each category. The Power 1 person can stand, the 2's kneel and the 3's sit to create a "pyramid."

● Power structures can be extended into writing. Use Power structures to help students develop simple paragraphs and to structure essay examinations (Sparks, 1982). Power writing provides a smooth transition from Power notes or maps to paragraph writing especially for younger students or for older students who have difficulty structuring their writing. These simple, structured paragraphs are the first step in the development of longer writing assignments.

One way to introduce students to paragraphing is to first have them develop Power outlines using words and phrases. Next, ask them to expand their ideas into sentences and then combine these sentences into a paragraph.

Begin with simple 1-2-2-2 structures.

> 1. I have several favorite sports.
>   2. Skiing in the winter is first on my list.
>   2. During the summer you will find me on my roller blades.
>   2. I love playing tennis.
> 1. My favorite sports keep my body and mind fit.
>
> (1) My three favorite sports, skiing, roller blading, and tennis, make me healthy and happy. (2) Skiing provides a great way to get through the winter. (3) I love the feel of gliding through the snow. (2) During the summer, however, you will find me on my roller blades. (3) Roller blading builds balance and strong muscles. (3) I really enjoy skating around town. (2) Finally, I love playing tennis. (3) It is so much fun to run around the court and hit the ball. (3) I always feel so good when I hit a clean shot over the net. (1) My three favorite sports keep my body fit and my mind sharp.

In the beginning stages, you may find it helpful for students to include the number of items or reasons in their topic sentence, e.g., "My three favorite sports. . ." After students have a good understanding of the Power 1 and 2 structures, they can begin adding Power 3 and 4 ideas and conclude with another Power 1 sentence.

Teachers can help students write essay questions by using a Power structure. Keep in mind that the structure will inform students about how much detail is necessary for a complete response.

Example:

What were the advantages of the North during the Civil War. Using complete sentences, complete the following Power structure. (The Power structure in itself could be the assessment, or students could readily use their outlines to write an essay.)

1. The North had several important advantages.
    2. The North had a larger population.
        3. The North had more men for their armies.
    2. The North had a better banking system.
        3. They had more money available.
    2. The North had better transportation systems.
        3. Railroads helped move products for the war efforts.
        3. The North had more ships.

The North had several important advantages during the Civil War. First, the North had a larger population, which gave them more men for their armies. In addition, the North had a better banking system. Wars are extremely expensive, and having a more efficient banking system provided needed funds for the war effort. Finally, the North had a better developed transportation system. The North had a more efficient railway system for greater ease in moving troops and supplies. The North also possessed more ships, necessary for transporting products and troops.

Keep in mind, however, that these structured paragraphs are only an intermediate step to freer forms of writing. Many students will not need such tight structures in order to develop coherent paragraphs. Over-structuring writing can hinder creativity and hamper students who have already internalized a sense of structure in their writing. Once students have an awareness of main idea and detail paragraph development, they will no longer need to think about their writing in the form of numbers.

In other words, as teachers, we must be careful not to be rigid about comprehension instruction. The goal of Power writing is to help students internalize structure. If individual students already have this ability, they must not be limited to a Power writing format.

Selective Underlining/Highlighting

Underlining, or highlighting, is probably the most used and the most abused study strategy. For underlining to work, students must be selective and have an idea of their purposes for reading. Otherwise, they will underline too much, hemorrhaging their yellow markers across the page without really transforming the information. In these situations, underlining isn't very effective. It only works when students take time to preview the material and skim or read the material first.

Underlining is particularly effective when used in conjunction with Questioning the Author. Students can underline portions of text they want to use in their discussions.

Introduction, Modeling, and Reflection

1. Explain to students that underlining and marginal notes are critical tools for understanding and transforming information. Talk about the importance of underlining selectively and having purposes in mind before reading. "Don't just start reading before doing some careful previewing and purpose setting."
2. Model how to preview the assignment. Show them how to read the introductory paragraphs and bold print headings, to examine the pictures and graphs, and to read the concluding paragraphs. "Stop and think about what you might learn from the selection and what you already know." Next, guide students in a discussion about developing purposes for reading. Finally, demonstrate how you selectively underline. Think-aloud as you demonstrate.
3. Use a transparency of an assignment to model how you underline selectively. With the students, develop some procedural steps:
   - Skim or read through the selection first.
   - Reread one paragraph at a time and begin underlining.
   - Underline selectively, never whole sentences.
   - Choose key words or phases from the sentences to highlight.
   - Organize main ideas and details by Powers or other types of notations.
   - Note main ideas with M or I or other types of notations.
   - Generate topics or categories for ideas and write them in the margins.
   - Justify underlined information with a partner.

4. Underline main ideas (Power 1) and details (Power 2 and 3) with different colored markers. For example, main ideas could be in blue while details are in red and green. When main points are not explicit, generate your own main points and jot them in the margins. Marginal notes might also contain queries for facilitating Questioning the Author discussions.

Comparing North and South

When the war began, both sides had advantages and disadvantages. How they would use those strengths and weaknesses would determine the war's outcome.

The North enjoyed the advantages of a larger population, more industry, and more abundant resources than the South. It had a better banking system, which helped to raise money for the war. The North also possessed more ships and almost all the members of the regular navy remained loyal to the Union. Finally, the North had a larger and more efficient railway network.

The North also faced disadvantages. Bringing the Southern states back into the Union would be difficult. The North would have to invade and hold the South—a large area filled with a hostile population. Furthermore, the Southern people's support for the war remained strong. Recalling the example of the American Revolution, when the smaller, weaker colonies had won independence from wealthy Great Britain, many believed the South had a good chance of winning.

One Northern advantage was not obvious until later. Both sides greatly underestimated Abraham Lincoln. His dedication, intelligence, and humanity would lead the North to victory.

One of the main advantages of the South was the strong support its white population gave the war. Southerners also had the advantage of fighting in familiar territory—defending their land, their homes, and their way of life.

The military leadership of the South, at least at first, was superior to the North's. Southern families had a strong tradition of military training and service, and military college graduates provided the South with a large pool of officers. Overseeing the Southern effort was Confederate president **Jefferson Davis,** a West Point graduate and an experienced soldier.

The South faced material disadvantages. It had a smaller population of free men to draw upon in building an army. It also possessed very few factories to manufacture weapons and other supplies, and it produced less than half as much food as the North. With less than half the miles of railroad tracks and vastly fewer trains than the North, the Confederate government had difficulty delivering food, weapons, and other supplies to its troops.

Source: Reprinted by permission Glencoe/McGraw-Hill.

---

5. Engage students in discussions about why selective underlining and marginal notes help them with comprehension. In particular, talk about how underlining guides them in analyzing the author's plan, as part of Questioning the Author, and for transforming information. These procedures help students become more metacognitive, particularly when given opportunities to talk about why they have underlined certain information.

Support and Extensions

- Provide students with opportunities to underline selectively. Use old text-books or photocopy sections of your assignments. Make transparencies of the selections for yourself. Talk about the author's plan and model underlining as students underline their own copies. Have students work with a partner to make decisions about what to underline.

- Divide students into groups of two or three. Give each group a transparency of a selection from their reading assignment. Have each group selectively underline the material on the transparency and present their highlighting on the overhead for class discussion.

- Provide students with clear transparencies that they can clip to a page of text and underline with washable markers. Before cleaning the transparency for the next page, students need to transfer the key ideas to their classroom notes. After a while, students will not need to underline with a transparency. They will be able to pull out main ideas directly and add them to their notes.

- Have students underline key ideas on tests or in their own notes.

- Continue to have process discussions about why underlining, when done selectively for specific purposes, demonstrates CRISS^{SM} principles and philosophy.

Pattern Puzzles

One active approach for understanding patterns and structure is to have students move sentences around to form well-organized paragraphs and essays. Pattern puzzles also work with any content that requires sequencing of steps and ideas.

Introduction, Modeling, and Reflection

1. With younger children, begin with a single paragraph that contains a well-developed topic sentence and supporting details. Select paragraphs that deal with simple concepts or spend necessary time developing background knowledge before beginning this activity. For older students, you may want to skip to Step 4.

2. Write each sentence on a separate strip of paper. Mix up the strips and demonstrate how to organize them into a paragraph. Talk about topic sentences and transition words. Encourage multiple solutions, as there are a variety of ways to organize any paragraph. Try out different sequences before deciding which sentence order seems to work best. The discussion about structure and content is always more important than the outcome.

   You might want to do the same modeling sequence using the overhead projector. Write the paragraph sentence by sentence on a blank transparency. Cut apart using a paper cutter. Mix up the sentence strips on the overhead, and lead a discussion about how to organize them.

3. Take multiple copies of another paragraph and cut apart, sentence by sentence. Put all the strips from each paragraph into an envelope and give one envelope to each group of two or three students. Instruct them to work together to organize the sentences into a well-written paragraph. Ask students to discuss why they organized the sentences into a specific pattern. Remind them about Power 1, 2, and 3 ideas.

4. With multi-paragraph selections, leave the first paragraph intact, but cut the remaining paragraphs into individual sentences. Make sure there is one sentence per slip of paper. Put all of the slips into an envelope and distribute to pairs of students. Then have the students place the paragraphs and the indi-

vidual sentences in the correct order. Suggest that they find sentences that contain Power 1 ideas. Then organize the Power 2 and 3 ideas appropriately. Make sure to bring out the students' prior knowledge before beginning this activity.

5. Use Pattern Puzzles to explore a variety of structures. Use paragraphs where main ideas are implied. Use poetry, math word problems, scientific journal abstracts, and newspaper articles.

6. Throughout, discuss why Pattern Puzzles are helpful for inspiring discussion and transformation of information-both key CRISS℠ principles.

Support and Extensions

- After completing a unit of study, have students list topics, subtopics, and bold print vocabulary on separate cards. Place in envelopes. As a post-reading activity, have students organize these into Power 1, 2, and 3 hierarchies.

- Have students write sentences, describing the main events of a sequence (scientific experiments, the steps to solve a math problem or a geometric proof, the plot of a short story). Cut the statements apart, and place the slips into envelopes. Have pairs of students organize them into correct order and then explain their thinking.

- As a revision strategy, have students working alone or in pairs take their own writing and cut it apart sentence by sentence and reorder. In this way, they can evaluate how well their writing is organized.

▶ Summary

In this chapter, we have focused on ways to help students construct meaning from text. When students know how authors structure their writing, they can more readily understand and remember what they read. Charting the author's style also makes text less intimidating, particularly, when readers question the author with queries that focus on the quality and depth of meaning. Selective Underlining, Power Thinking, and Pattern Puzzles are all designed to increase awareness of patterns and structure. With each strategy, we demonstrate, encourage, and model. Then, we gradually step aside and assist only when necessary. We teach a variety of strategies and then encourage flexibility and reflection so students can begin adapting these strategies to their own unique qualities as learners.

Research Conclusion	Reference
Readers who understand how authors structure their writing, more readily understand and remember what they read.	Goldman & Rakestraw, 2000

SECTION 1 The Two Sides

Guide to Reading

Main Idea

Both the North and the South had strengths and weaknesses that helped determine their military strategies.

Key Terms

border state, blockade, offensive, Rebel, Yankee

Reading Strategy

Classifying Information As you read the section, complete a chart like the one shown here by listing the strengths and weaknesses of the Union and the Confederacy.

	Union	Confederacy
Strengths		
Weaknesses		

Read to Learn

- why the border states played an important part in the war.
- how the North and South compared in terms of population, industry, resources, and war aims.

Section Theme

Government and Democracy The Southern states seceded from the Union to protect states' rights.

Preview of Events

1861 — 1862 — 1863

February 1861
The Confederacy forms

April 1861
Four more states join the Confederacy

Summer 1861
Confederate forces total 112,000; Union 187,000

June 1863
West Virginia joins Union

Confederate soldier, 1861

AN American Story

Union sergeant Driscoll directed his troops at Malvern Hill on July 1, 1862. The enemy fought fiercely, especially one young Confederate soldier. Driscoll raised his rifle, took aim, and shot the boy. As he passed the spot where the boy had fallen, Driscoll turned the daring soldier over to see what he looked like. The boy opened his eyes and faintly murmured, "Father," then his eyes fluttered shut, never to open again. A Union captain later wrote, "I will forever recollect the frantic grief of Driscoll; it was harrowing to witness. He [had killed] his son, who had gone South before the war."

Like the Driscolls, many families were divided by the war. Neither side imagined, however, that the war would cost such a terrible price in human life. During the four years of fighting, hundreds of thousands of Americans were killed in battle.

Choosing Sides

By February 1861, seven states had left the Union and formed the Confederacy. After the Confederate bombardment of Fort Sumter, President Abraham Lincoln issued a call for troops to save the Union. His action caused Virginia, North Carolina, Tennessee, and Arkansas to join the Confederacy. These four states brought needed soldiers and supplies to the Confederacy. For its capital,

460 CHAPTER 16 The Civil War

▶ Exhibit 1

Source: Reprinted by permission Glencoe/McGraw-Hill.

Understanding Patterns and Structure **47** ◀

the Confederacy chose **Richmond,** Virginia, a city only about 100 miles from the Union capital of Washington, D.C.

Four states that allowed slavery—Missouri, Kentucky, Maryland, and Delaware—remained in the Union. The people of these border states were divided over which side to support. Missouri, Kentucky, and Maryland had such strong support for the South that the three states teetered on the brink of secession.

Losing the border states would seriously damage the North. All had strategic locations. Missouri could control parts of the Mississippi River and major routes to the West. Kentucky controlled the Ohio River. Delaware was close to the important Northern city of Philadelphia.

Maryland, perhaps the most important of the border states, was close to Richmond. Vital railroad lines passed through Maryland. Most significantly, Washington, D.C., lay within the state. If Maryland seceded, the North's government would be surrounded.

Maryland's key role became clear in April 1861. A mob in Baltimore attacked Northern troops; Confederate sympathizers burned railroad bridges and cut the telegraph line to Washington, isolating the capital from the rest of the North. Northern troops soon arrived, but the nation's capital had suffered some anxious days.

Remaining With the Union

Lincoln had to move cautiously to avoid upsetting people in the border states. If he announced that he aimed to end slavery, for instance, groups supporting the Confederacy might take their states out of the Union. If he ordered Northern troops into Kentucky, Confederate sympathizers there would claim the state had been invaded and swing it to the South.

In some ways Lincoln acted boldly. He suspended some constitutional rights and used his power to arrest people who supported secession. In the end Lincoln's approach worked. The border states stayed in the Union, but many of their citizens joined armies of the South.

A Secession From the South

Most white Southerners favored secession. Still, pockets of Union support existed in parts of Tennessee and Virginia. People in the

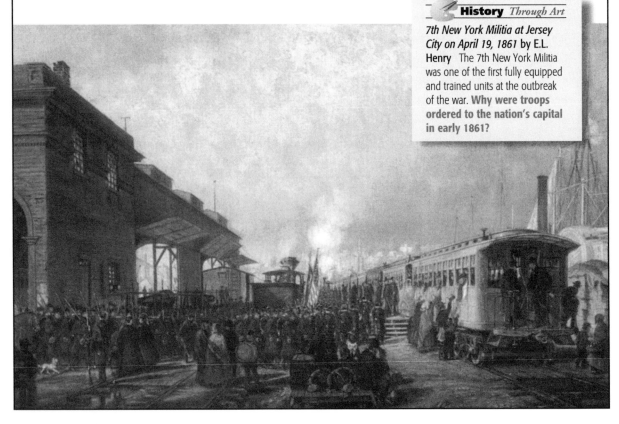

History *Through Art*

7th New York Militia at Jersey City on April 19, 1861 by E.L. Henry The 7th New York Militia was one of the first fully equipped and trained units at the outbreak of the war. **Why were troops ordered to the nation's capital in early 1861?**

▶ Exhibit 1 *(continued)*

Appalachian region generally opposed secession. In western Virginia a movement to secede from the state and rejoin the Union grew. In 1861, 48 Virginia counties organized themselves as a separate state called **West Virginia.** Congress admitted this state to the Union in 1863.

✓ Reading Check **Explaining** Why was Maryland strategically important?

Comparing North and South

When the war began, both sides had advantages and disadvantages. How they would use those strengths and weaknesses would determine the war's outcome.

The North enjoyed the advantages of a larger population, more industry, and more abundant resources than the South. It had a better banking system, which helped to raise money for the war. The North also possessed more ships, and almost all the members of the regular navy remained loyal to the Union. Finally, the North had a larger and more efficient railway network.

The North also faced disadvantages. Bringing the Southern states back into the Union would be difficult. The North would have to invade and hold the South—a large area filled with a hostile population. Furthermore, the Southern people's support for the war remained strong. Recalling the example of the American Revolution, when the smaller, weaker colonies had won independence from wealthy Great Britain, many believed the South had a good chance of winning.

One Northern advantage was not obvious until later. Both sides greatly underestimated Abraham Lincoln. His dedication, intelligence, and humanity would lead the North to victory.

One of the main advantages of the South was the strong support its white population gave the war. Southerners also had the advantage of fighting in familiar territory—defending their land, their homes, and their way of life.

The military leadership of the South, at least at first, was superior to the North's. Southern families had a strong tradition of military training and service, and military college graduates provided the South with a large pool of officers. Overseeing the Southern effort was Confederate president **Jefferson Davis,** a West Point graduate and an experienced soldier.

The South faced material disadvantages. It had a smaller population of free men to draw upon in building an army. It also possessed very few factories to manufacture weapons and other supplies, and it produced less than half as much food as the North. With less than half the miles of railroad tracks and vastly fewer trains than the North, the Confederate government had difficulty delivering food, weapons, and other supplies to its troops.

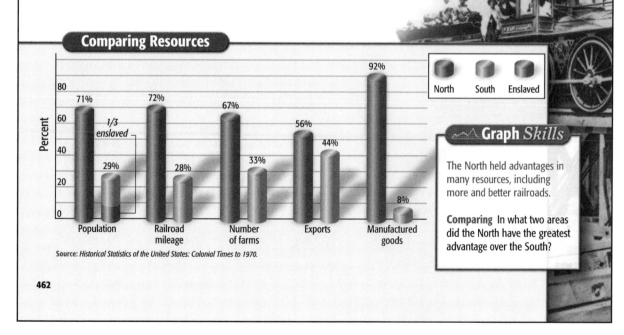

Comparing Resources

Percent

71% Population (North)
1/3 enslaved
29%
72% Railroad mileage (North)
28%
67% Number of farms (North)
33%
56% Exports (North)
44%
92% Manufactured goods (North)
8%

North   South   Enslaved

Graph Skills

The North held advantages in many resources, including more and better railroads.

Comparing In what two areas did the North have the greatest advantage over the South?

Source: Historical Statistics of the United States: Colonial Times to 1970.

462

▶ Exhibit 1 *(continued)*

The belief in **states' rights**—a founding principle of the Confederacy—also hampered the South's efforts. The individual states refused to give the Confederate government sufficient power. As a result, the government found it difficult to fight the war effectively.

War Aims and Strategy

The North and the South entered the Civil War with different aims. The main goal of the North at the outset was to bring the Southern states back into the Union. Ending slavery was not a major Northern goal at first, but this changed as the war continued.

The Union's plan for winning the war included three main strategies. First the North would blockade or close, Southern ports to prevent supplies from reaching the South—and to prevent the South from earning money by exporting cotton. Second, the Union intended to gain control of the Mississippi River to cut Southern supply lines and to split the Confederacy. Third, the North planned to capture Richmond, Virginia, the Confederate capital.

For the South, the primary aim of the war was to win recognition as an independent nation. Independence would allow Southerners to preserve their traditional way of life— a way of life that included slavery.

To achieve this goal, the South worked out a defensive strategy. It planned to defend its homeland, holding on to as much territory as possible until the North tired of fighting. The South expected that Britain and France, which imported large quantities of Southern cotton, would pressure the North to end the war to restore their cotton supply.

During the war Southern leaders sometimes changed strategy and took the offensive—went on the attack. They moved their armies northward to threaten Washington, D.C., and other Northern cities, hoping to persuade the North it could not win the war.

Reading Check **Explaining** What role did Jefferson Davis play in the war?

American People at War

The Civil War was more than a war between the states. It often pitted brother against brother, parents against their children, and neighbor against neighbor.

American Against American

The leaders from both North and South—and their families—felt these divisions. President Lincoln's wife, Mary Todd Lincoln, had several relatives who fought in the Confederate army. John Crittenden, a senator from Kentucky, had two sons who became generals in the war—one for the Confederacy and one for the Union. Officers on both sides—including Confederate general Robert E. Lee, and Union generals George McClellan and William Tecumseh Sherman— had attended the United States Military Academy at West Point, never dreaming that they would one day command forces against each other.

Who Were the Soldiers?

Most of the soldiers were young. The average age of a recruit was 25 years old, but about 40 percent were 21 or younger. Ted Upson of Indiana was only 16 when he begged his father to let him join the Union army. His father replied, "This Union your ancestors and mine helped to make must be saved from destruction." 📖 *(See page 603 for an additional primary source reading about Civil War soldiers.)*

▶ Exhibit 1   *(continued)*

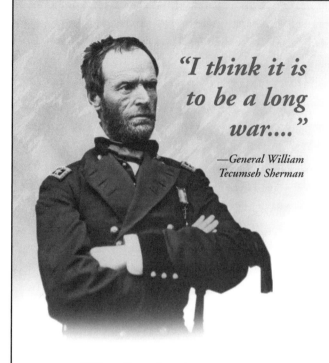

"I think it is to be a long war...."

—*General William Tecumseh Sherman*

William Stone from Louisiana rushed to join the Confederate army after the attack on Fort Sumter. His sister Kate wrote that he was

❝ . . . wild to be off to Virginia. He so fears that the fighting will be over before he can get there. ❞

Soldiers came from every region and all walks of life. Most, though, came from farms. Almost half of the North's troops and more than 60 percent of the South's had owned or worked on farms. The Union army did not permit African

Americans to join at first, but they did serve later. Lincoln's early terms of enlistment asked governors to supply soldiers for 90 days. When the conflict did not end quickly, soldiers' terms became longer.

By the summer of 1861 the Confederate army had about 112,000 soldiers, who were sometimes called Rebels. The Union had about 187,000 soldiers, or Yankees, as they were also known. By the end of the war, about 850,000 men fought for the Confederacy and about 2.1 million men fought for the Union. The Union number included just under 200,000 African Americans. About 10,000 Hispanic soldiers fought in the conflict.

False Hopes

When the war began, each side expected an early victory. A Confederate soldier from a town in Alabama expected the war to be over well within a year because "we are going to kill the last Yankee before that time if there is any fight in them still." Northerners were just as confident that they would beat the South quickly.

Some leaders saw the situation more clearly. Northern general William Tecumseh Sherman wrote, "I think it is to be a long war—very long—much longer than any politician thinks." The first spring of the war proved that Sherman's prediction was accurate.

✓ **Reading Check** **Comparing** Which side had the larger fighting force?

SECTION 1 ASSESSMENT

Checking for Understanding

1. **Key Terms** Write a short paragraph in which you use all of the following key terms: border state, blockade, offensive, Rebel, Yankee.
2. **Reviewing Facts** Why were the border states important to the North?

Reviewing Themes

3. **Government and Democracy** How did a strong belief in states' rights affect the South during the war?

Critical Thinking

4. **Predict** What do you think would be the South's greatest advantage in the war?
5. **Comparing** Create a diagram like the one shown here. Then compare Northern and Southern aims and strategies.

	North	South
Aims		
Strategies		

Analyzing Visuals

6. **Making Generalizations** Review the graph on page 462 and write a general conclusion based on the data presented in the graph.

Interdisciplinary Activity

Expository Writing You are a Southerner (or a Northerner) in 1861. Write a journal entry that explains your reasons for joining the Confederate (or Union) army.

464 CHAPTER 16 The Civil War

▶ Exhibit 1 *(continued)*

Section 6.2

Water and Diffusion

SECTION PREVIEW

Objectives

Relate water's unique features to polarity.

Identify how the process of diffusion occurs and why it is important to cells.

Review Vocabulary
homeostasis: regulation of the internal environment of a cell or organism to maintain conditions suitable for life (p. 9)

New Vocabulary
polar molecule
hydrogen bond
diffusion
dynamic equilibrium

Water—It's One of a Kind!

Finding Main Ideas Most of us take water for granted. We turn on the kitchen faucet at home to get a drink and expect water to come out of the faucet. We don't think about how important water's properties are to life. **Organize Information** *As you read this section, make a list of the properties of water. Next to each property, write how it is important in maintaining homeostasis in living organisms.*

Water is vital to the living world.

Physical Setting Connection

The structure of water molecules
Water is sometimes called the universal solvent because of its ability to dissolve a wide range of materials. This ability is related to the polarity of the water molecule, which is due to its "V" shape as well as the polarity of the hydrogen-oxygen bonds. Water molecules would not be polar if they were linear, with hydrogen atoms on opposite sides of the oxygen atom.

What do you need to know to understand this? Has the author explained this clearly?

— What does the author expect you to know here?

Water and Its Importance

Water is perhaps the most important compound in living organisms. Most life processes can occur only when molecules and ions are free to move and collide with one another. This condition exists when they are dissolved in water. Water also serves to transport materials in organisms. For example, blood and plant sap, which are mostly water, transport materials in animals and plants. In fact, water makes up 70 to 95 percent of most organisms.

Water is polar   What is the author talking about?

Sometimes, when atoms form covalent bonds, they do not share the electrons equally. The water molecule pictured in *Figure 6.12A* shows that the shared electrons are attracted by the oxygen nucleus more strongly than by the hydrogen nuclei. As a result, the electrons spend more time near the oxygen nucleus than they do near the hydrogen nuclei.

When atoms in a covalent bond do not share the electrons equally, they form a polar bond. A **polar molecule** is a molecule with an unequal distribution of charge; that is, each molecule has a positive end and a negative end. As illustrated in *Figure 6.12B*, water is an example of a polar molecule. Polar water molecules attract ions as well as other polar molecules. Because of this attraction, water can dissolve many ionic compounds, such as salt, and many other polar molecules, such as sugar.

What do we need to know to understand this?

What is the author trying to say? Does the author tell us why?

▶ Exhibit 2
Source: Reprinted by permission of Glencoe/McGraw-Hill.

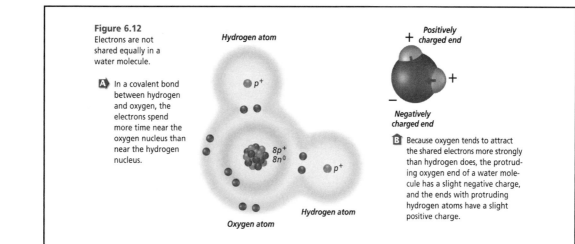

Figure 6.12
Electrons are not shared equally in a water molecule.

A In a covalent bond between hydrogen and oxygen, the electrons spend more time near the oxygen nucleus than near the hydrogen nucleus.

Hydrogen atom

$8p^+$
$8n^0$

Oxygen atom

Hydrogen atom

Positively charged end

Negatively charged end

B Because oxygen tends to attract the shared electrons more strongly than hydrogen does, the protruding oxygen end of a water molecule has a slight negative charge, and the ends with protruding hydrogen atoms have a slight positive charge.

Water molecules also attract other water molecules. The positively charged hydrogen atoms of one water molecule attract the negatively charged oxygen atoms of another water molecule. This attraction of opposite charges between hydrogen and oxygen forms a weak bond called a **hydrogen bond.** Hydrogen bonds are important to organisms because they help hold many biomolecules, such as proteins, together.

Also because of its polarity, water has the unique property of being able to creep up thin tubes. Plants in particular take advantage of this property, called capillary action, to get water from the ground. Capillary action and the tension on the water's surface, which is also a result of polarity, play major roles in getting water from the soil to the tops of even the tallest trees.

Water resists temperature changes

Water resists changes in temperature. Therefore, water requires more heat to increase its temperature than do most other common liquids. Likewise, water loses a lot of heat when it cools. In fact, water is like an insulator that helps maintain a steady environment when conditions fluctuate. Because cells exist in an aqueous environment, this property of water is extremely important to cellular functions as it helps cells maintain homeostasis.

Water expands when it freezes

Water is one of the few substances that expands when it freezes. Because of this property, ice is less dense than liquid water so it floats as it forms in a body of water. Use the *Problem-Solving Lab* on the next page to investigate this property. Water expands as it freezes inside the cracks of rocks. As it expands, it often breaks apart the rocks. Over long time periods, this process helps form soil.

The properties of water make it an excellent vehicle for carrying substances in living systems. One way to move substances is by diffusion.

Reading Check **Infer** why coastal communities usually experience milder temperatures than cities that are not located near large bodies of water.

Physical Setting Connection

Density of liquids Water is most dense at about 4°C. When the surface of a lake cools to 4°C, the surface water sinks and warmer water takes its place. This process continues until all the water has cooled to 4°C. Only then can the surface start freezing if it is cooled further. Even if the surface is frozen and air temperatures are well below freezing, the water near the bottom of the lake is at 4°C—warm enough for aquatic life to survive.

What does the author assume you already know?

Does the author tell us why?

▶ Exhibit 2 *(continued)*

Discussion: The Conversation of Learning

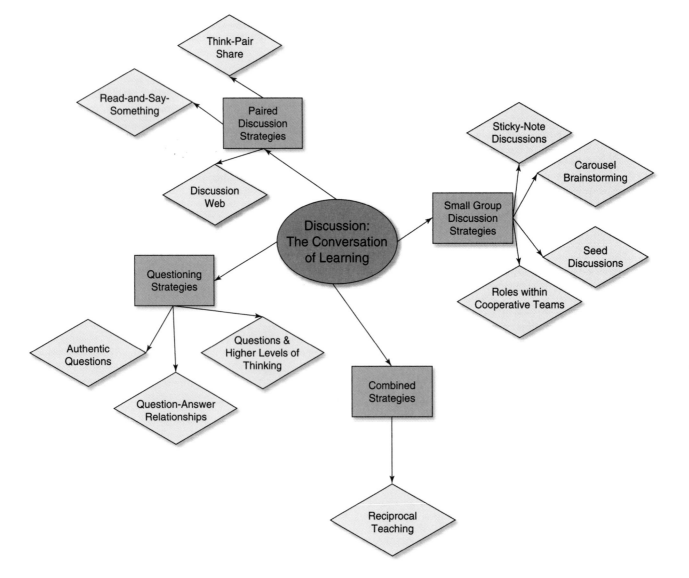

Students learn best when they engage in meaningful conversations about content. They cannot be expected to learn when they are not actively involved, grappling with the material. Students come to know their own social world by interacting with others. Each enters the classroom with some information, but no individual has the whole picture. By pooling their understandings and talking about what they think they know, students emerge from instructional conversations with deeper knowledge and a clearer focus for more learning.

Most of us will remember how it feels to be a student in a classroom dominated by teacher talk and interrogation. The teacher asks the questions. One-by-one, students reel off answers until someone hits on the correct one. The teacher remains the sole evaluator and controller of comprehension. Cazden (1988) calls this model of discourse IRE: the teacher initiates (I) talk by asking a question; a student responds (R); and the teacher evaluates (E) the response. This recitation model seldom results in an acquisition of knowledge that students can use to make their own inferences or draw their own conclusions. In these situations, teacher-student dialogue becomes a means of assessment rather than instruction.

Teacher-directed questions do have their place in our classrooms. But we prefer to create opportunities for students to initiate their own inquiries, to respond to one another, and to expand on previous responses. Therefore, we advocate a constructivist model of discussion in which students engage in instructional conversations to construct their own meaning (Goldenberg, 1993). As students talk, they test their ideas and consider the ideas of others.

Most research on discussion comes from work on literature-based reading instruction (Morrow and Gambrell, 2000). Researchers find discussion promotes deeper understanding of text, leads to higher-level thinking and problem-solving, and improves communication skills (Gambrell, 1996). Student-led discussions foster greater student participation than those led by teachers, and they improve communication skills—including the ability to take on different points of view. Such discussions also increase student sensitivity, encouraging recognition and acknowledgment of others in the group (Almasi, 1995). Moreover, effective discussions are more likely to occur in situations that embrace opportunities for participation by all students, that promote acceptance and value personal responses, and that include strategy instruction for enhancing discussion (Raphael et al., 1996). Finally, to be effective, discussants need focus; otherwise, student talk tends to drift.

Most CRISS^{SM} strategies, particularly those described in this chapter, help students learn how to participate more effectively in discussion groups. Many of these activities work well as part of cooperative learning groups. In fact, we recommend using cooperative learning models along with CRISS^{SM} strategies. Given that an understanding of the specific ways to implement cooperative learning models in the classroom is beyond the scope of this book, we invite you to explore the work of Spencer Kagan (1994).

Conversations about content occur naturally when cooperative groups focus on accomplishing a task, such as developing a character map or conclusion-proof notes. When students take a moment to write about what they are thinking before sharing their ideas with a partner or small group, they are more likely to participate in the discussions that follow (as in Think-Pair-Share, Sticky-Note and Seed Discussions). In other situations, the focus might be on "authentic" questions that individual students have recorded in their journals, or questions that teams develop for discussion with the entire class (e.g., Question-Answer Relationships and critical-thinking questions). Students can also assume specific roles in their discussion groups or participate in reciprocal teaching. This chapter contains a variety of discussion options in which student talk, rather than teacher talk, remains central.

Discussion Rules: Before using any discussion strategies, it is important to establish some ground rules for student-led conversations. Develop these collaboratively with your class. Begin by specifying several which you feel are critical. Here are a few ideas:

- Listen to what your discussion partners have to say.
- Let each person complete his or her thought; do not interrupt.
- Repeat the main points of the previous speaker before making your own comment. Repeating another person's idea will help you listen and will also let the speaker know that you have heard his or her message.
- Challenge or support ideas, not people.
- Support your ideas with examples and facts from the materials you are reading.
- Keep an open mind.
- Make sure that everyone has a chance to talk.
- Look at the person who is speaking.

Post these rules in your classroom, so they can be referred to when necessary during discussion periods. Refine them as needed.

For ease of presentation, we have organized the discussion strategies in this chapter into several overlapping categories: paired discussion strategies, small group discussion strategies, questioning strategies, and combined strategies.

Paired Discussion Strategies

Think-Pair-Share

Think-Pair-Share is a particularly powerful discussion strategy (Kagan, 1989) that allows every student to become an active participant. It works well as a pre-reading activity, as a problem-solving strategy, as a break in a lecture, or as a follow-up activity. In each case, the procedure is similar.

Introduction, Modeling, and Reflection

1. The teacher begins by suggesting a topic or asking a question.
2. Students "think" and write down what they know or have learned about a particular topic.
3. After students have written, have them "pair" with another student or with a small group of students and share their ideas.
4. Conclude with a whole-class "share" discussion.
5. Discuss how these strategies exemplify CRISS℠ philosophy. Consider background knowledge, purpose setting, writing, and discussion. "How did this strategy help prepare you to read this assignment? How might you use this on our own? What CRISS℠ principles have we put into practice?"

Support and Extensions

- Students generate their own questions or topics and use them within cooperative groups or with the whole class.
- Use Think-Pair-Share in place of brainstorming.
- Use this strategy to prepare students for a writing assignment.

Additional Paired or Small Group Discussion Strategies

Mind Streaming

Students work in pairs to bring out their background knowledge about a topic:

- Student A talks for one minute about the topic.
- Student B listens and encourages student A.

The roles reverse:

- Student B talks for one minute about the topic.
- Student A listens and encourages student B.

Mind Streaming also works effectively as a post-reading/listening strategy in which students do one-minute paired retellings of what they have learned from a reading assignment, video, or lecture. Also, use Mind Streaming as a component of Think-Pair-Share. Students could "mind stream" after they have written down what they "think" they know about a topic.

ABC Brainstorming

Ask students to write the alphabet on a sheet of notebook paper. Then, working with a partner, ask them to brainstorm, before reading or listening, their background knowledge that begins with specific letters. Students can be assigned certain letters or can brainstorm ideas for the entire alphabet. After reading or listening, ask students to return to their ABC brainstorming. What can they now add? What can they verify as correct information? ABC brainstorming also works well as a pre-writing tool. Once writers have listed what they know, they can begin to focus their ideas.

Three-Minute Pause (Buehl, 2001)

Students stop while reading, watching a video, or listening to a lecture and turn to their partner or group for a three-minute pause. They (1) summarize what they have learned, then (2) identify something they found particularly interesting, and (3) ask any questions about confusing information and/or make a prediction about what they might learn next. Explain to students that pausing about every 10 to 15 minutes helps them "fix" new information in memory. Take time to guide students in metacognitive conversations about why stopping and reflecting upon what they are learning helps them learn and store new information. Why is hearing and viewing information not enough for constructing new meaning? How did discussions with a partner help them construct meaning? How might this strategy be useful in studying for a test?

Concentric Circle Discussion
(Kletzien and Baloche, 1994)

This modification of Seed Discussion (see "Small Group Discussion Strategies," this chapter) works well for reviewing content in whole-class groups or in groups of six or more. Ask each student to prepare an index card. On the index card, he or she reviews or explains a key concept. Students stand facing each other in two concentric circles.

1. Each student in the inside circle pairs with a student in the outside circle.
2. Both students use their cards to explain the concept to one another. (Give students a time limit of one to two minutes per person.)

3. The partners ask questions to make sure they understand the information.

4. After completing both explanations, the two students trade cards. The outside circle moves clockwise one person, and each student is now paired with a new partner.

5. Students must now explain the information described on the new card to a new partner. The process is repeated and students again get a new partner.

6. With small groups, the conversation can continue until students get their original card back.

With little teacher intervention, the students can review key concepts, offer personal interpretations, and review vocabulary. This is an excellent way to review for a test.

Read-and-Say-Something

Read-and-Say-Something is effective for difficult materials. Rather than letting students struggle with the meaning alone, have them work with a partner so they can grapple with meaning together.

Introduction, Modeling, and Reflection

1. Have students read their assignment silently, paragraph-by-paragraph or page-by-page. (More difficult assignments probably call for paragraph-by-paragraph reading.) Use sticky notes on longer selections.

2. After students have completed the paragraph or page, have them turn to their partner and say something. They can say anything they want related to the article. They react to ideas, descriptions, images, and confusing sections.

3. You will find that conversations about the meaning of the article occur naturally. You may want students to conclude this session by writing down questions they would like answered by the whole class or other teams.

4. Talk about how Read-and-Say-Something worked for them as readers. "How did this strategy help you untangle meaning? Were you more actively engaged? Did it help you to be more metacognitive?"

Support and Extensions

● Use this strategy as a way for students to review class notes. Have them read through their notes with a partner and then say something to one another.

● Incorporate Read-and-Say-Something as part of problem solving in mathematics.

● Discussions can focus on specific topics. For example, a language arts teacher might have students talk about descriptive writing; a history teacher might have students pay attention to issues regarding human rights.

● Use Read-and-Say-Something as a small group activity. The group chooses a leader.

The leader is the first to read a section—paragraph, half page, or whole page. (If the classroom is confining, students can whisper-read the article while the group members follow along with the written text.) Students who are not comfortable reading aloud in front of their peers can pass. However, all students participate in oral discussion.

After the leader has finished reading, the person directly to his or her right asks a question or makes a comment related to the section read.

All students must listen and participate by saying something. Any person in the group can answer the question or further the discussion.

The role of the leader is to make sure the discussion remains focused within the time frame of the lesson. The person to the right of the leader continues to read the next section. Again, the person on the right of the reader "says something." Continue the process until the reading is completed.

Learning Strategy

Discussion Web

As teachers, we know that classroom discussions encourage students to think. But involving everyone is difficult. We don't want the debate monopolized by a few vocal students. We want everyone to have an opportunity to rethink a topic, to challenge viewpoints, and to acknowledge arguments. The Discussion Web (Alvermann, 1991; Buehl, 2001) helps students untangle different points of view by actively involving everyone. It also helps them understand opposing sides of an issue.

Guided Comprehension

Introduction, Modeling, and Reflection

1. Model as a whole class discussion. Make a transparency of the Discussion Web organizer (Blackline 3). Begin with a controversial and familiar topic, one that you know will generate some "heat."

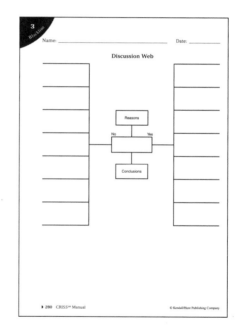

2. Write the question in the middle of the grid. (e.g., Should the Alaskan wilderness be opened for oil exploration? Should there be stronger gun control laws?) Then brainstorm opposing arguments (see example on page 60). Challenge students to take sides against their personal views.

3. Develop conclusions on both sides.

4. Then ask students to work in pairs and decide which conclusion seems more valid. Have each pair vote and come to a class consensus.

5. Conclude with a discussion about the strategy. "How did this strategy help you to analyse both sides of an issue? Were you able to take a more active role in the discussion? Did it help you organize your discussion?"

Discussion Web

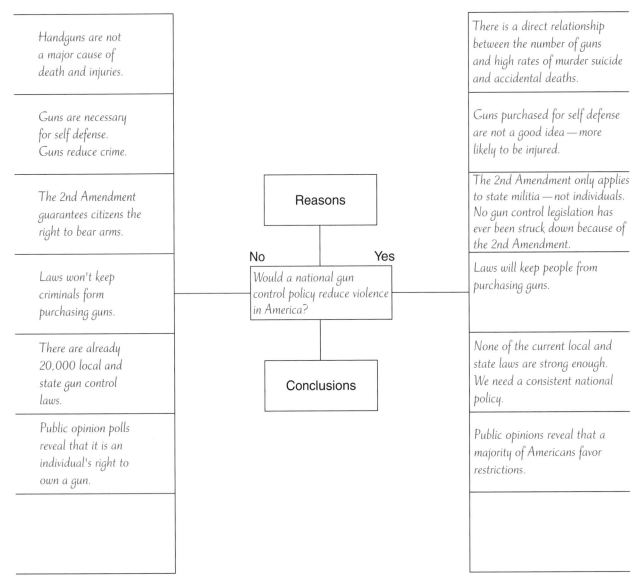

Support and Extensions

- Give students a reading selection containing opposing viewpoints and a copy of the Discussion Web to each pair of students. Activate background knowledge using strategies such as Think-Pair-Share or Mind Streaming.

  Provide a question over the selection that will generate opposing views. (Should gun control laws be strengthened? Should the United States government support subsidies to farmers? Should the state abandon state tests of mathematics and reading? Should wolves be protected?) Remind students to put aside their own opinions to ensure fair representation of both points of view.

  After students have completed their Discussion Web, itemizing support for both points of view, tell them to join another student pair. Working in groups of four, ask students to develop several conclusions or one conclusion which they think is most reasonable.

Then ask each group to present one conclusion to the whole class. They must explain the reasoning that led them to the conclusion.

Students can then use their notes to write an analytic essay.

❱ Small Group Discussion Strategies

Strategy

Learning

Sticky-Note Discussions

Sticky-note discussions work effectively when students are working in literature groups, reading word problems in mathematics, or dealing with challenging science and social studies materials. Ask students to use sticky notes as they read or after they have read a selection to mark the places they want to talk about. These might be sections about which they have questions, sections they especially enjoy, humorous bits, or an interesting or vivid description. Students should jot down on the sticky note some key words to help them remember why they marked the spot.

Guided Comprehension

Introduction, Modeling, and Reflection

1. Read aloud. When you come to a spot that you want to mark with a sticky note, explain why you are marking it. As you read and model, make a list of the kinds of things you noted. Some sample guidelines follow:

Guidelines for younger students in preparation for literature study groups:
- ❱ Questions that I have
- ❱ Parts that are beautifully written
- ❱ Places that make me sad, angry, laugh
- ❱ Parts that make me want to keep reading
- ❱ Parts where I learn more about the characters
- ❱ Places where I learn about where the story takes place

Guidelines for older students in preparation for literature study groups (elements of fiction):
- ❱ Tension: excitement, suspense, nervousness; anticipation that keeps us turning pages
- ❱ Character: conversations, actions; descriptions that teach us about the characters
- ❱ Place and time: descriptions that paint mind-pictures; sections creating time and place
- ❱ Mood: feelings of reader, characters; parts that arouse emotions
- ❱ Symbols: symbols contributing to mood, tension or resolution; what they represent
- ❱ Point of view: first or third person; how point of view influences thoughts and feelings about characters

---

Guidelines for non-fiction:
- ❱ Questions I have
- ❱ Places where I need more examples
- ❱ Powerful images to help me remember
- ❱ My opinions, feelings, reactions

---

2. Once students have the idea, you might suggest they mark one or two places per chapter. Limiting notes assists students in narrowing down significant areas and ensures that everyone participates more equally in sticky-note discussions. Students who have multitudes of items marked tend to dominate the discussion.

3. Begin sticky-note discussions as a whole class. Start by sharing a place that you have marked. Select one that will likely inspire the most discussion. Talk about why you marked it, and then ask students for any comments or reactions. This may launch a lively discussion, leading conversation to other ideas in and out of the text. Once the discussion is over, or if no real discussion has transpired, share another one of your noted areas.

4. Engage students in examining why sticky-note discussions help them become more involved in their reading than more traditional methods of teaching. "Would you prefer doing sticky-note discussions or reading the chapter and answering questions? How do you feel about discussing ideas in your groups? Do you understand the text better than if you had read it without any discussion?"

Support and Extensions

- Divide students into small groups and select one student to facilitate. After students have read and marked the selection, have the facilitator lead the discussion by going through the assignment page by page. Each student in the group talks about the parts he or she has marked.
- Have students use sticky notes to add to the author's text: illustrations, diagrams, examples from their own backgrounds, restatement of ideas.
- Use two or more colors of sticky notes:

    Argument notes: pink for information that supports opinion; blue for information that defeats opinion
    Vocabulary notes: pink for words they don't understand; blue for key math/science terms
    Question notes: yellow for questions to ask the author; blue for concepts that would make good test questions

Carousel Brainstorming

Carousel Brainstorming is a cooperative learning activity that involves students brainstorming in small groups. It can be used to bring out background knowledge and for review.

Introduction, Modeling, and Reflection

1. Pick about five related topics or concepts to determine your students' background knowledge. Write each topic on one piece of flip chart paper (at the top). Number the topics (1 through 5) and post them in order around your room.

2. Assign each student a number from one to five, then have all students move to the paper labelled with their assigned number. Give each group a different-colored marker to record their information.

3. Give the groups about one minute to write on the flip chart paper everything they know or have learned about the topic. If they are not sure about their information, they can write a "?" by it.

4. After one minute, the groups move to the topic with the next higher number (group 1 goes to topic 2, etc., and group 5 goes to topic 1). At the next topic,

they read what the other groups have written, make corrections or additions, and add any new information they know. As they move to each station, you might want to add a little more time for reading the preceding entries. All writing they do should be with their original colored marker (e.g., all of the groups 1's entries on the five topics are in red).

5. Continue this process until each group is back to its original number. After students have read what the other groups added to that topic, they move back to their seats, reading what has been added after their entry to each of the other four topics.

6. Have students reflect on what they have learned. Do they have questions of the other groups? Do they see connections between the topics? What else would they like to know? How did this strategy help them determine what they knew and did not know about the topic?

Support and Extensions

● Rather than having students write freely about their understanding of a concept, ask them to write a one-sentence summary over what they think is the most important information about each topic, and write on the chart. Follow the same carousel procedure until each group has added a summary sentence to the charts.

● Ask students to plan their own carousel brainstorming review. They determine the key topics, write them on the charts, and organize the groups.

Seed Discussions

One way to help students lead their own discussions is through Seed Discussions (Vallaume *et al.*, 1994). Students write down one important thing about what they are reading. Effective "seeds" grow into a discussion. Less effective seeds result in little discussion. Begin the discussion by having the author of the seed present the idea. Then everyone in the group comments on the idea before the next person presents a seed.

Introduction, Modeling, and Reflection

1. Explain to students that they will be leading their own Seed Discussions. Begin your introduction something like this: "While reading this book (assignment) you will be leading your own discussions. You aren't just going to answer my questions. Instead, you are to identify and develop topics important to your own thinking. As you read, think of one important thing to discuss. Write your discussion seed in your journal or on a card. We want strong seeds that will lead to lots of discussion about a topic. We'll do the first several seed assignments together."

2. Together, make a list of possibilities for seeds. Post them on a large chart so that students can refer to the suggestions:

   ❯ information or situations that I don't understand
   ❯ comments about what I have learned
   ❯ things that seem interesting or surprising
   ❯ vocabulary I want to know about
   ❯ descriptive writing I particularly enjoyed
   ❯ things that remind me of other things I know

3. Read aloud two or three pages and model your own discussion seeds. Model strong seeds and weak seeds. For example, seeds for the novel *Julie of the Wolves* might be:

Strong seed:
> I am not sure what this quote means: "Patience with the ways of nature had been instilled in her by her father." Discussions could center around what is meant by "ways of nature." How would patience relate to the "ways of nature?"

Weak seed:
> "Miyax is a pretty young girl." There is nothing to discuss here.

4. Begin the discussion by introducing one seed. Then have at least four students say something about the seed before the next one is introduced.

5. If little can be said about the seed, it means that the seed is not strong enough. Continue to model some strong and weak seeds.

6. Also model discussion behavior so students can respond to one another's comments:

> *"I really like what you said about. . ."*
> *"Do you have any other ideas about. . ."*
> *"I agree with you. . . but I also think. . ."*

7. Talk about the process. "How might Seed Discussions help you become a better reader? How did you feel about being a part of a Seed Discussion group? How does this strategy help you to become more actively engaged in your reading?"

Support and Extensions

● After modeling with the whole class, divide students into groups of four. Begin by asking one group to come to the front of the room and do a demonstration for the whole class; then have groups lead their own discussions.

Roles:

Leader—Responsible for calling on each person to share his or her discussion seeds.

Manager—Makes sure that everyone has all necessary materials for the discussion (books, journals, cards, etc.).

Checker—Makes sure that everyone has a chance to talk about his or her seeds. Everyone in the group comments on the seed before the next person presents a seed for discussion.

Communicator—Lets the teacher know when the discussion is complete. The communicator is the only person to leave the group.

● You might want to incorporate sticky notes along with the seeds. Students could put sticky notes on places that would make good discussion seeds.

Roles within Cooperative Teams

Harvey Daniels (1994) presents another tool for assisting students with discussion by assigning members of a discussion group specific roles. Roles combine a variety of strategies within a discussion group. Each group member takes on a role before reading and then comes to the group prepared to take on a specific task.

The chart on the following page shows a series of discussion roles modeled after Daniels' work, with modification to incorporate CRISS^{SM} strategies. This particular example was written by Steve Qunell, a social studies teacher who assigned roles to guide discussion about reading assignments in his government class at Montana Academy. In this case, his students read Orwell's *1984*. For a complete copy of his role sheet, adaptable to a variety of content situations, see Blackline 4. For elementary versions of role possibilities, see Blacklines 5–10.

Social Studies Adaptation

Role	Description
Discussion Director	Lead the group in discussion of questions assigned by the teacher or develop own questions.
Bridge Builder	Help the group make connections. What connections can you make between this reading and your own world? What bridges can you build? "This reminds me of. . ."
Quote Finder	Find important, memorable sections or quotes to read out loud to the group. These selections might be: well-written, confusing, powerful, surprising, interesting.
Illustrator	Provide a graphic or artistic response to the text through drawings, pictures, political cartoons. Show your picture to the others in your group. Ask them what they think it might mean. After everyone has had a chance to talk, tell them what you think.
Summarizer	Prepare a brief, written summary of (at least one full paragraph) the assigned reading. Present the summary to your group.
Vocabulary Expert	Find and share complicated or important words. Include at least five words from the reading; provide their definitions from the glossary, and explain how words were used in the text.

Introduction, Modeling, and Reflection

1. Teach and model each role with the whole class before using the roles in small group discussions. Students need to feel comfortable with all the roles you plan to use before they try them on their own in their discussion groups.

2. First, teach the role of Discussion Director to everyone. The Discussion Director develops four or five open-ended questions over the reading as a way to get the discussion going. In some cases, the Discussion Director might be responsible for engaging his or her group in a discussion of teacher-developed questions. (See Blackline 4)

3. Model how to develop questions from the reading. Remind students about QARs and authentic questions. (See "Questioning Strategies" in this chapter.)

4. Model how to use questions in small-group discussion. Bring four students to the front of the class and have each in turn ask one question to the rest of the group. When the discussion has run its logical course, divide the remainder of the class into groups of four and have them use their own questions to conduct discussions.

5. Follow a similar procedure for introducing the other roles you plan to use. Once students feel comfortable with roles you have selected, they are ready to apply them within their groups during or after reading their assignment.

6. Ask students how their discussion went.

Did everyone participate?
Was everyone prepared?
Were you willing to share tentative ideas?
Did you ask questions of one another?
Did you give reasons for your opinions?
Were you able to make connections with the world, with other texts, with yourself?

Support and Extensions

● Adapt the discussion roles for other contents.

Mathematics Adaptation

Role	Description
Discussion Director	Lead the group in discussion of questions assigned by the teacher or provided by the author, or develop your own questions over confusing concepts and processes.
Bridge Builder	Help the group make connections to math concepts which have been learned earlier in this class or in previous classes. What bridges or applications can you make between this information and the "real" world?
Example Finder and Creator	Find good examples that help clarify information in this section. Create your own examples for each concept.
Vocabulary Expert	Find and share complicated or important terms and vocabulary concepts. Have at least five words from the reading. When it is your turn to lead the discussion, have everyone find the word in their reading and then talk about what the word might mean. After your discussion, write down what you think the word means from context, and then add additional examples and/or information about the word from the glossary.
Process Server	Pay attention to processes and procedures in the section. Be prepared to share an application of the process or procedure that you have created.
Illustrator	Provide a graphic or artistic representation of the key ideas and processes in the text. Show your illustrations to the others in your group. Ask them to interpret your diagrams and tell how they relate to the major concepts and processes in the text.

- Have students develop their own roles and create their own role sheets. Encourage students to use CRISS^{SM} strategies as roles: developing opinion-support notes, problem-solution notes, or content frames. In other situations, one student might be prepared with sticky notes, another with a discussion seed, a visualization, authentic questions, or a summary statement. Practically all of the strategies described in this chapter would work well to define a role. The roles differ according to what students have experienced and the kind of assignment they are reading. Once students understand the different roles, each student in a group can take on a different role within the group. Ask students to give oral presentations using information from their discussions.

◗ Questioning Strategies

The role of questions in teaching has a rich research history that provides some intriguing insights useful for guiding our teaching. One conclusion deals with the sheer quantity of questions teachers tend to ask in their classrooms. Did you know that teacher questioning accounts for about 80% of classroom time? Yet most teachers remain unaware of just how much their own questioning dominates classroom interactions. For example, Nash and Shiman (1974), as reported in Marzano *et al.* (2001), found that elementary-school teachers, who thought they were asking 12 to 20 questions per hour, were actually asking from 45 to 150 questions an hour. Years later, Fillippino (1998), in Marzano *et al.* (2001), documented the same result.

Another insight comes from studies on the types of questions teachers tend to ask (Marzano *et al.* 2001). Researchers conclude that higher-level thinking questions—those that require students to apply knowledge or restructure information—produce deeper learning than questions focusing on lower-level factual information. These results seem logical. Unfortunately, researchers have also concluded that a majority of teachers ask mostly lower-level questions. So, the research tells us that teachers flood their classrooms with endless low-level questions, which tend to create passive, insipid learning. Kinda scary! Keep these results in mind.

Further insight comes from studies on the relationship between questioning and wait-time, which is the amount of time teachers wait for students to respond after asking a question. Longer is better! Not only is this common sense, but brain researchers have documented that our brains need time to retrieve and organize information. How many times have we caught ourselves quickly answering our own questions without giving students an opportunity to respond? Yet, when teachers pause several seconds after asking a question, allowing students time to think, their answers tend to be far richer and much more extensive. Wait-time also increases student-to-student interaction and stimulates more discussion (Marazano *et al.*, 2001). So we have to keep reminding ourselves not to jump in so quickly. It is okay to wait, even if the quiet feels a little uncomfortable.

One final issue focuses on who is asking the question: Which questioning approach leads to better comprehension? Should teachers ask the questions or should students generate their own? The best answer is: it depends.

If your goal is for students to know specific information from their reading, ask them a question about it. Teacher questions do help readers focus on particular content and lead to improved comprehension and memory for specifics.

However, if you seek more generalized improvement in comprehension—beyond the content of particular questions—and want students to become more independent, then teach them how to ask their own questions (Trebasso, 2002). When students generate questions about what they are reading (particularly *why* and *how* questions), they actively process text information and monitor their understanding. Some evidence suggests that teaching students how to ask their own questions leads to improvement on standardized test performance (Trebasso, 2002). Two implications arise from this body of research. First, question generation during reading is an important strategy for improving comprehension; second, students need to learn about effective questioning strategies. This instruction should include teacher modeling and guided practice, as well as opportunities for readers to practice developing questions with teacher feedback (Rosenshine *et al.,* 1996; Raphael *et al.,* 1982, 1984). With this brief overview, let's turn to some practical ways to implement effective questioning practices in our classrooms.

Strategy

Learning

Authentic Questions

In most situations, there is no one set of questions to ask every reader. Individual readers have their own ideas and their own questions. As students read or listen, have them record questions about material they do not understand. These are authentic or genuine questions that come to mind during reading. We want our students to know that all good readers have questions when they read. Having questions is not a sign of comprehension failure. It signifies a successful reader, who monitors his or her own comprehension.

Guided Comprehension

Introduction, Modeling, and Reflection

1. As you read aloud, talk about questions that come to mind. Explain that all good readers have questions when they read. Model a variety of questions that deal with (1) difficult vocabulary, (2) why a person did something or why something happened, (3) how a situation evolved, (4) what will happen next, and (5) who did what and why. As you continue to read and model, point out if the author answers any of your questions.

2. Ask students to read a selection and come up with questions. Accept every response.

3. Write some of their questions on the board and discuss possible answers. They may not be able to answer some of the questions.

4. Ask students to record in their journals or on a separate sheet of paper any unanswered questions as they read.

   Science Example.   As students completed a science experiment investigating mold, they developed questions leading to additional investigations.

   Would bread made with yogurt have different mold?
   Do different kinds of mold grow on fruit and vegetables?

Language Arts Example. In the example below, reading buddies reread a chapter in *Bridge to Terabithia* and wrote questions about things they did not understand. They asked their questions in cooperative team discussions.

Chapter	My Question
1.	Where do they live? city, state
2.	Where does his dad work? Washington D.C.
3.	Why does Mrs. Myers smile only on the first ³ the
4.	Why doesn't Leslie have T.V.? last
5.	Why does Janice Avery think she's so tough? Day?
6.	Why does Mrs. Aarons think Ellie is the Best?
7.	Why does Janice's Dad beat her?
8.	Why did Jess's dad get laid off?
9.	Why does Leslie call her parents by their 1st names
10.	How did Leslie die? ?
11.	Why did Jess say he didn't believe them?
12.	Why did Jess threw his present from Leslie in
13.	Why did Jess make Mary Belle Queen the creek
14.	of Terabitha
15.	Excellent questions Alison
16.	

5. Ask students why self-questioning is critical for all learning. "Why are the questions you have more important for your learning than another person's questions? How does self-questioning help you become more metacognitive? Were you a more active learner when you generated your own questions compared to answering another's questions?"

Support and Extensions

● Demonstrate the importance of student-generated questions by using them for discussions or essay questions. Once students realize their questions are taken seriously and that it's safe to ask questions, authentic questions will become more a part of their response to reading. As a result, discussions will become richer and more student-centered.
● Use authentic questions with all content areas.

Question-Answer Relationships

In the 1980s, Taffy Raphael (Raphael and McKinney, 1983; Raphael and Wonnacott, 1985) developed an important technique to help students identify sources of information for writing and answering questions. She considered this question: If students know how questions are written—in other words, if they understand the "craft of question-writing"—will they become more proficient at answering and asking questions? To test this, she ingeniously simplified the world of questioning into two broad categories: **In the Book**—text-explicit questions—and **In my Head**—text-implicit question. Information for generating text-explicit questions and answers is found directly in the text. She then distinguished between *Right There* and *Think and Search* text-explicit questions. Similarly, she classified text-implicit questions as either *Author and You* or *On my Own*. See Blackline 11.

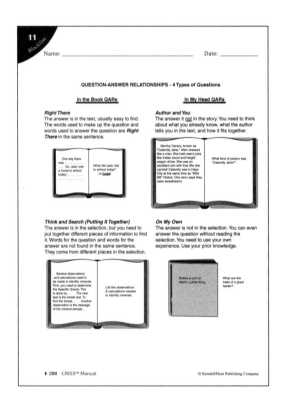

Raphael taught this system, which she termed **Question-Answer Relationships (QARs),** to her students. Once students became proficient in using **QARs** for writing and analyzing questions, they answered questions significantly better than students who lacked this understanding.

Introduction, Modeling, and Reflection

1. Introduce QARs with a reading selection. Use the "popcorn" example or a selection of your choice. Explain to students that you are going to teach them about questions. "There are four general types of questions. If you know these four general types, you will not only be able to ask better questions, but you will also be able to answer questions more easily."

2. Explain that you are going to be the "teacher" first and demonstrate how to develop questions based on the QAR framework. Make sure that each student has access to a copy of the framework (Blackine 11).

3. Go over the framework. Your explanation might sound something like this: "You can divide questions into two types—**In the Book** and **In my Head.** The answers to **In the Book** questions are found in the book.

   "Notice that there are two kinds of **In the Book** questions—*Right There* and *Think and Search.* The answers to *Right There* questions are found in one sentence in the selection. *Right There* questions are easy and require very little thought. You just have to find the relevant sentence in the book. (How is popping corn different from regular corn?)

"Another type of **In the Book** question is *Think and Search*. These are a little bit harder because to find the total answer you have to incorporate information from more than one place in the selection. You won't find it all in the same sentence. (Model an example: How can popcorn be a healthy snack? Or, why does popcorn pop?)

"**In My Head** questions force you to work harder than **In the Book** questions. There are two types of **In My Head** questions, *Author and You* and *On My Own*. To answer *Author and You* questions, you have to take what you know from the story and think about it. You can't find the answer in the book, but you have to read the story in order to answer the question. (For example: Why do you think popcorn has become such a popular snack in our country? Has the author convinced you to eat popcorn as a snack? Why?)

"The answers to *On My Own* questions come directly from your own head. It helps to read the story because it helps you think about what you already know, but you don't have to read the story to answer this sort of question. (Example: Why is it important to eat healthy snacks?) Point out to students that *On My Own* questions are useful for bringing out background knowledge before reading.

4. After modeling several questions of each type, explain to the students that you are not going to lead the discussion over the selection. They are. Explain that it is better for them to ask their own questions than to answer your questions. They will understand more and become better readers by asking questions. Ask them to take turns being the teacher, leading their own discussions over the selection.

5. Select a few pages of content text. Divide students into cooperative teams. Have each team produce examples of the four types of questions. Then have each team present their questions to the class. Use the following steps:
   a. Have one team read the question without telling what type it is.
   b. Don't ask for the answer first. Ask the class to tell you the type of question it is.
   c. Make sure students tell you why it is a certain type of question. Ask them to justify their answer by explaining why the question fits into one of the four categories.
   d. Finally, have students answer the question.
   A discussion of the type of question is more important than the answer. So make sure that students explain why a question fits a certain category before they answer it. Remember—the type of question determines the type of answer.

   Justifying the answer always produces lively debate, particularly if the question happens to be a *Think and Search* or *Author and You* type. Often students have valid arguments supporting a question as both. In the end, it does not really matter if a particular question fits within a specific category. It is the thinking that occurs in justifying answers that is important. The process is far more important than the end result. If students are upset with the ambiguity, have them rewrite the question so it can only be interpreted one way.

6. Throughout these teaching sequences, encourage students to talk about how QARs help them become more proficient in analysing and in asking questions. QAR's take the mystery out of responding to the comprehension passages on state assessment tests and on the ACT and SAT college entrance exams.

Support and Extensions

- After students understand how to develop questions and have practice holding discussions as a whole class, small groups are ready to begin leading their own discussions.
- Have students prepare questions individually as they read. They should bring their questions to group discussions.
- If students are writing questions in their journals as they read, they can go back and classify the types of questions they have written. The QARs provide students with a system for evaluating their own questions. If students find that most of their questions are *Right There* and *Think and Search,* challenge them to come up with other higher-level questions as they read. Most students will realize that authentic questions are usually *Author and You.*
- QARs work well for content materials as shown in the following math/science example.

Students formulated QARs from a graph developed from a coordinated project in science and math classes. Students surveyed 116 students in four math and science classes about recycling in their homes. After compiling the data and summarizing it in a graph, students developed questions following the QAR format for discussion.

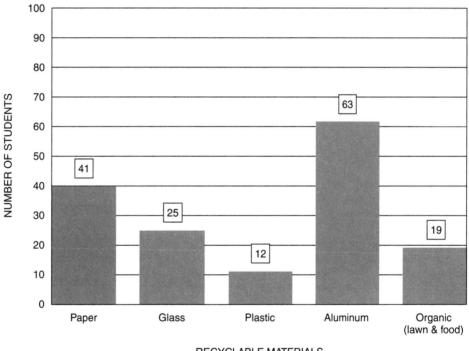

Right There: How many students reported that their families recycled glass? (The answer is found in one place on the graph.)

Think and Search: What are the different materials that people are recycling in this town? (The answer is directly in the graph, but from different locations on the graph.)

Author and You: How many more people recycle aluminum than plastic? (The author doesn't give you this answer. You have to use your own knowledge and the process of subtraction.)

On my Own: Why do you think more people recycle aluminum than other re-cyclable materials? (The answer is not on the graph. You have to use your own background knowledge to answer this question. Answers will vary.)

QARs also work for the humanities as shown in the following examples in art and music:

	Art	**Music**
Right There	What is the subject of the painting?	What kind of music is this—band, orchestra, piano?
Think and Search	What colors did the artist use?	What instruments do you hear throughout this piece?
Author and You	How did the painter show perspective in this piece? What feelings do you think the artist was trying to convey?	What feelings do you think the composer was trying to convey? How did the composer create feeling?
On Your Own?	If you made a living as a painter, what medium would you use? Why?	If you could play any instrument, what would it be and why?

● The definitions of QARs can be altered for specific needs. For example, McIntosh and Draper (1995) modified the four types of questions to make them more applicable for mathematics students.

Right There—The answer is right there in the text in the same sentence. Ex-ample: "State the slide model for addition." Ans. "The slide model for addi-tion is. . ." (right from the text)
Think and Search—The question is just like an example in the text, only the numbers are different. Example: The text shows an example of how to simplify $-3 + -x + 7$. The Think and Search QAR would be, "Simplify $-2 + y + -9$"
Author & You—The author has given you information in the text that you have to put together with what you already know (perhaps from previous sections or chapters) to get an answer. Example: After learning how to simplify (as in the Think and Search example above), the author shows students how to solve simple equations like $x + 6 = 10$, and $17 - y = 12$. An Author and You ques-tion might be, "Solve $-3 + t - 4 = 0$"
On My Own—The answers to these questions are not in the book at all. These questions ask you to think about and use your own experience. Example: "Negative numbers appear on television in many situations. What real situa-tion might each negative number represent? a) -1.32 in stock market aver-ages, b) -9 in rocket launches, c) -3 in golf."

● QARs can help students prepare for standardized tests. Include QARs in preparing for state assessments. Have students practice categorizing ques-tions on sample tests. Knowing the type of questions used on standardized tests helps students perform better and reduces test-taking anxiety.

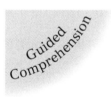

Questions and Higher Levels of Thinking

Consider using a modified version of Bloom's taxonomy as a system for teaching students to ask their own questions. Rather than eight levels of thinking, there are five (recall, analysis, comparison, inference, and evaluation), and each of these can be readily taught to students.

Recall. Recall means recognizing or remembering key facts, definitions, rules, and principles. Recall questions require one to retell or repeat information. (*Right There* questions are examples of recall.)

Analysis. Analysis means dividing a whole into smaller parts. This might be separating main ideas and details or organizing information into clusters and frames. (*Think and Search* questions require analysis.)

Comparison. Comparison means explaining similarities and differences between two or more things.

Inference. Inference involves predictions, requiring both deductive and inductive reasoning. In deductive tasks, there is a general statement and details that relate to it. Main ideas followed by supporting details constitute a *deductive* task. *Inductive* tasks involve the opposite sequence. One generates or induces the main idea from the details. With inductive thinking you have the evidence or details and must come up with the generalization. (*Author and You*)

Evaluation. In an evaluation, one arrives at a conclusion and then provides supporting reasons and evidence. (*Author and You*)

Introduction, Modeling, and Reflection

1. Introduce students to the taxonomy. Give students the description of the levels of thinking or post an abbreviated version of the definitions on a chart.
2. Explain that you will be teaching them a system for asking questions that taps into higher levels of thinking. Then, using a common reading selection, model several questions representing each level.
3. Hold process discussions about how higher level questions help to focus on the essential understanding rather than superficial information.

Support and Extensions

● You can also post or give students a copy of action words to use as question starters. Students can use these words to develop their own higher-level questions.

- Give small groups a copy of the question frames (Blackline 12). Have them choose a topic they know about (e.g., sport, hobby, music). Using this topic, have each team develop five questions to present to the whole class.
- Students can use these frames to develop questions about a reading assignment.

Name: _____ Date: _____

Question Starters & Frames for Higher-Level Questions

Recall: *who, what, list, repeat, identify, name, when, define*

What is _____ ?

Define _____ .

Identify the _____ .

Who did _____ ?

Analysis: *summarize, categorize, divide, separate*

What is the main idea of _____ ?

List the main events of _____ .

What are the parts of a _____ ?

What is the topic of _____ ?

Comparison: *differentiate, compare, contrast*

Compare ___X___ to ___Y___ . In what ways are they similar?

How does ___X___ differ from ___Y___ ?

Inference: *predict, conclude, what if, anticipate, infer*

What do you think will happen next in _____ ?

What do you conclude about _____ ?

Predict what _____ will do.

What would happen if _____ ?

Evaluation: *judge, defend, prove, assess, evaluate*

What is your opinion of _____ ?

What is the best solution to the problem of _____ ?

Evaluate the writing of _____ .

Defend your opinion about _____ .

© Kendall/Hunt Publishing Company   CRISS™ Manual 289 ◀

▶ Combined Strategies

Reciprocal Teaching

Learning Strategy

It is no accident that we introduce reciprocal teaching as the final strategy in this chapter. It includes a transactional model of teaching in combination with four powerful comprehension strategies: summarizing, questioning, noting difficult parts, and predicting. Reciprocal teaching is one of the most promising instructional paradigms to emerge in the last twenty years.

Ann Marie Palinscar and her colleagues (1984, 1986) have evaluated this procedure in a variety of content settings. In all instances, they found that students who participated in reciprocal teaching made far greater gains in reading comprehension than did students who used more traditional approaches. A decade later, Rosenshine and Meister (1994) conducted an extensive review of recent work on reciprocal teaching and found that its effectiveness increased as students progressed. It appears that multiple strategy instruction becomes increasingly important as students face escalating academic demands. Moreover, weaker students benefit most from reciprocal teaching (Trebasso and Bouchard, 2002).

The positive effects of reciprocal teaching also transfer to peer teaching. Teachers trained seventh-grade tutors to carry out these four activities with their tutees. Tutors and tutees both made substantial gains in comprehension. Palinscar and her colleagues also found that the tutors became very effective in modeling and in providing specific feedback to their tutees.

The teacher begins by doing much of the work, but instruction shifts as the reader takes on more and more responsibility. The teacher continues to provide support as needed through praising, prompting, additional modeling, and coaching. When students become more adept at these four skills, they instruct one another. The reading materials are the students' own content texts or materials.

Introduction, Modeling, and Reflection

1. Begin with a section of your content text which contains a series of well-written paragraphs.

2. Tell students that you are going to demonstrate four different strategies: summarizing, questioning, noting difficulties, and predicting.

3. Read through the first paragraph. In two sentences, summarize the gist of the material. Talk about how you developed your summary.

4. Ask a question about the paragraph's content. Discuss what you did to come up with your question.

5. Note any difficult vocabulary or unclear statements in the paragraph, and comment about what you think they mean. Ask students if they have any other questions that need clearing up.

6. Predict what you think you might learn in the next several paragraphs.

7. Continue modeling over a period of several days until students are comfortable with the strategies.

8. After modeling, ask a student to be the teacher and do the four-strategy sequence with the next paragraph. Provide feedback about the summaries, questions, and predictions.

9. Other students and the teacher answer the questions and provide alternative questions, summaries, and predictions.

10. Students take turns being teacher until the reading assignment is complete.

11. Have students work in pairs and take turns using the four strategies.

12. Take time for process conferences. "How did reciprocal teaching help you read and understand better? How does reciprocal teaching help us become more metacognitive? How does discussion and collaboration help you understand more? What have you learned from our work with reciprocal teaching that you can immediately apply when reading on your own?"

Support and Extensions

- Include Question-Answer Relationships in a reciprocal teaching paradigm. Students take turns asking one another questions following the QAR model.
- Use reciprocal teaching as a whole class, with small groups, and in one-on-one tutorials with students who need extra help with reading. Use reciprocal teaching as a component of Special Education and Title 1 programs.
- Use reciprocal teaching on sample tests in preparation for state reading assessments and standardized exams such as the SAT and PSAT. After students have processed a reading selection using reciprocal teaching, have them answer the test questions.

▶ Summary

Discussion enriches comprehension. When readers have an opportunity to discuss their interpretations, meaning is made for all. True discussion is an open exchange of ideas and questions, which may not have easy answers. These exchanges are quite different from teacher-directed recitation in which instructors ask the questions, do most of the talking, and limit student-to-student conversation.

The strategies described in this chapter assist students in leading their own discussions. Think-Pair-Share, Sticky-Note Discussions, Read-and-Say-Something, Seed Discussions, and the Discussion Web inspire students to take the lead in instructional conversations. Additional strategies focus more directly on helping students develop their own questions for discussion. Authentic questions, QARs, and questions highlighting different levels of thinking assist students with their own critical inquiries. Reciprocal teaching incorporates an instructional model that exemplifies CRISS^{SM} philosophy as teachers guide students in taking more and more responsibility for their own strategic comprehension. When students have opportunities to untangle meaning from text and to talk about their insights and questions, you will have "grand conversations" in your classroom (Peterson, 1990).

Research Conclusion	Reference
Discussion promotes deep understanding of text, leads to higher-levels of thinking and problem solving, and improves communication skills.	Gambrell, 1996
Student-led discussions foster greater student participation than those led by teachers, and such discussions improve communication skills, including the ability to take different points of view.	Almasi, 1995
Effective discussions are more likely to occur in situations where students learn discussion strategies.	Raphael, et al., 1996

CHAPTER

5

Active Strategies for Learning

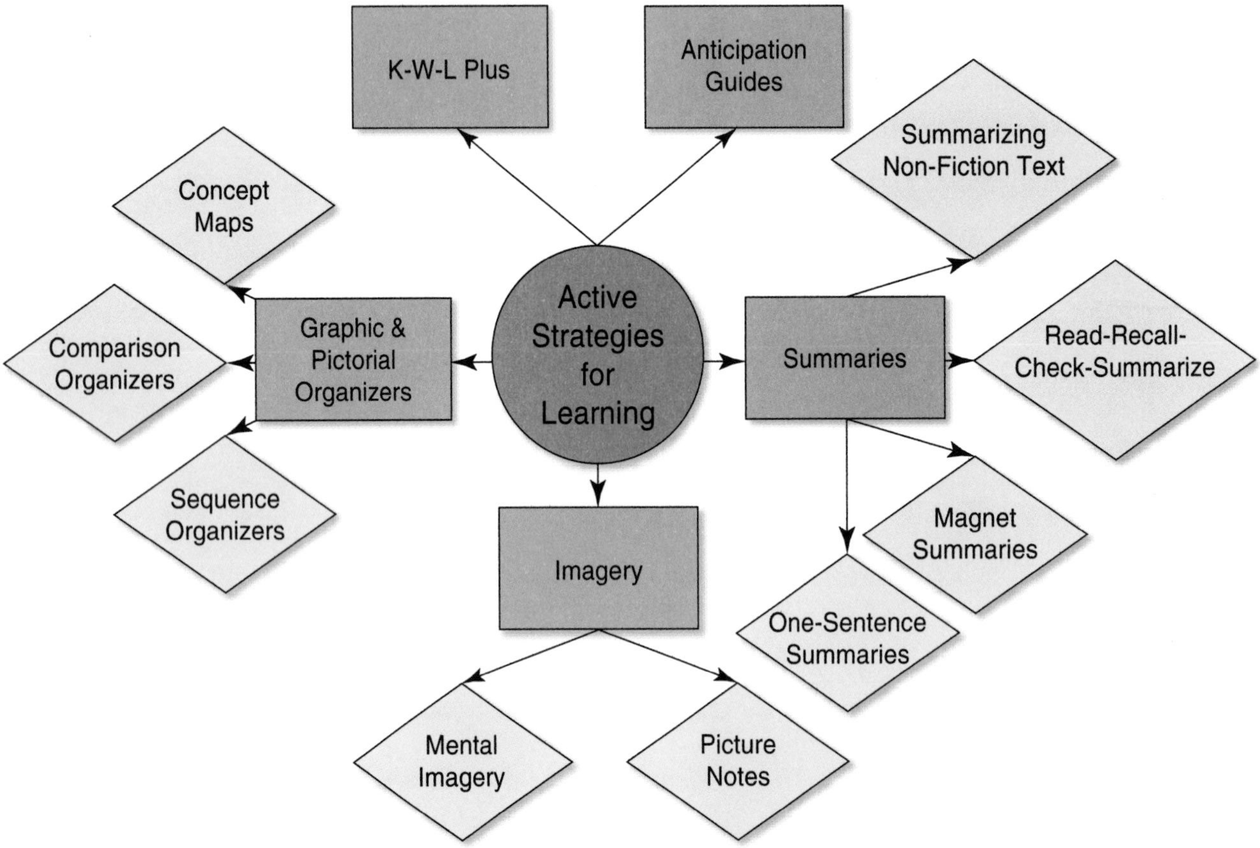
K-W-L Plus
Anticipation Guides
Summarizing Non-Fiction Text
Concept Maps
Active Strategies for Learning
Graphic & Pictorial Organizers
Summaries
Read-Recall-Check-Summarize
Comparison Organizers
Sequence Organizers
Imagery
Magnet Summaries
One-Sentence Summaries
Mental Imagery
Picture Notes

Before beginning a discussion of comprehension and learning strategies, let's take a moment to think about Dolores Durkin's classic article on reading comprehension published in *Reading Research Quarterly* in the late 1970s. Her research uncovered how little comprehension instruction actually occurred in classrooms. Teachers assigned, questioned, and lectured students about the content, but did little to show them how to understand and learn new information. They assessed, but did not teach, comprehension. Durkin's study helped initiate a boom in research and instructional efforts that continued through the 1980s and early '90s—a boom which focused on instructional strategies for helping students comprehend and retain information from their reading. The effects were particularly striking with poor readers. When students had opportunities to learn *how* to comprehend and learn, they did far better on all kinds of reading and learning tasks.

Two decades of research provide overwhelming evidence that students can be taught how to use comprehension strategies. Has this led to changes in classroom instruction? One would assume so, given this convincing evidence and the pressure of high-stakes assessments, which focus primarily on reading comprehension. Yet, the data tell us otherwise. Michael Pressley and his colleagues (Pressley, 2002) note that little has changed since the time of Durkin's study. In extending Durkin's work, Pressley and his colleagues noted many effective literacy practices, but hardly any comprehension instruction. Even teachers identified as exemplary did little teaching of comprehension.

We all know that assigning activities is not the same thing as teaching them. CRISS^{SM} is strategic teaching!

It is difficult to present the strategic strategies in this book as a cohesive whole, rather than as discrete skills. CRISS^{SM} is a teaching philosophy, not a compilation of strategies that students learn one-by-one. But in order to explain the strategies which comprise CRISS^{SM}, putting its principles into practice, we have to present them one at a time. Don't be confused about this. Just keep in mind as you read this book that CRISS^{SM} strategies become ways of philosophically transforming classrooms. They mix and flow together as part of the CRISS^{SM} Strategic Learning Plan. Always think about how these strategies might work before, during, and after students read.

To put strategic instruction into a classroom context, we start this chapter with a picture of what strategic instruction looks like in a classroom. Beginning with the whole helps to show how the various pieces fit together. So, let's step inside Sue Dailey's classroom and see what the whole looks like.

Sue, one of our National Trainers, teaches Montana History to seventh graders in Kalispell, Montana. She has developed an innovative curriculum particularly conducive to teaching students how to comprehend and learn. She aims to create in her seventh graders a desire to read and learn content. She knows that students must be engaged in what they are learning, or they won't choose to comprehend. And comprehension cannot be forced.

Therefore, Sue clusters the material in her curriculum into broad themes of study, such as explorations, ranching, and homesteading. Thematic study offers students an opportunity for in-depth learning focusing on big questions—which are far more interesting than leaping from topic to topic, detail by detail in a social studies text. For each thematic area students explore essential questions by reading a variety of engaging texts, including fiction and nonfiction literature, old newspapers, and journals. Students enjoy reading these complete works more than excerpted literature or textbooks.

She starts by directly teaching her students CRISS[SM] theory. In fact, she presents the same information we give to teachers in our Level 1 CRISS[SM] workshop. Sue wants her students to understand fundamental principles of learning, so they can think metacognitively about how background knowledge, active learning, organization, writing, and discussion influence their learning.

As part of the curriculum, Sue incorporates teacher modeling and guided practice of learning strategies. For example, she models how to preview assignments, how to activate background knowledge, and how to organize background information into categories and purpose questions. She shows students what good readers do when they comprehend by making explicit what is too often implicit. Sue models her own active reading by generating questions, clarifying ideas, and summarizing key information. She demonstrates how she stops to make predictions and to write down important information. After teaching a particular strategy, she guides students as they practice in small groups. In her classroom, talk about process is as important as talk about content.

Using a transparency of a reading selection, Sue models how to reduce information to essential ideas by underlining and summarizing, and by distilling information from a variety of texts into concept maps and charts. She then shows her students how to predict exam questions and test themselves over content. As students practice strategies, they talk and write about what they are learning as well as how they are learning it.

With CRISS[SM] philosophy and strategies in mind, let's think about what Sue does to infuse her curriculum with the teaching of comprehension skills and study strategies. Before students read, she asks them to talk and write about what they know about the themes and topics they are about to study. Asking about what they already know helps engage students and provides an organizational framework for new information.

During and after reading, Sue models a variety of ways to organize or transform new information. Organization strategies (such as two-column notes, charts, concept maps, or conclusion-support papers) require students to process new information actively as they fit it into old organizational schemes or create new schemes to make sense of the new information.

Throughout this process, Sue explicitly teaches students how to test themselves in order to measure the information they have mastered. Self-testing requires that they use their personal backgrounds and perspectives to integrate a variety of materials. Students also write position papers, poems, and plays, incorporating their new knowledge. Continual process conferences allow Sue to guide students as they talk about how they are using CRISS[SM] principles in their own learning and how particular strategies are working for each of them.

As shown in this example, CRISS[SM] teaching goes beyond the presentation of a series of strategies. CRISS[SM] shows how to use strategic instruction to help students engage in texts and learning before, during, and after reading. Strategies intertwine and flow cradled in CRISS[SM] philosophy and principles. With this in mind, we are now ready for this chapter's presentation of CRISS[SM] strategies.

Know–Want to Know–Learned Plus (K–W–L +)

Donna Ogle's K-W-L+ (1986, 2002) is a classic in strategy instruction. Teachers from all content areas successfully incorporate and modify K-W-L+ in their elementary and high school classrooms. This lesson sequence incorporates every aspect of CRISS℠ theory as part of three reading phases: (1) Students brainstorm what they **know** (K) about the topic, (2) generate questions about what they **want** to know (W), and then record what they **learned** (L). Students then do the "plus" part of the sequence, transforming the information into a concept map and writing a summary. The K-W-L chart (see Blackline 13) is a graphic organizer that can be used with a whole class, small group, or an individual as a pre-reading, during-reading, and post-reading study guide.

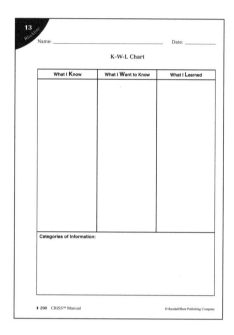

After completing the K-W-L + process, the teacher leads students in a discussion, helping them to analyze the framework's effectiveness. Students can readily see the strategy exemplifies the major tenets of the CRISS℠ philosophy: generating background knowledge (**K**now); setting purposes (**W**ant); transforming information, writing, and talking (**L**earned). Students also talk about how the Learned portion of the chart provides a natural way for them to monitor their comprehension. Finally, by transforming the information again through construction of a concept map (+) and writing (+), students do an additional metacognitive check.

Process conferences such as these transfer ownership from the teacher to the student. They're essential!

Introduction, Modeling, and Reflection

1. Choose a reading selection from your class materials.
2. List the topic (Power 1) and/or key vocabulary from the reading assignment on the board or chart as in the health example that follows. (You might want to use a chart similar to Blackline 13 for generating and organizing information.)

3. Ask students to tell what they know about a topic (Power 3 information). List their ideas on the overhead or in the first column (K) of the chart (Blackline 13). Alternatively, incorporate "Think-Pair-Share" (see Chapter 4), in which students write down what they know in their journals and then share their ideas with a partner. After partner sharing, initiate a whole-group discussion.

In the example that follows, Peggy Johns asked ninth graders to read an article, "Fruits and Vegetables, the Healthy Snack." They brainstormed the following information:

Topic: Fruits and Vegetables

What I **Know**	What I **Want to know**	What I **Learned**
▶ Many different fruits and vegetables available ▶ Contain many vitamins ▶ Vegetables and fruits should be eaten every day ▶ They are good for your body ▶ They are low in fat and calories ▶ Can be found fresh or canned ▶ Can be found in solid or juice form ▶ Found all over the world		

Categories of Information:

4. Categorize this Power 3 information. Find ideas that go together. Come up with Power 2 headings or categories (see Chapter 3) that describe the ideas. Place these categories on the K-W-L Chart.

Topic: Fruits and Vegetables

What I **K**now	What I **W**ant to know	What I **L**earned
▶ Many different fruits and vegetables available ▶ Contain many vitamins ▶ Vegetables and fruits should be eaten every day ▶ They are good for your body ▶ They are low in fat and calories ▶ Can be found fresh or canned ▶ Can be found in solid or juice form ▶ Found all over the world		

Categories of Information:

Sources

Nutrients

Daily recommended allowance

Benefits

5. Next, ask students for additional information they might know about each category, and list that information on the chart.
6. For each category, have students generate questions about what they would like to know. List their questions in the second column of the chart.

Topic: Fruits and Vegetables

What I **K**now	What I **W**ant to know	What I **L**earned
▶ Many different fruits and vegetables available ▶ Contain many vitamins ▶ Vegetables and fruits should be eaten every day ▶ They are good for your body ▶ They are low in fat and calories ▶ Can be found fresh or canned ▶ Can be found in solid or juice form ▶ Found all over the world	***Nutrients:*** ▶ What fruits and vegetables contain the nutrients necessary for a healthy body? ***Daily Recommended Allowance:*** ▶ How many fruits and vegetables should a person eat each day? ***Benefits:*** ▶ What are the health benefits if a person eats a lot of fruits and vegetables?	

Categories of Information:

Sources

Nutrients

Daily recommended allowance

Benefits

7. Have students read or listen to the selection. As and after they read and listen, have them write down what they have learned in the third column. Encourage them to develop new categories of information.

Topic: Fruits and Vegetables

What I **K**now	What I **W**ant to know	What I **L**earned
▶ Many different fruits and vegetables available ▶ Contain many vitamins ▶ Vegetables and fruits should be eaten every day ▶ They are good for your body ▶ ~~They are low in fat and calories~~—not all! ▶ Can be found fresh or canned ▶ Can be found in solid or juice form ▶ Found all over the world	**Nutrients:** ▶ What fruits and vegetables contain the nutrients necessary for a healthy body? **Daily Recommended Allowance:** ▶ How many fruits and vegetables should a person eat each day? **Benefits:** ▶ What are the health benefits if a person eats a lot of fruits and vegetables?	**Sources:** ◆ spring, summer, fall and winter fruits **Nutrients:** ◆ vitamin C—citrus, tomatoes, cantaloupe ◆ vitamin B2—green leafy vegetables ◆ vitamin A—yellow vegetables ◆ calcium—green leafy vegetables **Daily Recommended Allowance:** ◆ 3–5 servings of vegetables per day needed ◆ 2–4 servings of fruits per day needed **Benefits:** ◆ antioxidants—help blood vessels ◆ fiber for digestion ◆ vitamins for healthy heart, eyes, hair, teeth, gums ◆ many are low in fat and calories, but not all, e.g., bananas, peas

Categories of Information:

Sources

Nutrients

Daily recommended allowance

Benefits

8. Discuss as a whole class what the students learned and recorded in the third column. Ask them to revise their charts, making changes in their pre-reading knowledge. Often students will have misconceptions about a topic. Ask, "Do we need to change any information from our first list?" Together mark ($+$) information verified in the selection. Use minus signs ($-$) to indicate incorrect information, or cross it out.

9. After completing the chart, extend the learning process by adding the "Plus." Ask students to transform the information on the K-W-L chart by developing a concept map or other organizer. Talk about why transforming the information again helps them generate additional information and discover new interrelationships. Concept maps also provide a useful tool for writing and presenting information orally (the final step in "plus").

10. Now, have students use the map to write a summary of the selection.

11. Lead a discussion that focuses on how this strategy helped students better understand and remember the reading assignment. Ask, "How well did K-W-L+ fit within what we know about how we learn? What CRISS℠ philosophical principles does it incorporate?"

Support and Extensions

● Do K-W-L charts as part of cooperative teams. Each team does the pre-reading and creates part of a concept map. Then, the groups develop questions that focus on what they want to learn.

● Ask students to bring in sample K-W-L charts from other classes. If you are a science teacher, ask them to show you a sample from their history class. Take time to talk about how this strategy works for all subject areas.

● Have students preview their assignment and make an outline of topic headings. Have them use these headings to develop two or three questions they think will be answered in the selection.

● Before students read a selection, have them read the introduction, bold-print headings, and summary. Then, list key concepts on a chart. Have students brainstorm about what they already know and what they expect to find out from reading a chapter. In the following example, Shirley Jensen and Kathy Theis (1993) changed the K-W-L to K-E-L (What we **K**now, What we **E**xpect to find out, What we **L**earned). They found that this subtle change helped students focus more on text structure. The categories of information matched the main themes presented in their Western Civilization text. After students read, they used two-column notes to document what they had learned.

Category	What We KNOW	What We EXPECT To Find Out	What We LEARNED
Region			
Politics/Government			
Geography			
Social Issues			
Economy			
Culture			
Technology			

Name: _____

Topic: _____

- When multiple resources are used, add a fourth column that lists the resources from which the information was obtained.
- You can convert the chart into a scientific inquiry grid by including a fourth section for more questions (Schmidt, Gillen, Zollo and Stone, 2002).

What I **Know**	What I **Want to Know**
What I **Learned**	More **Questions**

Resources:

- Use K-W-L with videos. An Illinois varsity football coach asked his players what they knew about the team they were to play the next week. He listed this "K" information on a K-W-L chart. Then, he asked them what they wanted (or needed) to know (W) so they could defeat the team. He listed their questions, and added some of his own in the "W" column of the chart. As the team watched the videos of their competition, the coach had them write down the answers they discovered in the "L" column. After the videos, they had a great discussion.

Anticipation Guides

Anticipation Guides (Herber, 1978; Buehl, 2002) are an effective way to activate background knowledge about a topic before reading a selection. Based on their personal thoughts and experiences, students respond to several statements that are related to the selection or topic. They must either agree or disagree with each statement, and they should be able to explain or defend their positions to a partner or a group. This strategy provokes students' curiosity to find out if they are right or wrong and to investigate further the topic. Teachers should remember that Anticipation Guides are not designed to teach content, but to "hook" students into wanting to read and learn more. These guides can be used in all content areas and with a variety of learning materials, including videos.

This procedure creates interest, guides students in setting purposes, and inspires learners to higher levels of thinking. After reading or listening, they return to the statements to decide whether or not they still agree with their original choices. Did they have any misconceptions about the content? Do they still agree or disagree with each of the statements or do they need to change their opinion? Why or why not?

Guided Comprehension

Introduction, Modeling, and Reflection

1. Identify five or six major concepts to be learned in the material (film, lecture, text, science experiment). Keep the following guidelines in mind:
    When writing these statements, think about what students might already know about the concepts, paying particular attention to common misconceptions.
    Write statements that reflect large segments of texts rather than specific details. Otherwise, students will simply skim to find the answers.
    Avoid simple true and false statements.
    Word statements to provoke critical thinking.

2. Present the Anticipation Guide on the overhead or as an individual handout.

Example

Extended Anticipation Guide for Partners and Small Groups

Topic: The Restless Decade

Part I

Directions. Read each statement. If you agree with the statement, put a check in the Agree column. If you don't agree with the statement, put a check in the Disagree column. Discuss your answers with a partner. The teacher will be asking the class before reading the story how the class as a whole marked their papers.

Agree   Disagree
1. _____ _____   The lowest point of the Great Depression occurred during the 1920s.
2. _____ _____   The "flapper" was an airplane part Charles Lindbergh used to make his plane fly across the Atlantic Ocean during this decade.

3. _____ _____ A "speakeasy" was a place where people went to use a newly-invented telephone system.
4. _____ _____ The 1920s has long been remembered as an era of change.
5. _____ _____ The word "cataclysmic" means far-reaching and expanding.
6. _____ _____ Charles Lindbergh, a hero of this time, is known for his solo flight from Paris to New York.
7. _____ _____ "Bootleggers" were cowboys and farmers who kept America stable and secure.

Are you curious to find out if you are right or wrong?

---

3. Have students read the selection and refer to the Anticipation Guide to see if they have changed their minds.
4. Have students return to their small groups, and ask them to develop a consensus about the answers and complete Part II of the Anticipation Guide. (See following example.) Remind them to provide evidence "in your own words" to convince others.

Part II

Directions. Now you will read the article, "The Restless Decade," which contains information related to each of the statements in Part I. If you find information in the article that supports your response in Part I, put a check in the Support column; in the In Your Own Words column, write a summary of the information you found to support your response. If you find information that disproves your response, put a check in the No Support column, and summarize the correct information. You should have seven true statements in the In Your Own Words column when you have finished.

Support   No Support   In Your Own Words
_____   _____   1. _____
_____   _____   2. _____
_____   _____   3. _____
_____   _____   4. _____
_____   _____   5. _____
_____   _____   6. _____
_____   _____   7. _____

5. Have a whole class discussion
6. Talk about what the Anticipation Guide did for your students as learners? Did they have a purpose for reading? Did it help them realize what they knew and didn't know about the topic before reading? Were they more interested in reading the selection? Ask, "How might the Anticipation Guide help you identify your misconceptions about the topic?"

Support and Extensions

- Assign groups of students to prepare their own Anticipation Guides. Then, ask them to trade with another group and complete them. The very act of developing a guide motivates students to process and to define the essential ideas in a selection.
- Ask students to underline or place sticky notes by evidence in the selection that supports or refutes a statement.

- Develop Anticipation Guides from different perspectives. For example, give students a role such as an environmentalist or a logger. How would they respond to this Anticipation Guide before reading an article on "clear cutting"? How would they defend their point of view?

Environmentalist	Logger	
_____	_____	Clear cutting is the most economical way to log.
_____	_____	It is essential that logging companies have unlimited access to our national forest.
_____	_____	It costs our government more to build roads in roadless areas than the companies take out in profits.
_____	_____	Logging is essential for preventing forest fires.
_____	_____	Logging has devastated America's forests.

▶ Graphic and Pictorial Organizers

One way to instill active comprehension and dynamic discussion is through graphic and pictorial organizers. These organizing strategies help students transform information from one form to another. Researchers have found that graphic organizers, such as concept mapping, help students effectively read poorly-structured texts (Goldman and Rakestsraw, 2000). In a comprehensive review of research, Trabasso and Bouchard (2002), found that teaching students to use graphic organizers to structure textual information benefited comprehension and retention, particularly in the areas of science and social studies. In this section, we describe a variety of graphic and pictorial organizers.

Learning **Strategy**

Concept Maps

Through concept mapping, a concrete representation of the relationship among ideas, readers organize the superordinate and subordinate components of a concept. Students find concept maps useful before, during, and after reading and as a procedure for organizing and remembering information. Mapping works particularly well with materials that lack cohesive structure, those in which the relationship of main ideas to details is difficult to determine. It also is an excellent summarizing procedure in conjunction with other strategies such as K-W-L and Two-column Notes.

Guided Comprehension

Introduction, Modeling, and Reflection

1. On the board, write a word or concept (Power 1 idea) that relates to the topic about which you want your students to learn.
2. Open the discussion with a brainstorming session in which students discuss all the information they know or think they know about the topic. Write the

brainstormed information on the overhead. Follow the strategy outlined for K-W-L: brainstorm what they know and want to know; then categorize the information into a pre-reading map. The pre-reading map for the nutrition example on page 85 might look something like this.

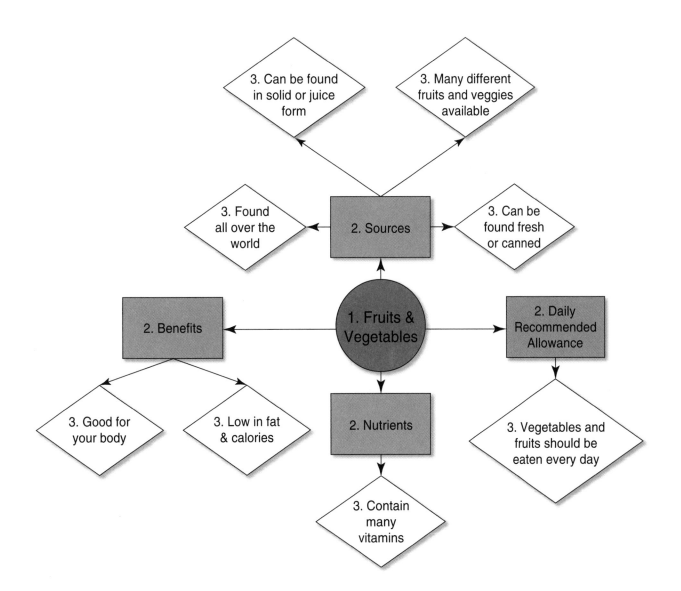

3. Have students read and add information to the pre-reading map. In the following health example, the new information is in the Power 3 boxes.

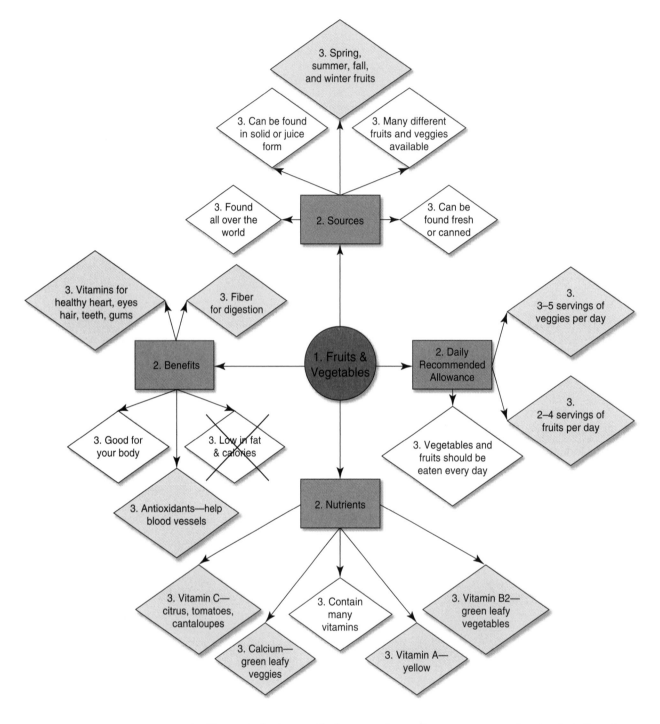

4. Have students use their maps to write a summary about what they have learned.
5. Lead a process conference about how this strategy sequence exemplified key CRISS^SM principles.

Support and Extensions

- Conducting research. Mapping provides an effective structure for organizing information for research and for narrowing topics to specific areas. For example, each arm on the map (the Power 2 categories), becomes a topic of research. Students can use these "arms" for organizing their notes.

  Record one Power 2 category on each note card. For instance, in the nutrition example, students would have four different note cards, one for each topic (Sources, Nutrients, Daily Recommended Allowance, and Benefits). Then, they use their cards for taking notes. Only notes about benefits are written on the "Benefits" card. By keeping topical information separated in this way, the task of organizing their papers becomes easier.

Sources
spring fruits/vegetables
summer fruits/vegetables
fall fruits/vegetables
winter fruits/vegetables

Nutrients (Vitamins, Minerals, Trace Minerals)
Vitamin A—yellow vegetables
Vitamin C—citrus, tomatoes, cantaloupes
Vitamin B2—leafy green vegetables
Calcium—leafy green vegetables

Daily Recommended Allowance
3–5 servings of vegetables per day
2–4 servings of fruit per day
serving equals...
1 medium apple
1/2 cup chopped, cooked, or canned fruit/vegetable
3/4 cup 100% fruit/vegetable juice

Benefits
Antioxidant—helps to prevent wear and tear of the blood vessels
Fiber—helps move food through the digestive system; helps you feel full when eating; reduces blood cholesterol
Vitamins—production of DNA, RNA
normal red blood cells
metabolism
healthy nerve cells
heart, eyes, hair, teeth, and gums

Consider doing research projects as cooperative team efforts. One student from each team researches one or two topics from the map. Then, the team comes back together and shares information, drafting a group report or class presentation.

If mapping is used for a cooperative team report, ask students to use large sheets of newsprint or chart paper to develop their maps. Have them add to the map as they learn more about each topic. Encourage students to draw pictures and add graphics to clarify information. Then, students can use their maps for their presentations. Because mapping has helped students to organize their thoughts, these oral reports surpass those presented without this tool.

● **Character/Biography Mapping.** Character mapping works well for taking notes about special people. Students can use character maps to record the main events of a person's life while reading a novel or a biography or while studying a famous person in history. They can then use their notes for writing.

Learning Strategy

Comparison Organizers

Venn diagrams provide students with a structure for making comparisons. The area within the overlapping circles is for recording similarities; information about differences belongs in the rest of the diagram. This format helps students untangle similarities and differences among concepts, characters, and events. See Blackline 14.

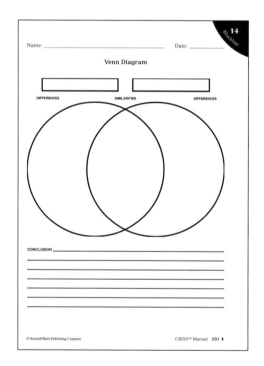

Introduction, Modeling, and Reflection

1. Introduce the Venn diagram by inviting two students to the front of the room. Interview them, and note similarities and differences on the Venn diagram. The following Venn diagram was used to introduce students to each other in a Spanish II class.

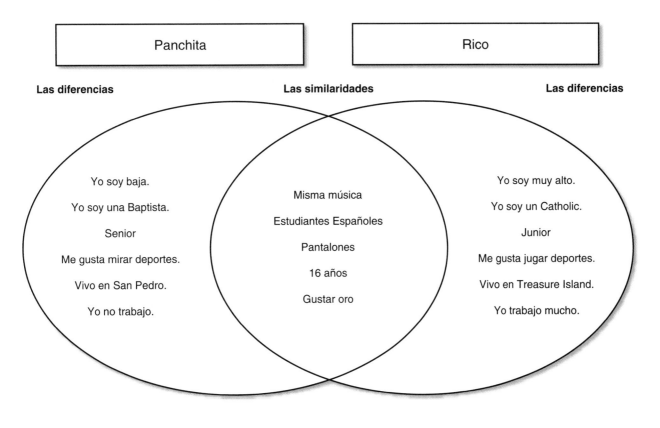

Panchita		Rico

Las diferencias   **Las similaridades**   **Las diferencias**

Yo soy baja.

Yo soy una Baptista.

Senior

Me gusta mirar deportes.

Vivo en San Pedro.

Yo no trabajo.

Misma música

Estudiantes Españoles

Pantalones

16 años

Gustar oro

Yo soy muy alto.

Yo soy un Catholic.

Junior

Me gusta jugar deportes.

Vivo en Treasure Island.

Yo trabajo mucho.

2. Model how to use the Venn diagram to compare characters or specific information in your content area. In the following example, algebra students compared rational and irrational numbers.

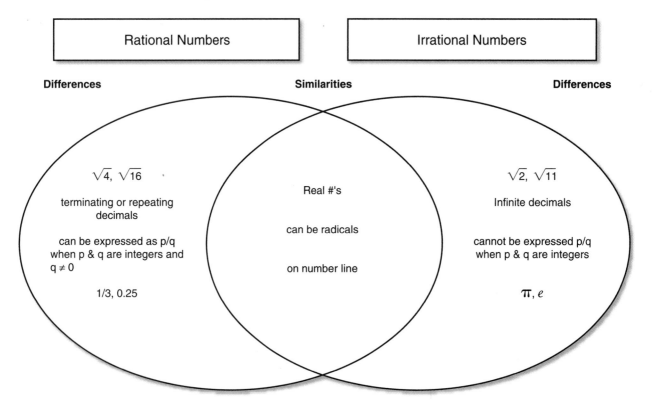

In this example, biology students used a Venn diagram to clarify their understanding of DNA and RNA.

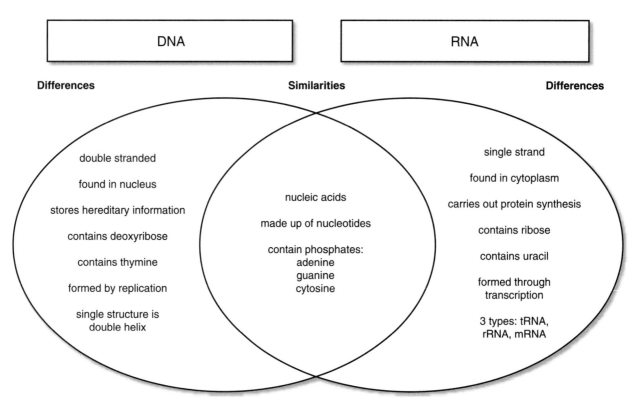

3. Ask students how Venn diagrams work for them. "Did they help focus the discussion? Did they help you transform ideas and review important concepts? How might you apply the Venn diagram to other material you are studying?"

Support and Extensions

● The Venn diagram is an effective assessment tool. Add a column to the left of the two circles to indicate the categories of information you want the students to explain. Having them draw a conclusion from their entries provides additional information for assessment. The following science example includes both of these modifications.

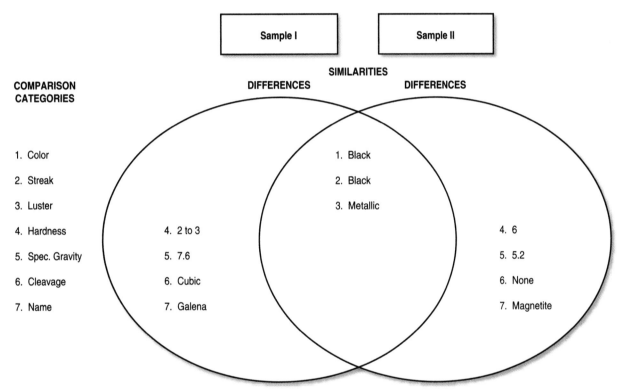

COMPARING UNKNOWN MINERALS

| Sample I | Sample II |

SIMILARITIES

COMPARISON CATEGORIES

DIFFERENCES   DIFFERENCES

1. Color
2. Streak
3. Luster
4. Hardness
5. Spec. Gravity
6. Cleavage
7. Name

Sample I	Similarities	Sample II
	1. Black	
	2. Black	
	3. Metallic	
4. 2 to 3		4. 6
5. 7.6		5. 5.2
6. Cubic		6. None
7. Galena		7. Magnetite

CONCLUSION: Although at first the two samples looked a lot alike, after I did the tests, I found sample II was much harder and not as dense as sample I. Because the samples were about the same size I didn't notice the cleavage at first. I'm sure sample I is galena and pretty sure II is magnetite. If I had a magnet to test sample II with, I'd be sure.

● The Venn diagram can by used to compare three topics, as in the following example.

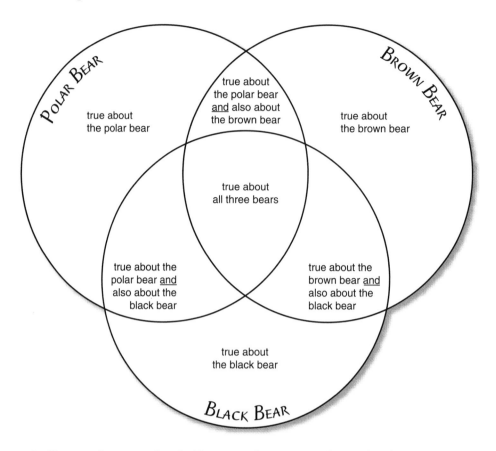

● Have students use visuals. For example, a geography teacher had her students do reports on European countries. When they were done, each student paired with another student who had selected a different country. They compared their two countries using a Venn diagram; however, instead of two circles, or ellipses, the students overlapped the outlines of their two countries.
● Have students use color in their diagrams. The overlapping circles or images can be of different colors, and the writing within can correspond. In a physical education class, students compared racketball to tennis. They wrote the racketball information in red inside a figure that represented a racketball racket, the tennis information (placed on a tennis racket) in blue, and the similarities where the two rackets overlapped in purple.
● Have students use other comparison formats.

The Contrast and Compare Chart. This chart provides a way to categorize all information. In accordance with brain research, the differences are listed first. This is particularly important when comparing two items or concepts which might easily be confused. See Blackline 15 for a blank chart.

CONTRAST & COMPARE CHART

1. "THE FAWN"	2. "THE MEADOW MOUSE"

HOW DIFFERENT?

1.   *With regards to...*   2.

1.	With regards to...	2.
Rhymed	Form	Free verse
Observes; no capture; animal mother; see the escape	Content	Capture; is mouse's parent; don't see escape
Uncertainty; room for hope	Theme	All are doomed
Optimistic	Tone	Naturalistic; pessimistic

HOW SIMILAR?

With regards to...

1. & 2.

	1. & 2.
Attitude toward nature	Love of nature; feel part of it – connected
Content	Babies alone; nests; escapes
Type of poetry	Lyric poems
Poem structure	Stanzas

Conclusion:	Both poems express a love of nature through the lives of animals, but "The Fawn" is much more optimistic and upbeat than "The Meadow Mouse."

The Triangular Comparison Diagram. This helps students identify the similarities and differences among three concepts or items. This comparison diagram can be extended to compare more concepts by choosing polygons with more sides (e.g., a square figure can compare four subjects; a pentagonal diagram can compare five subjects). See Blackline 16 for a blank diagram.

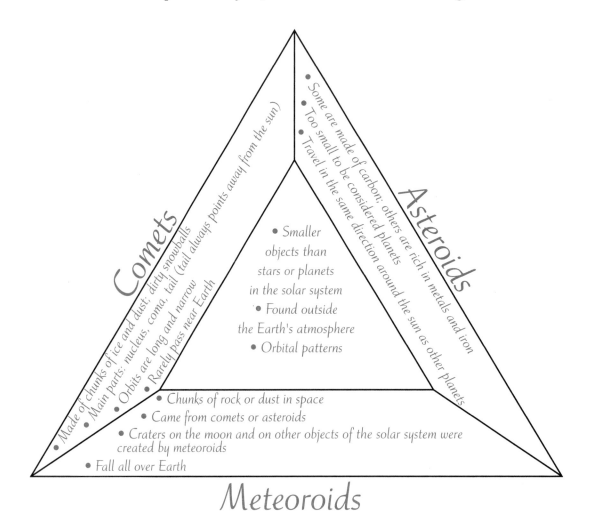

Inspiration® Software. Inspiration® provides several comparison templates. In addition to the Venn diagram, you will find the following comparison organizer.

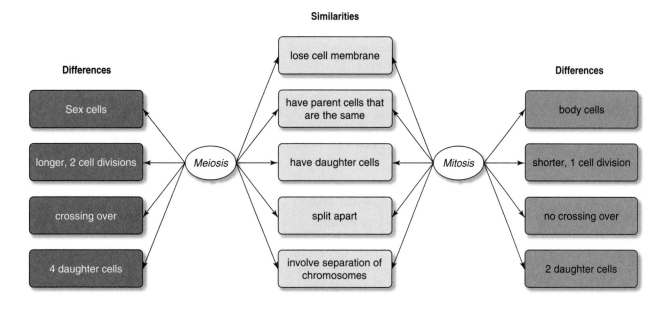

Sequence Organizers

Sequence organizers provide a structure for analyzing story events, determining character changes, identifying the sequential processes of a scientific investigation, and solving a mathematics problem. The format changes, depending upon the task. Information contained in sequence organizers flows naturally into writing.

Introduction, Modeling, and Reflection

1. Begin with familiar topic.
2. Choose a framework that works for the topic (e.g., comic strip, flow chart, timeline).
3. Develop the sequence together.

   In the following example, a physical education teacher asked her tennis students to itemize the steps in negotiating a top-spin.

Using small steps, move toward the ball.	Move the head of the racket downward, below your elbow.	Begin shifting your weight forward, keeping your elbow close to your body, and moving your hips and arms together.	Move your back swing up, hitting the backside of the ball, spinning it three or four feet over the net.	Complete your swing, making sure your weight is forward, but stable. Your arm should be pointed in the direction of the ball.

4. Discuss how frameworks help identify each component of a process. Talk about how brainstorming each step leads to a clearer understanding of the whole.

Support and Extensions

- Maureen Danner, a middle school English teacher, asked students to divide a large sheet of paper into eight squares. Students then reproduced the main events of a myth in comic strip format. She challenged them to include information about characters, symbols, and the moral of the myth.
- Seventh graders working in cooperative groups used modified computer programming symbols to come up with their own sequence maps for solving word problems. They shared their flow charts with the class, and asked their peers to evaluate how well they worked to solve simple problems.

Sequence Map to Solve Math Word Problems

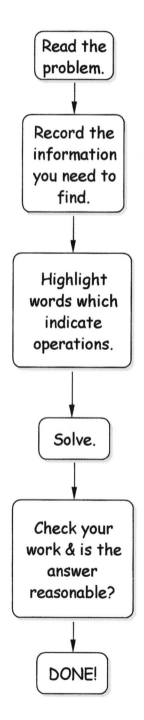

Read the problem.

↓

Record the information you need to find.

↓

Highlight words which indicate operations.

↓

Solve.

↓

Check your work & is the answer reasonable?

↓

DONE!

❱ Imagery

"A picture is worth a thousand words"—so goes the old saying which may explain why comprehension is enhanced by mental imagery and by depicting thoughts in sketches, symbols, or diagrams. Although little research has been done on transformation through actual drawing, there is a great deal of experimental support for mental imagery (i.e., the reader making mental pictures while reading and listening). See Gambrell and Koskinen (2002) for an extensive review of this literature.

Indeed, researchers provide ample evidence that creating mental images while reading or listening enhances comprehension and retention for both children and adults (Gambrell and Koskinen, 2002). Imagery seems to help students integrate information across text, and encourages more active engagement while assisting readers in monitoring their understanding. Imagery turns out to be particularly effective with less proficient readers.

There is much less data on the relationship between comprehension and having students represent what they read by physically creating pictures. However, in developing Project CRISS[SM], we have conducted many classroom studies, finding a consistent and positive relationship between image production and comprehension. Students, who read a selection, then worked in a small group to transform the information into pictures, learned the information better than students who just read and discussed it. The effects on long-term retention are most impressive. After a week's delay, students who explained key concepts in physics by drawing remembered them significantly better than students who did not transform the information through art. So, when we want students to process and learn difficult information, Picture Notes becomes our strategy of choice. With this brief overview of research, let's examine how to work with Mental Imagery and Picture Notes in the classroom.

Learning Strategy

Guided Comprehension

Mental Imagery

Introduction, Modeling and Reflection

1. Trigger visualizations through Guided Imagery (Buehl, 2001). When your eighth-grade health students are ready to study the human heart, for example, use Guided Imagery as a pre-reading strategy. It might sound something like this:

   "Close your eyes, relax, use your imagination. Imagine that you are an arthroscope—a medical instrument for seeing beneath the skin. You are peering inside of your chest, reaching in just to the left and underneath your sternum. What do you hear? See? You see your heart, a pulsing, writhing mass of muscle. Imagine its color, its size—about the size of your fist. Once every second, watch the wall of your heart contract. Move inside one of its chambers or rooms. The chamber opens; blood rushes in. Now it closes and squeezes the blood out. Watch it open, fill, close, and empty; open, fill, close, and empty. Feel its rhythm. With each pump, blood spurts from the heart into a tube-like vessel."

2. Ask students to talk about their images. What questions came to mind? What do they want to know?
3. After students read, have them imagine their own heart again. What additional pictures do they see?
4. Read aloud an excerpt of a high-imagery story, poem, or informational text. Stop and share mental images.
5. Once students understand the concept of imagery, provide them with background knowledge about research. Your conversation might go something like this: "Making pictures in your mind can help you understand and remember. It helps to clarify meaning and to monitor comprehension. Think about why

it works for you. How does imagery help you become more engaged with the material?"

Support and Extensions

- Divide students into pairs. Ask them to read, stop, and share images.
- Have students develop their own Guided Imagery scripts and lessons.

Strategy

Learning

Picture Notes

Picture Notes, which involve students reading, talking, and then drawing their own representations of meaning, work well as a small-group activity. In the first example that follows, small groups worked together to explain key concepts in a biology unit (*photosynthesis*). After developing their representations, they gave oral interpretations of their drawings to the class. Afterwards, they wrote explanations. Reading, talking, drawing, presenting, and then writing helped these students do multiple transformations of content.

Guided
Comprehension

Introduction, Modeling, and Reflection

1. After students have read an assignment, organize them into small groups. Give each group a large sheet of paper and a set of colored markers. Tell them to determine the important ideas in their reading assignment and to come up with a way of representing their ideas on paper through words, pictures, and diagrams.

2. Explain that the quality of the artwork is secondary to the thinking processes involved in discussing content and deciding how to organize it. The only criterion is to represent main ideas and their interrelationships to each other and to supporting details. Encourage students to use words, pictures, phrases, circles, squiggles, or whatever creative endeavor they feel best portrays their analysis. (Changing words into pictures encourages active synthesis of ideas.) No two productions will be the same. Several student examples are usually sufficient to launch the rest into creating their own unique representations.

3. The teams share their productions with the class. Decorate your classroom, attaching the representations to walls and bulletin boards.

In the following example, biology students used Picture Notes to explain photosynthesis:

4. After several days, ask students to recall the content of their Picture Notes or give a more formal test over the material. Ask, "How did your picture notes help you understand and remember the material? What did you have to do to transform what you were learning into pictures? How might you use this strategy on your own?"

Support and Extensions

● Use picture notes for reviewing content for tests. Different topics can be assigned to groups who then review their topics for the whole class.

● Ask students to transform their notes into images. Use Inspiration® software and clip art for students who are uncomfortable with drawing their own images.

● Use Picture Notes as a pre-reading activity to bring out prior knowledge.

● Have students create images to help them remember key vocabulary terms or concepts. Title I high school students created the following images to remember the meanings of words found in short stories read at Halloween time.

PHOBIAS   LABYRINTH   FIGMENT

● "Review a book in an hour." In groups, students create a pictorial representation of one chapter in a book. The students in each group only read their one chapter. Images are shared in sequence. Each group must relate their segment to previous chapters. Save the last chapter for everyone to read or review.

● Create a "Book in a Bag." Instead of pictures, use concrete items to represent information in a book or reading selection. Put all items in a bag labeled with the book title (e.g., toy bus in a bag for a book on Rosa Parks).

▶ Summaries

Reducing information to essential ideas is critical to comprehension. Masses of information bombard us every day. In order to remember and understand this volume of information, we have to combine and reorganize details into a meaningful message. Teaching students this skill is a challenging task, but research confirms its importance to student learning.

A review of research indicates when students learn how to summarize and can use the strategy effectively, a positive effect on comprehension and recall of textual information occurs (Trebasso & Bouchard, 2002). This positive effect only holds if students have *explicit* instruction about how to summarize. Just *telling* students to do so is not enough. When students learned *how* to write brief summaries or annotations in the margins of their texts, for example, their comprehension and retention improved (Nist & Simpson, 2000).

Before describing strategies for teaching summarization, let's go back to an early study conducted by Taylor (1984), who observed behavioral differences between those who can and cannot summarize. Taylor found that those who wrote poor summaries tended to read over the assignment quickly and begin writing immediately. They spent little time rereading and thinking about the selection before they wrote. They did nothing observable in the way of note taking or underlining to organize their thoughts. In contrast, the expert summarizers continually monitored their writing progress, checking back to the original selection to ensure their efforts preserved its gist. This behavior differed markedly from that of the poor summarizers, who rarely referred to the original.

Share this information about successful and unsuccessful summarizers with your students. Then model the steps for developing summaries.

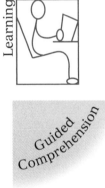

Learning
Strategy

Guided
Comprehension

Summarizing Non-Fiction Text

Introduction, Modeling, and Reflection

1. Begin by reviewing any structural aids such as titles, bold faced headings, vocabulary, discussion questions, and illustrations. Remind students to notice transition words (e.g., first, second) that indicate main points. Note the presence of key vocabulary, repeated ideas, and clue phrases (e.g., the main point is . . ., most important).
2. Make predictions about what you think you will learn from the selection.
3. Read the selection and describe your own thinking processes (teacher think-alouds) for sorting through main ideas and details. Reread and take notes on the board, including key words from topic sentences that express the main points of each paragraph. Or read and model how to annotate the text with brief notes in the margins.
4. Organize your ideas from your notes. You might cluster ideas that seem to go together or organize your ideas into a concept map (see the mapping sections of this chapter).
5. Write your summary. As you write, cross out any information that does not seem important. Be sure to verbalize your thoughts. Choices about what to exclude are as important as decisions about what to retain.
6. Ask students to think about the process of summarization. What does it entail?

Support and Extensions

- Summarize together. Do this as a whole class, or divide students into cooperative teams. Students read through the selection first, underlining main ideas and details. (See Chapter 3 for information on teaching underlining.) Then, on a separate sheet of paper, have students take notes to use for developing their summaries. Have them convert their notes to summaries. Ask them to reread their summaries and cross out any unnecessary words or ideas. Groups exchange summaries and evaluate.

- After students have practiced as a whole class or in small groups, some may be ready to develop their summaries independently. Do not expect students to become totally independent immediately. Summarizing always depends on the difficulty of the material. If the material contains unfamiliar content or is poorly written, you will need to continue to work together. With well-written and familiar material, some students will begin developing summaries independently.

Read-Recall-Check-Summarize

Introduction, Modeling, and Reflection

With Read-Recall-Check-Summarize, students first read the selection and then recall important information. Their recall becomes the basis of their summaries (Karnes, 1992).

1. Read a selection together. Then, as a whole class, recall information you've read. List the information on the board.
2. Reread the piece to check for accuracy of recalled information.
3. Cluster the recalled material into logical groupings using Powers and/or a Concept Map.
4. Delete any unimportant ideas from this information.
5. Write the summary together.
6. Discuss how this type of summary is similar to or differs from other summary processes.

Support and Extensions

- Pair students, and have them read another selection. They recall and record the information. Then, check back for accuracy. Each pair writes a summary. Students present their summaries to the whole class.

Magnet Summaries

Doug Buehl's Magnet Summaries (2001) help students "rise above the details to construct meaningful summaries in their own words." Students identify magnet words—key concepts and terms from their reading—relate appropriate details to each magnet, then combine the ideas in writing.

Introduction, Modeling, and Reflection

1. Doug suggests introducing the idea of "magnet" words with an analogy: "Just as magnets attract metal, magnet words attract information." Read a short, familiar passage to your students and pick out one or two magnet

words. Show your students how the various details "attach" themselves to the magnet words

2. Next, write magnet words on an overhead transparency. For example, in an article on Indonesia, the magnet word for the first part of the article might be *population.*

3. Ask students to recall details, expanding the concept. For the topic *population,* responses might be: fourth most populous nation (225 million people), diverse religions, poverty, political unrest. Ask students to write the magnet word and details on an index card:

4th most populous nation	political unrest
POPULATION	
Diverse religions	poverty

4. Model how to combine these words into a summary (e.g., Indonesia, the fourth most populous country in the world, is characterized by poverty, diversity of religions, and political unrest.

5. Continue by distributing three or four cards to each student. Read, stop, and talk about possible magnet words and details. Then, help the students create a one-sentence summary for each card.

petroleum	textiles
ECONOMY	
Subsistence farming: Rice, cassava, peanuts	mining

One-sentence summary: Indonesian economy is poor, primarily based on petroleum, textiles, and mining with most people working as subsistence farmers raising rice, cassava, and peanuts.

religious problems	ethnic strife
POLITICAL UNREST	
Muslim fundamentalist	300 different languages

One-sentence summary: Indonesians struggle to live together peacefully because of religious differences, language barriers, and the increasing threat of Muslim fundamentalism.

6. Arrange the sentences into a logical order to create an initial draft of the selection summary.

7. Model for the students how to edit the draft into a finished summary.

   Example: Indonesia, the fourth most populous country in the world, is characterized by poverty, diversity of religion and political unrest. While some people make a living in the petroleum and textile industries, most work as subsistence farmers raising rice, cassava, and peanuts. One of the main problems for Indonesians is the struggle to live together peacefully because of religious differences, language barriers, and the increasing threat of Muslim fundamentalism.

8. Ask students to think about the relationship between summarizing and active reading. How did this strategy help them get to the essence of the author's message?

Support and Extensions

● Have students use Magnet Summaries to transform and review notes.
● Divide students into groups. Have each group take a section of a chapter and develop Magnet Summaries to teach their text section to the class.

Strategy

Learning

One-Sentence Summaries

One-Sentence Summaries guarantee active student participation and provide excellent feedback for the teacher. These brief writings clearly indicate the level of understanding of concepts. These condensed summaries work best after students have had some experience with paragraph and Magnet Summaries. One-Sentence Summaries are typically used to encapsulate essential ideas or the big understandings from a reading selection, lecture, or video. To encourage brevity, ask students to write their summaries on 3″ × 5″ cards.

Introduction, Modeling, and Reflection

Procedure A: Read, Set Aside, and List

1. Read a selection aloud.
2. Put the selection aside and list four or five ideas/words from it.
3. Model how to combine these ideas/words into a One-Sentence Summary.
4. Delete any extraneous words from the summary.
5. Ask students, "How did putting the material aside and writing down key words help you begin transforming the information?"

Procedure B: Selective Underlining and Two-column Notes

1. After modeling selective underlining (Chapter 3), go through the selection and highlight key ideas (Power 1 ideas).
2. Show students how to combine these ideas into a One-Sentence Summary.
3. Alternatively, after developing two-column notes, have students take the ideas on the left and use them to write a summary sentence.
4. Delete any extraneous words.
5. Ask students, "How does a combination of strategies work for you? Why was summarizing easier once you had underlined or taken notes on the material?"

Procedure C: Content Summary Chart

1. Present students with the following chart for developing a One-Sentence Summary.

Identify the topic being summarized.	Tell what it begins with.	Tell what's in the middle. Use words such as: covers, discusses, presents, continues with.	Tell what it ends with.

2. Summarize familiar content using the chart.
3. Write summaries together based on the information in the chart. Delete extraneous words.

Language Arts Example. The Shakespearean play *MacBeth* <u>begins with</u> witches setting an ominous tone, <u>continues</u> by developing the changes in MacBeth's character due to his ambition, and <u>ends with</u> MacBeth's downfall from the throne.

Math Example. To multiply two fractions, I <u>begin by</u> changing mixed numbers to improper fractions, <u>continue by</u> multiplying the two numerators to get the numerator of the answer and multiplying the two denominators to get the denominator of the answer, and I <u>end by</u> simplifying the answer, first through reducing it to lowest terms and then by changing it to a mixed number if it is an improper fraction.

4. Under what circumstances might you use this chart to help you summarize information?

Procedure D: One-Sentence Summary Frames

1. Make an overhead transparency of One-Sentence Summary Frames as shown below and on Blackline 17 (Cope, 1991).

One-Sentence Summary Frames for Common Text Structures

Description	1. A _____ is a kind of _____ that ....
Compare/ Contrast	2. ___x___ and ___y___ are similar in that they are both ..., but ___x___ ..., while ___y___ ....
Sequence	3. _____ begins with ..., continues with ..., and ends with ....
Problem/ Solution	4. _____ wanted ..., but ..., so ....
Cause/Effect	5. _____ happens because.... *or* _____ causes ....

2. Model how to develop a summary sentence using several of these frames.
3. Ask students if they found these frames helpful. Which of these summarizing strategies worked the best for them? Why?"

Support and Extensions

- Students reduce paragraph summaries to one sentence by deleting less important information and by combining similar ideas.
- After listening to a lecture on a topic, students combine key ideas from their notes into a summary.
- Students write One-Sentence Summaries about videos.
- Include summaries in examinations. List three or four key concepts, which students combine into a paragraph or a one-sentence summary.
- Students write telegrams. Explain to students they have $1.50 to spend. Each word costs $.10, and they are to write a telegram expressing the main ideas of the selection. Have them compete for the best, complete message.
- At the end of a class period, students write a One-Sentence Summary explaining what they learned during the period.
- Before students read, view a video, or listen to a lecture, they write what they already know about the topic in a One-Sentence Summary.

◗ Summary

The strategies described in this chapter help our students better understand the Project CRISS[SM] philosophy—particularly the principles of background knowledge and transformation. Strategies like K-W-L+ and Anticipation Guides build a deeper awareness about background knowledge and purpose setting. Our students don't arrive as blank slates. When we take time to learn about what they know before asking them to read, the momentum of our lesson changes. Students become more curious about reading. By brainstorming what they think they know, talking with peers about their ideas, and then coming up with questions about the topic, students begin to have a stake in their own learning. They become engaged and want to learn more.

We also gain a deeper understanding of transformation. Students don't learn much by just listening to our lectures or by simply reading our assignments. They must transform information so it becomes their own. Concept mapping, Venn diagrams, imagery, picture notes, and summaries are some of the tools that facilitate knowledge transformation.

Finally, the strategy presentations are all nested in an instructional framework of teacher modeling and guided practice. CRISS[SM] teachers don't just test comprehension, they teach it.

Research Conclusion	Reference
Teachers tend to assign, question, and lecture students about content, but do little to teach students how to understand and learn new information.	Durkin, 1979; Pressley, 2002
The explicit teaching of strategies improves comprehension.	Pressley, 2002

Organizing for Learning: Two-Column Notes, Frames, and Story Plans

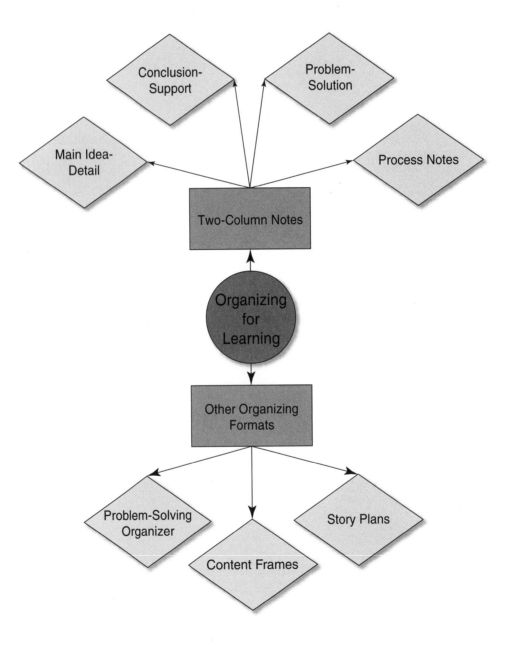

In this chapter, we present a number of approaches that help students organize and remember information. Students need to know about a variety of study procedures before they can develop their own flexible systems. To gain this expertise, they must not only experience many different ways to organize and write about information, but have an **awareness** of the author's purpose and style of writing.

Development of personal systems depends upon knowledge about a variety of organizing strategies, flexibility, and self-monitoring. Good readers know how to use different systems and know which strategies produce the most effective reading. Poor readers are far more rigid, sidestepping challenging reading because they don't know what to do. They give up, shut down, and avoid assignments. Or, in situations where they do attempt an assignment, they skim it searching for answers to end-of-chapter questions. They remain unaware of the need to transform, to self-monitor, and to think consciously about how to learn. Successful students watch over themselves as they learn. They know *when* they know and what to do if they *do not* know. They constantly transform information to make it their own (Paris, Wasik, and Turner, 1991; Duke and Pearson, 2002).

As we teach strategies, we must help students become more metacognitive by having frequent "process" discussions. After a test, lead a discussion that focuses on how the students learned the material. Categorize approaches leading to successful and less successful outcomes. Have students keep learning logs in which they record their study behaviors and test performances. Are there trends? Talk about why one strategy works better than another. Ask process questions similar to the following: "Do some approaches to learning seem more effective than others? Why is this so? Is it because the more successful strategies tap into Project CRISS[SM] principles and philosophy more readily than others? Is test performance better when using a form of Two-Column Notes? What learning processes are involved for developing and using notes?" This discussion will help students uncover what they are doing to be successful.

The particular organizational *scheme* a student chooses to use depends upon their learning goals and how the author crafted the piece. If expository materials happen to be fairly well-structured with obvious main ideas and details, Two-Column Notes work well. When materials have less obvious structure—where authors have scattered information throughout a piece—Concept Mapping makes more sense for obtaining key points and details. If readers want to untangle the author's arguments, analyze problems, or do problem-solving in mathematics, the strategies of choice would be Conclusion-Support, Problem-Solution notes, or Process Notes.

The type of *strategy* readers use depends upon how an author has presented the information. Has the author organized the information according to problem-solution relationships, cause and effect relationships, a chronology of events, or a series of comparisons? Or does the author present an argument using propositions and supportive information? The organizers described in this chapter provide students with a way of thinking about different forms of text structure; they also help students learn from challenging, confusing, and poorly written text.

The organizational *frameworks* also vary according to the material's structure. Formats used in expository subjects, such as main idea-detail notes, make little sense for narratives. Instead, we need frameworks that focus on the elements of fiction or that help students analyze characters and theme.

So, keep in mind as you explore the strategies in this chapter, all are not equally applicable. The purpose of reading and the author's craft must guide your selection.

Finally, the organizing strategies work best if students already have some familiarity with the content. Many readers find them particularly helpful when used for organizing information around essential ideas after reading. If used as during-reading strategies, take time for students to brainstorm background knowledge, to preview the assignment, and to develop purposes for reading. Otherwise, students will have difficulty sorting the wheat from the chaff.

▶ Two-Column Notes

Two-column notes can take a variety of formats, depending upon the subject area, instructional goals, and the nature of the text. We include four different types in this chapter: (1) Main Idea-Detail notes, (2) Conclusion-Support, (3) Problem-Solution, and (4) Process Notes. Two-column notes can also be adapted to situations demanding higher levels of thinking. These include adaptations for developing opinions and persuasive papers, for analyzing problems, and for improving process skills in science and mathematics.

Strategy

Learning

Main Idea-Detail Notes

Main idea-detail notes help students organize main ideas and details from subject area reading assignments. This format works particularly well with text that is structured around concepts and definitions. Students divide their papers into two columns; they record main ideas in the left column and details on the right. Main points can take the form of questions or key words. Students can then use their notes as a study guide. Covering the information on the right, they test themselves with key words or main idea questions on the left.

Guided Comprehension

Introduction, Modeling, and Reflection

1. Make a transparency of a selection, and demonstrate how to underline key points. Photocopy the selection for students to underline and make marginal notes as you model.
2. Preview the assignment. Read the introduction and bold print headings, examine visuals, and read the summary and end-of-chapter questions. Brainstorm background knowledge and develop a purpose for reading. "Why do you think the author wrote this selection? What do you think some of his/her big ideas might be?" Consider using Questioning the Author as a during-reading strategy.
3. Use the author's clues to main ideas to develop two-column notes. For example, if the author happened to develop main ideas through bold print and rhetorical questions, your discussion might be similar to the following: "We can use the author's clues to develop notes over the important information in the selection. In our notes we want to be sure to include the main ideas asked through rhetorical questions. In addition, we want to include bold print vocabulary and main points from the pictures and diagrams."
4. Model how to convert these clues to notes. Together, develop the notes on the transparency while students write down their own notes at their desks. Talk about how to abbreviate the questions and other key points. "Do not use complete sentences in your notes. Use brief phrases to summarize ideas. It takes too much time to write sentences." Model how to include main ideas and vocabulary essential to content in the left column. In the right column, record information that elaborates on main points. "Write the author's information in your own words. Making the author's message your own ensures better comprehension and retention."

5. Demonstrate how to use the notes for self-testing and for reviewing information. Show students how to cover the right-hand column with a sheet of paper. Model how you self-test by using the questions and key words on the left. "Now watch me as I use my notes to study. I cover all of my notes to the right and use the ideas on the left as triggers to test myself. I first ask myself how much information is needed (e.g., *two* causes for . . ., *three* steps in. . . ., etc.)." Next, I ask myself what the information is. After reciting what I know, I uncover my notes and check. Finally, I ask what else I know and draw some conclusions or make applications to other situations." Point out that this last question is your metacognitive check. "If you can't add anything to the information, you probably don't *know* it. It has only been memorized. Go back to the original and reread." After the demonstration, ask students to work alone or in pairs and use their "triggers" in the left-hand column to test themselves.

Nature's Clean-Up Organisms: Scavengers & Decomposers	
Scavengers What are they?	large and small animals
Examples:	big animals—coyotes, lions vultures smaller—slugs, beetles, tadpoles, grubs
Habitat	litter: dark, moist food—note: one rotting apple can have 100,000 roundworms, also found in cow manure
What do they do?	begin clean up—eat dead matter
Decomposers What are they?	microscopic, fungi, bacteria, microscopic animals 1000s of different kinds
Examples	mushrooms
Habitat	different decomposers in each ecosystem
What do they do?	change litter and waste back to basic materials
Decomposition	Breakdown of dead material into basic materials by decomposers

6. The 12-Minute Study encourages brief, but frequent, studying in preparation for a test. Students self-test for 12 minutes by covering information on the right and trying to picture and recall it. Challenge students to study for 12 minutes

at least twice each day before the test (class time, study hall, after school, evening)—no more than 12 minutes! Talk about why frequent brief study sessions tend to clinch information in memory better than longer, less intense sessions. It is hard for minds to wander when you only have 12 minutes!

7. After students practice using their two-column notes for studying, lead a discussion about what a test over the material might look like. Plan the test together.

8. Next, give the students a test. Use questions developed previously in your discussion. Do not give the test until you are sure that students know the material. Everyone deserves to experience success.

9. After students complete their test, allow time for a process conference to help students begin to internalize study strategies. "How well did you do on your test? Why do you suppose you did so well? What did you do to learn this material?" Then, as part of this discussion, list the strategies. Your list might look something like this:

   a. We previewed the material and thought about what we already knew about the topic.
   b. We came up with several big ideas or purposes for reading.
   c. We figured out how the author presented main ideas.
   d. We summarized the main ideas and details in two-column notes.
   e. We studied our notes by testing ourselves.
   f. We predicted the types of questions that would probably be asked on the test.

After listing the steps, continue your discussion. "The next time you study for a test, what are you going to do to learn the material?" Talk about these strategies as working for practically any content material.

Support and Extensions

- Continue modeling how to take and use two-column notes throughout the year. Each selection students read will probably be structured differently, and they will need help in understanding how their text is written.

- Have students incorporate QARs in the left column of their two-column notes. Encourage them to use mostly *Think and Search* with few *Right There* questions. *Think and Search* questions encourage students to put details together. *Author and You* questions can be added to get at higher levels of thinking. You will need to model the use of these questions (see Chapter 4).

- In the content subjects, students will always need help distinguishing important from unimportant information. As part of every pre-reading activity, provide your students with some ideas about what they should be looking for in their reading assignments. "As you read your social studies text, make sure to take notes on these topics . . ." You may even want to list important ideas on the board so students know to include them in their notes.

- Have students work together on their notes. You may want to assign small groups the same or different parts of a reading assignment. Each team could then present their notes to the class for discussion.

- Use two-column notes as part of discussions and lectures. As you present, develop two-column notes using a blank transparency on the overhead projector. In the beginning, develop a complete set of notes with the main points of your lecture on the left and details on the right. Then begin to write down less information allowing students to fill in more of the details as you talk.

● Consider incorporating Power Structures as part of two-column notes:

Chapter 4: The New England Colonies

Main Ideas	Details

1. *Puritans in Massachusetts*
    2. Who were the Puritans?
	3. Wanted to reform Church of England
	    4. Wanted simpler service, do away with customs taken from the Catholics
	3. Different from Pilgrims who wanted to separate from the Church

2. Reasons for leaving England	3. They felt uncomfortable and unsafe in England
	    4. England's King Charles did not like Puritans' ideas. Took away their business charters, had them kicked out of schools, and even had some jailed.
	3. In 1629, royal officials gave Massachusetts Bay Co. (formed by Puritans) a charter so they could form a colony in New England.
	    4. Colony based on laws of God
	    4. Not watched by England, so had some freedom
	    4. Many non-Puritans joined to get land and a new start

● Use two-column notes for students to record reactions, questions, and reflections as they read novels.

Questions you have while reading. What surprised you?	Reflect on meaning. Make connections. Comment on the journey.

● Add a third column for studying, pictures, notes from films, and class discussions that relate to key ideas in the left-hand columns.

Book Notes		Class Discussion
Advantages of the North	More people More factories and mills	People were also clustered in more urban areas easier to pull together (more soldiers) More people to produce goods South had to get goods from Europe
Advantages of the South	Defensive war Better generals, Robert E. Lee was far better, many surprise moves	Defensive war—people very protective of their homes, makes them fight harder

Conclusion-Support Notes

Conclusion-support is a two-column format in which students develop and support arguments with evidence (Santa, Dailey, and Nelson, 1985). This approach stresses critical thinking skills with both expository and narrative text. Students write down their thesis or conclusion in the left-hand column, and use the space in the right-hand column for recording evidence from their reading. They then use their notes to develop persuasive written arguments.

Once students know how to develop single paragraphs using the Conclusion-support format, they can use the same procedure for developing longer papers. An argumentative paper, in effect, combines several conclusion-support paragraphs.

Introduction, Modeling, and Reflection

1. Find a selection that will inspire strong reactions from the students. Conclusion-support is particularly effective with controversial characters or issues. An issue in our own high school was whether or not students should leave campus for lunch. Pick a similar issue in your school.
2. Divide the class and assign pro and con positions. In these roles, students discuss the issue from two to five minutes.
3. Then have a whole class discussion and together develop pro and con conclusion-support notes:

Conclusion	Support
Students should be allowed to eat off campus	1. Supports local lunch business 2. Gives students a break from school—come back feeling recharged 3. Teaches students more responsibility
Students should not be allowed to eat lunch off campus	1. School cafeteria would lose money 2. Causes problems for neighbors near school 3. Creates tardies to afternoon classes

4. Conclusion-support notes evolve naturally into persuasive writing. Demonstrate how the thesis or the conclusion statement becomes a topic sentence, which students support with sentences taken from their notes. Conclusion-support notes can also be used for longer papers. The notes in the previous example can readily be woven into an argument paper following the spool format (see Chapter 8). In this case, the introduction presents two points of view. The following paragraphs present each conclusion along with support; the paper concludes with a comment about which of the two opinions seems to make the most sense.

5. Provide opportunities for students to talk about how this strategy works for them. "How does it help you think through an issue? How might Conclusion-support help with questions on the state assessments? How did it help you write a better persuasive essay?"

Support and Extensions

- Conclusion-support works well as part of cooperative group discussions and debates. Ask students to form an opinion about a character or issue and develop Conclusion-support notes. Then ask them to bring their notes to small group discussions. Each student presents his or her conclusion and support to the group. Team participants ask questions leading to clarifications of opinions. After students discuss their ideas, they write persuasive papers.

- To support conclusions, students find exact quotes in a selection and mark them with sticky notes. Clarifying statements can be written on the notes.

- Students can create character Conclusion-support notes through pictures. They draw or write about their opinion and the qualities of the character that prove their opinion. In the example below, students developed Picture Notes supporting their opinions about famous people in history.

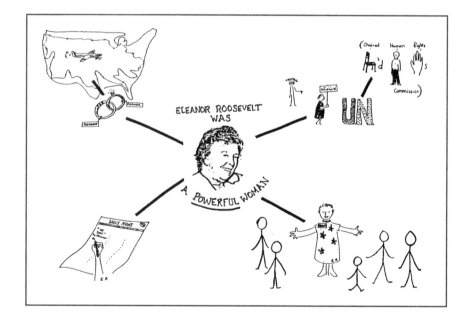

- Combine with Power Thinking (see the example about Napoleon on page 124). With some Power 1 issues, students can elaborate with Power 2 and 3 information. Power 3 details are the *why* statements. Often students can list evidence to support their opinions, but they do not explain why the evidence is supportive. Making the Power 3's *why* statements helps students remember to explain their evidence.

● Use Conclusion-support to tease out issues in content subjects. In the following example students conducted research about Napoleon. They read several library sources and took Power notes on two points of view. They found evidence that he was a good leader and evidence that he was not. They used their notes to develop argument papers.

Conclusion	Support

1. Napoleon was a great leader	2. Ended revolution
	   3. Established police force
	   3. Allowed nobles to go home
	2. Drew up new constitution
	   3. Gave men right to vote
	2. Fair taxation
	   3. Rich had to pay taxes
	2. Government workers chosen for ability

1. Napoleon was not a great leader	2. Many lives lost 2. Tried to rule the world 2. Only men got to vote

Student example:

Some people think Napoleon was a great leader. Others disagree and think he was not such a great leader.

Those who thought Napoleon was great liked the way he brought an end to the revolutionary fighting in France and then established a national police force to keep peace. He told all the nobles who had fled the country during the fighting that they could return home. Napoleon also drew up a new constitution that gave all male citizens the right to vote. All citizens, including the rich, were made to pay taxes, and the government workers were chosen for their ability. It did not matter who they were. He also led the military to many victories.

Others said that he wasn't so great. So many people died during all those wars when he tried to rule the world. The people who had run away during the revolution could only come home if they supported him. The others had to stay away. Also, he only allowed men to vote as if he didn't think women were smart or could do a good job.

Napoleon probably was a great leader, but he did not always think about the people. I am glad he is not living now. I wouldn't like him.

After writing their papers, students conferred in pairs, using the following revision rubric.

Features	Score 3	Score 2	Score 1
Format of notes	My conclusion-support notes are correctly organized with conclusion to the left and proof statements to the right.	Some of my conclusion support notes are correctly organized with opinions to the left and support statements to the right.	My conclusion-support notes aren't correctly organized with conclusions to the left and support statements to the right.
Support	My conclusions have three or more support statements.	My conclusions have at least two support statements.	My conclusions have no more than one support statement.
Elaboration	My persuasive paragraphs contain a lot of detail.	My persuasive paragraphs need a few more details to be convincing.	My persuasive paragraphs have very few or no details.
Structure	My persuasive paper has a well-developed introduction, body and closing paragraph.	My paper has two of the three parts: introduction, body and closing.	My paper has one or none of the three parts: introduction, body and closing.
Conventions	My paper has no more than 2 spelling, structure, or punctuation errors.	My paper has 3 or 4 spelling, structure, or punctuation errors.	My paper has 5 or more spelling, structure, or punctuation errors.

- Use Conclusion-support as a way for students to prove their opinions. In the following example middle school students read the book, *Maniac Magee* and then worked in groups to analyze the qualities of the main character.

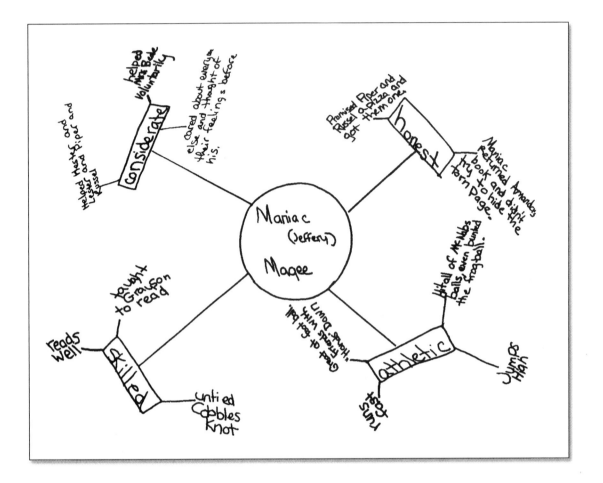

- Use the Conclusion-support strategy to prepare students to take state assessments and other standardized tests of reading comprehension. Have students take conclusion-support notes on practice selections before answering the questions.

In addition, use this framework to prepare students to write persuasive essays—a prevalent feature in most state assessments. On some state assessments, such as Florida's FCAT, students are given a conclusion in the item stem for short and extended response questions. Students must find support for the conclusion within the text and in their own words paraphrase the evidence.

Example: Chief Joseph Article

According to the author, Chief Joseph was both a peace chief and a military genius. Use details and information from the selection to support these conclusions.

Conclusion	Support
1. Chief Joseph was a peace chief	2. 2. 2.
1. Chief Joseph was a military genius	2. 2. 2.

This is an excellent test-preparation strategy, for students who are not allowed to use their background knowledge or form opinions. The task is to find evidence within the text to support the conclusion they have been given.

Adaptations

Proposition-Support (Buehl, 2001).   Proposition-support is a more advanced form of conclusion-support. As students progress through school, they need to become increasingly adept in analyzing an author's point of view. The Proposition-support framework helps older students critically analyze an author's conclusions or propositions by identifying different ways to build a case using facts, statistics, examples, expert authority, and logical reasoning. By untangling the various dimensions of argumentation, students can more readily analyze oral and written text containing differing viewpoints, opinions, hypotheses, and theories. This framework guides students in writing persuasive papers, in preparing speeches and debates, and in conducting research. Completed notes also prepare students for more focused classroom discussions. In addition, Proposition-support notes provide a superb way to analyze political and environmental issues.

Steps:

1. Begin by explaining the term proposition—a statement expressing a judgment or opinion. Then choose a text containing a clear proposition and various forms of argumentation.
2. Read the selection together, using the "Questioning the Author" strategy to arrive at the author's intended point of view or proposition.
3. Next, analyze and categorize the varying arguments.

   Does the author make a convincing case?
   Do you reject or accept the proposition?
   Has the author used one form of argumentation more than another?
   Scrutinize how the author might do a better job of supporting the proposition?
   Are the arguments logical?
   Are they based on research and examples?
   Is one or more expert authorities cited?

In the process of analyzing these questions, students become far more astute thinkers, writers, and debaters.

In the example on page 128, high school health students read an article about the safety of the food we eat ("How Safe?" *National Geographic* magazine, May 2002) and organized their notes into a Proposition-support outline.

Proposition-Support Outline

Proposition: Much of the food we eat is unsafe (*National Geographic*, May 2002)	Support
Facts	1. Salmonella—from contaminated pork 2. Fish, cattle, broiler and laying chickens now raised in food factories—conditions favor contamination 3. E-coli wide spread in cattle herds 4. Families eat out more often; more chance of contaminated food
Statistics	1. The Center for Disease Control and Prevention (CDC) reports 76 million people each year suffer from food born diseases 2. CDC reports 5,000 people die per year 3. FDA took samples of food in Washington DC; 20% samples had Salmonella bacteria 4. Study by consumer's union—2/3 of chickens in U.S. grocery stores contain campylobacter that causes extreme abdominal pain and vomiting in people.
Examples	1. Uncooked eggs and egg products (Caesar salad, eggnog) 2. Rare cooked meats 3. Pâté, blue cheese, cambembert 4. Poorly washed fresh vegetables
Expert authority	1. Patricia Griffin (CDC) increasing risk of eating contaminated food 2. Frederick Angulo (CDC) animals eat contaminated food that they carry in their bodies 3. Carmela Velazquex—handwashing is essential
Logic and reasoning	1. Change eating habits—fewer fast foods 2. Need better disposal of animal wastes 3. Food cannot be made risk-free 4. Insist on cleaner meat, poultry, eggs, and vegetables

Adaptations

Hypothesis-Evidence.   Hypothesis-evidence notes help students think like researchers. The analysis of written materials according to theoretical assumptions and evidence is integral to the research process.

Steps:

1. Make a transparency of a research article.
2. Talk about how researchers present their hypothesis or theory in the opening paragraph and dedicate the rest of the paper to presenting evidence that supports the theory.
3. Read through the article, underlining the theory and evidence.
4. Then, develop the notes together.

5. Finally, have students evaluate whether or not the evidence is convincing and write their comments on their notes.
6. Once students have an idea of how to take Hypothesis-evidence notes, find articles that have different theories on the same topic. Divide students into teams and have each team take notes supporting one hypothesis. Then have each team present its Hypothesis-evidence notes.

Hypothesis	Evidence

Question: Why did dinosaurs disappear?
 	
1. Hypothesis: An asteroid, six miles in diameter, hit the earth.
	2. Tremendous amount of dust in atmosphere
	   3. Rise in temperature
	   3. Changed weather
	2. Dust block off light
	   3. Plants died
	   3. Destroyed food supply
	2. Extinction happened quickly

Agree or disagree with hypothesis:	Seems far fetched No evidence of spot on Earth where it hit Would like more evidence

Model how to use the notes for writing a summary paragraph. Sometimes a paragraph frame will help students develop summaries from their notes:

The author in this article concludes . . .
First, the author says . . .
Next, . . .
Finally, . . .
I think . . .

Student example:

The author concludes that dinosaurs disappeared because of a giant asteroid that hit the earth. First, the author says that the asteroid probably caused a rise in the temperature of the earth. The rise in temperature may have caused the dinosaurs to die because the weather changed quite drastically. Next, when the asteroid hit, it created a lot of dust and particles. The dust probably kept the sun from shining so that plants couldn't grow. The dinosaurs could have starved. Finally, the dinosaurs died quickly. A huge asteroid might have caused them to die fast.

I think the theory might be true. They would die if they didn't have any food and that would have happened pretty fast. I am not in total agreement with the theory though. There should be some gigantic hole some place where the asteroid hit the earth.

Problem-Solution Notes

The Problem-solution format is organized so that students list four questions in the left-hand column: (1) What is the problem or issue? (2) What are the effects of the problem? (3) What are the causes of the problem? (4) What are the solutions to the problem? Answers to the questions are recorded on the right-hand column of the page. This format provides students with a guide for thinking and writing about issues in novels and in content subjects. The format works well as a discussion guide and for taking notes from reading assignments. It is particularly effective for analyzing social issues, ecological issues, current events, and conflict in short stories. Students can also use the structure for analyzing personal problems. Some school administrators have students who receive disciplinary referrals complete Problem-solution frameworks before meeting with them. The administrators report this is a good way to prevent the incidents from recurring since the students have to determine solutions. Also, administrators and counselors use the framework for dealing with feuding students. Students must work together to complete the Problem-solution frame. This helps the students to see both sides of the problem and to resolve their issues more effectively.

Guided
Comprehension

Introduction, Modeling, and Reflection

1. Model with a discussion about a current issue.
2. Develop a problem statement and write it in the right-hand column, opposite the question.
3. Brainstorm possible effects, causes, and solutions to the problem, and record them in the right-hand column opposite the appropriate questions.
4. If reading an article, skim the article first to determine the problem being discussed. Write out the problem in the Problem-solution guide. Next, read through the article more carefully and underline the effects, causes, and solutions. You can label them in the margins of the article with an "e," "c," or "s" to keep the underlined information straight. Next, write the information in your Problem-solution guide. These sample Problem-solution notes are based on an article about erosion.

1. What is the *Problem* or *Issue*?	America's topsoil is eroding away at an alarming rate.
2. What are the *Effects*?	ugly ditches cut through the hillsides creek beds choked with topsoil soil can't produce as many crops more land will have to be put into production
3. What are the *Causes*?	one crop on the same field over-tilling the soil not rotating crops
4. What are the *Solutions*?	no-till farming new fertilizers strip farming

5. Model how to use the notes to write a Problem-solution paper. The first paragraph identifies and explains the problem. The next paragraphs cover the effects, causes, and solutions.

Example:

A huge problem for the American farmers is erosion. Topsoil is eroding away at an alarming rate. This problem must be stopped.

You can see the effects of erosion any time you drive into the countryside. After a rain, deep, ugly ditches cut through the hillsides where the rains have washed the top soil away. Our creek beds become choked with soil as the water sweeps the soil away. Too much soil in streams destroys animals and plant life in our streams. In addition, the remaining topsoil in the fields becomes thin and can't produce abundant crops. This means that more land will have to be put into production, which leaves little left for supporting native plants and animals.

There are several factors that lead to the problem of soil erosion. Farmers like to plant one crop on their land so there is nothing to stop whole hillsides from eroding away. After a crop is harvested, farmers plow the soil until it is too fine which makes it easy for the rain to wash the soil away or for winds to blow it away.

How can the problem be solved? Farmers need to do strip farming, where different crops are planted next to one another in strips. There might be a strip of winter wheat next to a strip of green peas. If the water starts to flow through the land planted in peas, it will stop when it comes to the wheat crop. Another idea is to use no-till farming, where farmers just plant into the stubble rather than cultivating it first. There are many things that can be done so that farmers keep their land productive.

5. Discuss why this strategy is helpful for analyzing problems and solutions. "How did identifying the ingredients (problem, effects, causes, and solution) of problem solving help you analyze it? How did this framework help you with discussion? With writing?"

Support and Extensions

- Problem-solution notes can serve as a basis for small group discussions. Students work together identifying problems and solutions, and then present their ideas to the whole group.
- Problem-solution notes also work well with personal problems and issues.

PROBLEM: Husband and wife both working outside of the home.	
EFFECTS:	**CAUSES:**
1. Increased need for child care	1. Neither parent home to take care of children
2. Changing of traditional roles	2. In order for family to operate smoothly, household chores have to be shared. Wife may have to chop wood, husband may have to fix dinner.
3. Stress in marriage	3. Less time for each other. Difficulty being super-parent, super-spouse, and super-worker.
4. Higher standard of living	4. Two incomes

SOLUTION: Counseling for husband/wife or for family
Legislation for more quality child care facilities
Lowering expectations
Hiring others for jobs like cleaning and household maintenance

• These notes can help students think about problems confronting characters in novels and short stories. Students can take brief notes from each chapter using a Problem-solution format. This note-taking strategy works well for literature because chapters usually build around one or two problems that the main character or characters need to resolve. Asking students to take Problem-solution notes individually and to bring their notes to cooperative team discussions works as an effective discussion strategy.

Mickey Conway, a teacher from Lockport, Illinois, used the following modified framework to assist her sophomores in reading and discussing *The Scarlet Letter*. Students brought their completed reading guides to their literature discussion groups.

What characters have we met so far?	What seems to be the main conflict/problem at this point?	Questions I had while reading:	My predictions about what will happen next:
Chapters 1–3			
Chapters 4–6			
Chapters 7–9			
Chapters 10–12			

Adaptations

Cause-Effect Two-Column Notes.   Another way to examine issues is by analyzing causes and effects in a two-column format. While reading *Sadako and the Thousand Paper Cranes,* students examined the effects of the atomic bomb dropped on Hiroshima.

Cause	Effect
Because the atomic bomb was dropped on Hiroshima, Japan ...	1. No one could live there until the radidation left. 2. Many Japanese people got a disease. 3. Lots of people were killed from the explosion 4. Hiroshina was disrayed 5. People are still dying today of the effects 6. It ended a war 7. We know how horrble it can be 8. It was a nightmare at the time. 9. We are making treaties to ban atomic bombs

Problem-Analysis.   Students in George Rusnak's American history class, used the following Problem-analysis template (also Blackline 18) to take notes, discuss, and write about agricultural problems in the 1920s.

Problem Analysis

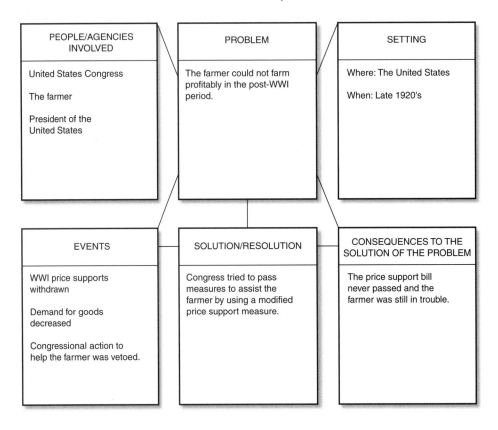

Student example:

In the late 1920s after World War I, agricultural problems arose in the United States. Farmers were finding it harder and harder to make a profit as a result of their work. Price supports were withdrawn, and equipment became fancier and more expensive while the demands for products decreased. Members of Congress introduced the McNary-Haugen Bill to restart price supports. The bill was vetoed. Agriculture in the United States was in just as much trouble as it had been before the war.

Problem-Solution-Graphic Structure. Another format that teachers have found useful for generating discussion and writing is found in Blackline 19 (Cope, 1991).

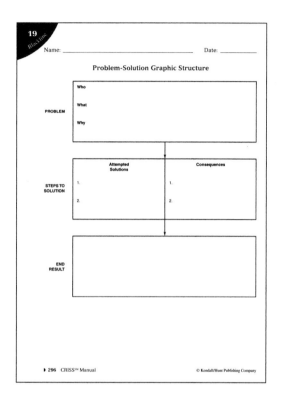

History-Change Frame (Buehl, 2001).   History texts appear to be an endless flood of names, dates, and events with authors mentioning one fact after another. Buehl's History-change frame helps students begin to make more sense of history—namely that it is a story of change and people's reactions to change. Change forces us to rethink old ways and creates new problems for us to resolve. This framework helps students begin to think about how changes affect groups of people, and it guides students to go beyond the facts and think about bigger ideas or essential issues.

Settling the American West

Group American Indians	Group Farmers	Group Cattle Ranchers
What problems did they face? ▶ land was being taken ▶ could no longer live on the open land/ different ideas of land ownership ▶ no longer freely hunt ▶ destruction of native culture ▶ violence	What problems did they face? ▶ challenging farming conditions ▶ isolation ▶ debt ▶ American Indian attacks ▶ conflicts with cattle ranchers	What problems did they face? ▶ conflicts with farmers on rights to land ▶ conflicts with American Indians ▶ transportation of products ▶ over production led to overgrazing
What changes led these problems? ▶ railroad ▶ different ideas about how land should be used ▶ Oregon Trail/mass settlement ▶ Lewis & Clark Expedition opened up possibility of settling the West ▶ Homestead Act	What changes led to these problems? ▶ opening of the West ▶ unclear about use of public lands	What changes led to these problems? ▶ destruction of buffalo emptied land for cattle ▶ railroads/opened up the west to more settlers
What did they do to resolve the problems? ▶ moved to reservations ▶ Dawes Act gave separate plots of land to each native American Indian family	What did they do to resolve problems? ▶ more farm machinery to make farming easier ▶ building of roads ▶ many settlers quit farming	What did they do to resolve problems? ▶ cattle ranching on smaller scale ▶ American Indians moved to reservations ▶ fencing the plains with barbed wire

Source: Adapted from Buehl, 2001.

Process Notes

Students seldom realize that they use processes daily to achieve results in all aspects of their lives. They seem to think that they get from one point to another by random acts or, maybe, just by luck. Whenever students need help learning how to do a step-by-step process, consider process notes as a guide. Process notes help students work through the steps and procedures for negotiating a multitude of tasks such as conducting scientific experiments, building furniture in a woodworking class, and solving those dreaded word problems in mathematics.

In fact, mathematics teachers find process notes particularly helpful for guiding students through the steps in solving word problems. Word problems become far less intimidating. Two of our national trainers, Jim Divine and Sally Hunt, have explored a variety of ways of using process notes in mathematics. The following are some of their ideas.

Sally Hunt notes that even her best math students struggled with word problems. "They'd freeze and lose confidence because they had difficulty breaking down the information from word problems—they wanted to do everything in one step." Therefore, she and her algebra students developed mathematics process notes, which made problem solving less intimidating while assisting them in becoming better problem-solvers (see example on page 138).

Introduction, Modeling, and Reflection

1. Give students a blank copy of the Word Problem Process Notes (Blackline 20).
2. Model each type of problem students need to solve.

Name: _____ Date: _____

Word Problem Process Notes

Write the question.	
List clue words and facts.	
Identify the variable(s).	
Make a drawing.	
Choose a strategy.	
Solve the problem.	
Write your answer in a complete sentence that answers the question.	
Checks: Credibility (Does your answer make sense?) Mathematical	

© Kendall/Hunt Publishing Company   CRISS™ Manual 297

Example:

Problem (page 199, #37): **Movies.** When rating movies, movie critic Ms. Taylor gives four thumbs up to every five thumbs up given by movie critic Mr. Leshnock. If Ms. Taylor gives thumbs up to 68 movies, how many movies does Mr. Leshnock rate favorably?

WORD PROBLEM PROCESS NOTES

Write the question.	How many movies does Mr. Leshnock rate favorably?
List clue words and facts.	Clue words: "four thumbs up to every five" - indicates a ratio. Fact: Ms. Taylor gives 68 thumbs up.
Identify the variable(s).	T = Number of Ms. Taylor thumbs up L = Number of Mr. Leshnock thumbs up
Make a drawing.	Movies 1 2 3 4 5 T L T L T L T L T L
Choose a strategy.	Set up a ratio of favorable Ms. T. picks to favorable Mr. L. picks. Solve the proportion by using the product of the means equals the product of the extremes.

Solve the problem.	$\dfrac{T}{L} = \dfrac{4}{5} = \dfrac{68}{L}$, $4L = 5 \times 68$ means = extremes [cross products]
	   $L = \dfrac{340}{4}$ divide by 4
	   $L = 85$ simplify

Write your answer in a complete sentence that answers the question.	Mr. Leshnock rates 85 movies favorably.

Check
   Credibility (Does your answer make sense?)
 	
   Mathematical
	Credibility: The answer makes sense, since Mr. L. would rate one-fourth more movies favorably than Ms. T. would.
	
	Mathematical:
	$\dfrac{68}{85} = .8$ which is the same as $\dfrac{8}{10}$ or $\dfrac{4}{5}$

Source: Excerpted from *Algebra I, Interpretation, Applications, Connections,* 2000. Reprinted by permission of Glencoe/McGraw-Hill.

3. As you model, students follow along and complete the process notes in their notebooks.

4. Model other types of problem-solving formats; students record in their note-books. Students refer to these models when doing their assignments. The following is an example from geometry:

Two-Column Notes
Mathematics

Geometry: A lot for a new house is shaped like a trapezoid, with two right angle corners. If the third corner is an 80 degree angle, what is the measurement of the fourth angle?

Main idea: *What is being asked for?*	*To find the measure of the fourth angle*
List the important facts. *What facts are necessary to solve the problem?*	*lot shaped like a trapezoid* *has two right angles (90 degrees + 90 degrees)* *3rd angle is 80 degrees* *sum of all angles should be 360 degrees*
Draw a picture of the situation.	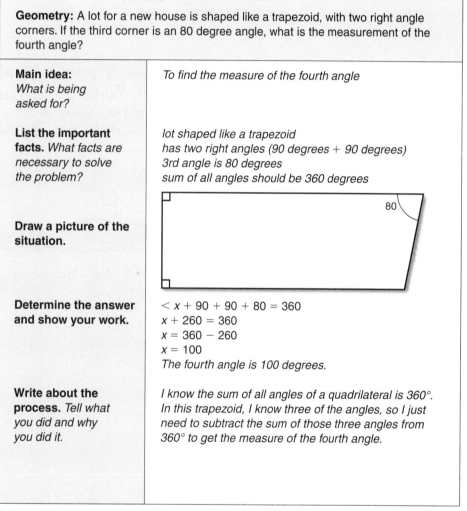
Determine the answer and show your work.	$< x + 90 + 90 + 80 = 360$ $x + 260 = 360$ $x = 360 - 260$ $x = 100$ *The fourth angle is 100 degrees.*
Write about the process. *Tell what you did and why you did it.*	*I know the sum of all angles of a quadrilateral is 360°. In this trapezoid, I know three of the angles, so I just need to subtract the sum of those three angles from 360° to get the measure of the fourth angle.*

Source: Meints 2001

5. Students work in pairs or small groups using process notes to complete their assignment.
6. Ask students how the process notes helped them tackle word problems. How did the notes help them internalize the steps needed to solve the problems?

Support and Extensions

● The following example is an elementary version of Process Notes:

A boat sailed 750 miles from Vancouver to San Francisco, another 412 miles to Los Angeles, and on to Panama 3,000 miles away. What was the total length of it's journey?

```
  750
  412
 3000
 ----
 4162
```

main idea	To find the total of miles in trip. From Vancuver to Panama
important facts	750 miles from V. to S.F. 412 miles to L.A. 3,000 mi to Panama
Clues	total
Picture	
Predict Any second step needed	makes to have bigger number NO
Do the work Check	see above

● You can adapt two-column notes for students to record information from scientific explorations. In the left column, list the steps involved in an investigation. In the right, students record answers based on their experimentation and observations.

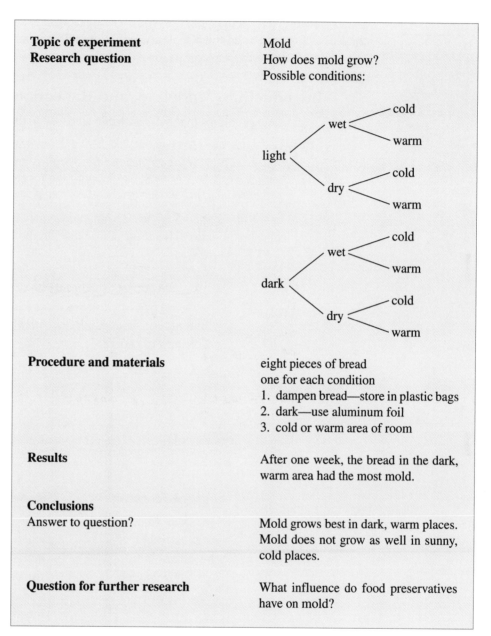

Topic of experiment **Research question**	Mold How does mold grow? Possible conditions:
Procedure and materials	eight pieces of bread one for each condition 1. dampen bread—store in plastic bags 2. dark—use aluminum foil 3. cold or warm area of room
Results	After one week, the bread in the dark, warm area had the most mold.
Conclusions Answer to question?	Mold grows best in dark, warm places. Mold does not grow as well in sunny, cold places.
Question for further research	What influence do food preservatives have on mold?

Students can then use their notes for writing a scientific report.

Example:

In this experiment, we studied mold. We wanted to know what makes mold grow. We used eight slices of bread. We put water on half of the bread and then stored all pieces in plastic bags. Some bags were in light places. We put tin foil around some of the bread to keep out the light. After one week, we decided which pieces of bread had the most mold. The wet bread kept in tin foil had the most.

Other Organizing Formats

Problem-Solving Organizer

Jim Devine developed the Problem-Solving Organizer as a way to help fifth, eighth, and tenth graders prepare for the Florida Comprehensive Achievement Test (FCAT) in mathematics. Students were not only asked to solve a problem, but also had to explain the process. The explanation part of the assessment presented, especially for grade 5 teachers, a unique challenge. Jim developed this Problem-solving organizer in response to teachers' pleas for help (also Blackline 21).

Guided Comprehension

Introduction, Modeling, and Reflection

1. Select problems that have multiple steps, as in the sample problem below.

   Anna's allowance is $5 a week. She can earn more by doing extra chores. She can earn $1 per day for walking the dog and $1 per day for doing dishes. How much can Anna make in four weeks if she does every chore? Show how you figured it out and write a brief explanation of your process.

2. For the first step, model how to paraphrase the question. What does the problem ask you to do? This information goes in the box at the top of the page.

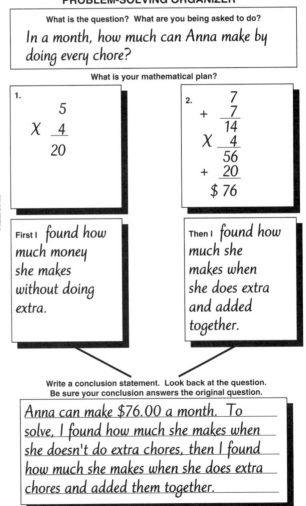

3. In the boxes numbered "1" and "2," write your mathematical plan using numbers and symbols. Come up with several different plans, demonstrating that there is more than one way to solve the problem.
4. Below each step in the mathematical plan, develop a written explanation for what you did.
5. In the last box, model how to synthesize the information into a concluding statement that includes the answer to your original question.

    This organizer prompts students to begin by paraphrasing the question, then asks them to refer to the same question again as a writing prompt for their concluding statement.

6. Talk about the different methods for solving this and other problems. "How did the Problem-solving organizer help you think through multiple methods for solving the problem?" Jim Devine notes that the organizer also helps teachers better understand student thinking processes. Consequently, they can provide more precise feedback about how a student might approach a problem more effectively.

Support and Extensions

- Pair students, and give them several copies of the organizer. Challenge them to solve problems in a variety of ways and record on their organizers.
- A more advanced form of the Problem-solving organizer is presented on Blackline 22.

Content Frames

Frames, or charts, provide another way to organize and compare information. Armbruster, Anderson, and Meyer (1991) conducted a series of investigations with middle school children that demonstrated the positive effects of framing on comprehension and retention of science and social studies materials. They also noted that involving the readers in producing the frames is an important factor in the success of the technique.

Frames work well in situations where students analyze the inter-relationship of ideas. Consider using frames with material that is structured so that main topics are compared with similar subtopics. For example, Julie Johnson's biology students organized information about genetic disorders into a Content Frame. First, as a class, they examined the organization of their textbook chapter and determined the categories of information presented and the subdivisions into which the categories were divided. Then, as they read, they recorded the information to complete their frames.

Content Frame

GENETIC DISORDER	CHROMOSOME ERROR	DOMINANT OR RECESSIVE	SYMPTOMS (HOW IT AFFECTS A PERSON)
Albinism	# 11	RECESSIVE	no melanin, pigment in hair or skin, sensitive to light
Cystic Fibrosis	#7	Recessive	Respiratory + digestive problems., delayed growth ↳ thick mucus builds up b/c of sodium channels of cells. males = infertile, pale stools, coughing, weight loss. Most fatal inherited disorder affecting Caucasians in USA.
Tay-Sachs Disease	#15	RECESSIVE	Usually in Jewish people. start to appear @ 3-6 mos. progresses Rapidly + death = 4-5 yrs. deafness, dementia, seizures, Paralysis, loss of muscle function, delayed mental growth
Sickle-Cell Anemia	blood disorder #6	RECESSIVE	joint pain, fatigue, breathlessness, rapid heart rate, delayed growth, ulcers on lower legs, jaundice, bone pain, attacks of abdominal pain, fever, excessive thirst & urination, chest pain. ⊃ = R.B.C. norm ⊃ = s.c. African Am.
Phenylketonuria (PKU)	#12 bad PAH enzyme	RECESSIVE	severe mental retardation. can be tested for & prevented w/special diet. ↳ low-protein diet "diet for life."
Huntington Disease	#4 mutated gene	dominant	on set = middle age (late 30's - 40's) kills brain cells, loose control of muscles, c.n.s. break down. European client death w/in 15 yrs. of onset. -mood swings, depression, loss of movement, memory

Introduction, Modeling, and Reflection

1. When developing a frame, ask your students two questions: What are the important categories of information? How might these categories be subdivided? With content materials, model how you can use headings, subheadings, introductions, and summaries for clues to frame categories. Then build your chart together.

2. Read through the material together. Question the author. Selectively underline. Note topics and details. Note Power 1 ideas or topics, and underline Power 2 ideas or subtopics (see Chapter 3). When necessary, write topics and subtopics in the margins.

3. Together, build a frame of the information. Then read through the material to fill out the chart. Talk about whether or not your chart works for each topic. Make changes or additions in the frame as necessary.

4. After the frame is complete (you may need more than one resource), model how to use it for self-testing.

5. Talk about how developing the frame helps to organize information logically and to see interrelationships of ideas.

Support and Extensions

- As part of pre-reading, have students make some decisions about the best ways to organize information. Ask students to think about these questions:

  What does the author want us to learn?
  How does the author structure his/her writing for presenting main points?
  How is the material organized?
  How should I transform the information?
  Are there categories of information that reflect the major concepts in the materials? If so, perhaps a frame might work better than other transformation strategies.

- Have students work in small groups or in pairs. Have each team design a frame they feel works for the materials. Teams present their frames and explain how they represent the structure of the material.

- The following examples represent some sample frames from a variety of contents:

Literature

Character	Personality Traits	Actions that Support Trait	Conversations by or about the Character that Illustrate Trait

Mathematics

Name	Symbol	Label	Key Word	Definition (own words)
Plane			2-D or Flat	A plane is a flat surface like the top of my desk.
Point	•	•M	dot	A point has no dimension, just a location. Group together to make lines.
Line	←——→		straight	A line is a set of points, determined by any 2 points. It is horizontal, vertical or oblique (angle).
Line Segment			endpoints (R&S)	A part of a line with points on the ends to show where it ends.

Science

Biomes	Location	Climate	Plants	Animals
Tropical rain forest				
Grassland				
Desert				
Temperate forest				
Taiga				
Tundra				

Social Studies

Political Party	Environment	Education	Social Programs	States vs. Central Government
Democrats				
Republicans				

● Semantic Feature Analysis is a modified Content Frame designed to help students gain greater understanding of a concept and to relate vocabulary within a selection (see Chapter 9).

Story Plans

Story Plans (also called story grammars) are organizers used for understanding narrative structure. Teaching students about the plan or structure of a story leads to improved comprehension. In his review of research on story structure instruction, Trebasso (2002) found that teaching students to analyze stories improved comprehension as measured by performance in answering questions and in recalling of information. In addition, knowledge of story structure led to higher standardized test performance, particularly for less able readers in grades 3–6.

Story Plans characterize the general structure of stories by defining what most have in common. They are, in effect, a summary of the plot and setting of a narrative. When students understand the architecture of fiction, they can use these generic frameworks in comprehending literature and in drafting their own stories. In addition, they are effective props for story retellings.

Story Plans usually contain the following key elements: major characters, setting (time and place), problem (characters attempt to solve problems), goal (character's plan to solve the problem), main events of the story, and resolution (see Blackline 23).

Story Plans provide a concise way of summarizing stories because readers choose only the events that lead directly to the resolution of the problem. If students first define the problem and resolution, they will have a way to sort through the story details. They can narrow down details to those that directly lead to the solution of the problem.

Guided Comprehension

Introduction, Modeling, and Reflection

1. Explain that most stories have certain elements in common, and understanding these components leads to improved comprehension.
2. On the overhead, model how to develop a story plan with a simple story such as *The True Story of the Three Little Pigs,* by A. Wolf, as told to Jon Scieszka. Guide the discussion with questions.

Setting questions: Where did the story occur? When did the story occur?	
Character questions: Who is the main character? Whom is this story most about?	
Problem and goal questions: What major problem does the main character face? What does this character hope to achieve?	
Resolution questions: Does the character solve the problem? Is the character defeated by the problem? Does the character learn to live with the problem?	

3. A completed Story Plan for *The True Story of the Three Little Pigs* might look something like this:

Setting	Wolf's neighborhood, way back in "once upon a time"
Characters	Wolf, three pigs, reporters, police
Problem	Wolf doesn't have any sugar for Granny's cake
Goal	Make a birthday cake for Granny
Events	1. Wolf visits first neighbor pig in straw house to get sugar—no answer; wolf sneezes, house falls down and accidentally kills pig; wolf eats it 2. Visits next neighbor to get sugar; house built out of sticks; pig tells him to go away, he sneezes, house falls down, accidentally kills second pig; wolf eats it 3. Visits third neighbor pig; house built with bricks, pig is obnoxious, tells him to go away, makes fun of his granny, wolf tries to destroy house, goes to jail
Resolution	Wolf in jail; doesn't get to make cake

4. Together use the Story Plan to write a summary.
5. Talk about how Story Plans help with analyzing narratives. "How might Story Plans be used as part of book discussion groups? How might they be used to help in the writing of original stories? Why are Story Plans an excellent way to summarize narratives?"

Support and Extensions

● Once students have a basic understanding of a Story Plan (Blackline 22), extend their understanding by explaining that problems in stories are resolved in one of three ways. The character can solve the problem, the problem defeats the character, or the character simply learns to live with the situation. Use the Story Plan map example below as a format for analyzing the three possible resolutions. Students can use this format for thinking through problem-resolution in class novels and in their independent reading.

Who has the problem? _____

_____

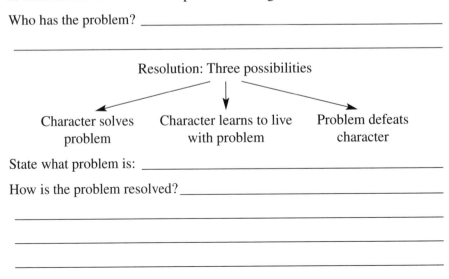

Resolution: Three possibilities

Character solves problem   Character learns to live with problem   Problem defeats character

State what problem is: _____

How is the problem resolved? _____

_____

_____

_____

- Have students use Story Plans as notes for oral book reports.
- Have students do several different Story Plans for a selection. Each plan should have a different problem statement. For example, with *The True Story of the Three Little Pigs* the problem statements might be:

The Wolf is misrepresented in the original story of the *Three Little Pigs.*
A Wolf has a bad cold.
A Wolf is a murderer.

After students have brainstormed different problem statements, divide them into groups. Have each group work out a Story Plan for one problem statement. Then have groups present their plans and convince other class members the story events and the resolution provide evidence that their problem is developed in the story.

- Have students develop Story Plans for media presentations—television, movies.
- Have students use Story Plans for drafting their own stories. Before students write, encourage them to think about the characters, setting, problem, and solution.

Use Story Plans for revision conferences. After students have drafted their stories, they can use a checklist similar to the following for making decisions about revision or a rubric similar to the one presented below.

> Will the reader be able to describe the setting?
> Who is the main character?
> What is the main character like?
> What problem does the main character need to resolve?
> How is the problem resolved? Do we know?

If students find out they do not have these components in their stories, they will have some specific ideas for revision.

Story Plan Rubric	Wow—I did it! 3 points	I did most of it! 2 points	I need to do better. 1 point
I have completed every part of my Story Plan.			
I have the names of the main characters.			
I have complete notes about the setting.			
I have told about the main problem.			
I have explained how the problem was solved.			
I have listed the events that led to the solution.			
I have used my best handwriting.			
I have checked my work for conventions (spelling, punctuation, grammar).			

Adaptations

Modified Story Plans can be used for non-fiction situations.

History.   After reading about an event in history or a current event article, have students work in pairs or cooperative groups to fill out the following Story Plan from the perspective of one of the parties involved. In the Teapot Dome scandal example below, students filled out the frame from Secretary Albert Fall's perspective.

Event	Teapot Dome Scandal
Setting	Washington, D.C. & Teapot Dome, WY—1923
Characters	Pres. Warren G. Harding, Interior Secretary Albert B. Fall
Problem	Oil rich land in Wyoming is to be used by the Navy
Goal	Secretary Fall wanted to get rich
Events	Harding, overwhelmed by presidency, gives Cabinet positions to friends Profitable oil reserves found in Wyoming—earmarked for Navy Fall, one of the "friends," sells off drilling leases to private companies (illegally & secretly) Fall gets cash, stocks, and cattle as bribes from the companies Congress discovers the fraud Harding becomes ill and dies before all is resolved Fall is convicted and sent to jail
Resolution	Fall loses everything and goes to jail

Mathematics.   Use the modified Story Plan to help students solve open-ended math problems or as an organizer for developing their own written problems.

> *Your mother sends you to the store with $5.00 and asks you to buy fruit for a fruit salad she plans to make. She doesn't care what you get as long as you get at least <u>three</u> types of fruit, and so long as it makes enough for <u>exactly 10 people</u>—she wants to have enough, but no leftovers. She gives you the information in Chart 1 to help with your selections. You discover the information in Chart 2 when you get to the store.*

Chart 1: Single serving size for various fruits	
Fruit	**Serving Size**
Orange	1
Apple	1
Kiwi	3
Banana	1
Strawberries	½ pint
Raspberries	½ pint

Chart 2: Grocery store prices for fruit	
Fruit	**Cost**
Oranges	3 for $1.00
Apples	4 for $1.00
Kiwis	4 for $1.00
Bananas	6 for $1.00
Strawberries	1 pint for $1.50
Raspberries	1 pint for $3.00

The store allows you to buy oranges, bananas, apples, kiwis, and bananas one at a time, but the smallest amount of either strawberries or raspberries is one pint. How much money do you return to your mother, and what is your fruit salad recipe?

Setting	**Kitchen and grocery store**
People/things involved	**Mother and me**
Goal	**Make a fruit salad that costs $5.00 or less, serves exactly 10 people, and contains at least three kinds of fruit.**
Important information or "givens"	**How much fruit provides enough for one serving (see Chart 1)** **Cost of the individual types of fruit (see Chart 2)**

Steps to solution	1. **Since the raspberries are so expensive, I don't think I will use them.**
	2. **I will try to use the remaining fruits and a similar amount for each.**
	3. **Since I can't divide the strawberries, I will buy 1 pt., which serves 2 people and costs $1.50.**
	4. **I have four fruits left and need eight more servings, so I will try two servings of each and see how the money comes out.**
	    2 oranges @ .33 = $0.66
	    2 apples @ .25 = 0.50
	    2 × 3 kiwis @ .25 = 1.50
	    2 bananas @ .17 = 0.34
	                $3.00 plus $1.50 for strawberries makes a total of $4.50

Solution	**Return $.50 to mother. Salad contains 2 each of oranges, apples, and bananas, 6 kiwis, and a pint of strawberries.**
Check solution	**I went back and rechecked my calculations. The answer seems reasonable to me since I have lots of fruit, and I did not go over the $5.00 Mom gave me.**

Science: The Story Plan can be modified to serve as a format for a laboratory investigation.

Science Example

Process	Process topic
Setting	Conditions for the process (temperature, humidity, vacuum, etc.)
Components	Necessary materials or elements
Goal	End product
Steps	Steps of process
Results	Results

Process	Photosynthesis
Setting	Daylight, time of year when plants are not dormant (some photosynthesis actually happens in dark too)
Components	any green plant (having chlorophyll), light, carbon dioxide, water
Goal	Changing light energy into chemical energy
Steps	Carbon dioxide and water are taken in by the chlorophyll-bearing cells in a plant. When light energy is added, oxygen and glucose are formed. $$6\,CO_2 + 6\,H_2O \xrightarrow{\text{light energy}} C_6H_{12}O_6 + 6\,O_2$$ (carbon dioxide) + (water) (glucose) + (oxygen)
Results	The glucose the plant forms is used as a source of stored energy for the plant. The chemical energy is used also by animals that eat the plant. The oxygen that is a bi-product is used by animals for breathing.

▶ Summary

In this chapter, we explored a variety of ways to organize and structure text information. We know successful readers glean main points from their reading assignments and have specific strategies such as Main Idea-Detail Notes and Content Frames for organizing information they have read. In order to succeed, students must organize and apply information from their reading.

In addition to helping our students understand the main ideas from their reading, we encourage higher levels of thinking. The instructional strategies for evaluating opinions, problems, and issues help students think critically about their reading. Students develop support for opinions, define propositions, analyze problems, identify processes, and analyze the literary elements in narratives. As teachers, we must model options and teach for competence in these strategies so students have the confidence to develop their own individual study plans.

Research Conclusion	Reference
Good readers are metacognitive; they not only experience many different ways to organize and write about information, but also have an awareness of the author's purpose and style of writing.	Duke and Pearson, 2002
Poor readers remain unaware of the need to transform, to self-monitor, and to think consciously about how to learn.	Paris, Wasik, and Turner, 1991

Informal Writing to Learn: Learning Logs

During the first weeks of school, we ask our students to purchase a loose-leaf or spiral notebook to use as a learning log. These logs become a regular part of our classroom routines. Students use logs for free writing, for explanations, for letters about their reading, for scientific observations, and for simply collecting personal thoughts.

The reasoning behind logs is simple. Students become better writers and more active learners when they write often (Atwell, 1998; Zinsser,1988). When people write about something, they learn it better. Learning logs provide students with a safe place to speculate, seek, discover, and figure things out. This is more about thinking than polished writing. Writing also prepares students for discussion. When they write about their thinking before they talk in their groups or with the whole class community, discussions become richer and more interactive.

We recommend introducing logs by explaining why writing is essential for learning. Explain that entries may include questions about vocabulary, difficult concepts, or lab results. These entries are often messy, with thoughts scratched out and arrows indicating added information.

Students might write in their logs two or three times during a class period. Pause frequently during lectures to allow students to write down ideas and questions. Then let them share their responses before moving on to the next part of your lecture. Mixing writing with listening helps to energize students. It is harder to stare blankly when you know you are expected to write about and discuss information from a lecture.

Sometimes entries have focus; in other situations, they are completely open-ended. Free-writes, dialogue, and perspective entries generate more open-ended responses than those where students write explanations, develop pre- and post-reading entries or write about their observations. The response depends upon the content and goals of a lesson.

This chapter offers a variety of options.

Learning Strategy

Free-Write Entries

Whenever students read and then write without a teacher's specific direction about what and how to do it, they are making free-write entries. By design, free-writes help students to react emotionally and to think more deeply about their reading. Readers learn to trust their own instincts while they speculate, question, and find meaning as they write. Free-writes help students connect with the piece and untangle challenging ideas.

Guided Comprehension

Introduction, Modeling, and Reflection

1. Make a transparency of a series of quotations from a novel, newspaper article, non-fiction book, or poem. Display the first quotation. Explain that students are to "write freely about anything that comes to mind. Express your own opinions, ideas, and questions. No one is going to grade your responses."
2. Model your own response with items crossed off and words tumbling across the page. Your model will help everyone feel safe about taking risks.
3. After a few minutes, ask students to finish their last idea. Display the remaining quotations one at a time, allowing students two or three minutes to write about each one.
4. After students have responded to all the quotations, invite them to reread their responses. "Mark any phrases, questions, words, or ideas that you find promising. Note ideas that could be developed further. Talk about some of these possibilities with your partner. Are there excerpts or ideas that you might want to share with the whole group?"

5. Take time for students to think about the free-writing process. "How do free-writes help you become more engaged in reading? How did this strategy work for you? Did it help with your discussions? How did it aid your understanding of the selection. Did it help you become more metacognitive?"

Support and Extensions

● Use free-writes during novel studies. Students might be reading a novel as a class or as part of a literature study group. At the end of a reading period, ask students to write non-stop. For less able writers and younger students begin with five-minute writings, gradually working up to ten minutes. Use a timer. Next, ask students to share their free-writes with the class. Accept their ideas. Listen intently. Repeat back what the writer says. If it seems right, delve more deeply: "I am interested in what you said about . . . What made you say this?" Your modeling and interest show that you really do care about their ideas. Gradually, students will begin to trust their own ideas and thinking.

In the following example, a fifth-grade reader responds to a chapter in the novel *Kavik, the Wolf Dog.*

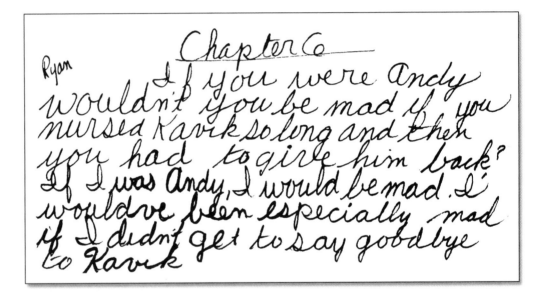

● Encourage free-writes in the form of questions. Begin by explaining that good readers constantly question the text—before, during, and after reading. Model questions that come to mind as you read a literary excerpt, a current events article, or a math problem.

Stop and let students do the same thing.

In the following example, high school government students wrote freely about a political cartoon illustrating the 94th Congress. Questions naturally emerged in the writing.

What is the cartoonist saying about the 94th Congress? I'm not sure. Are the representatives like soldiers just following orders? Why are the people all dressed up like English soldiers? Are they trying to be tyrants? Is the cartoonist saying that the representatives are afraid to do anything on their own? It shows that the representatives can't lead or make any decisions. . .kind of scary when you think about it.

- As a pre-reading activity, have students examine pictures relevant to the upcoming topic and write about their feelings and ideas. In the following example, middle school students, before reading, looked at the picture on the front cover of Gary Paulsen's *Tracker* and explored their interpretations.

> This is a weird picture. The only explanation that I can come up with is that this person cares more about the environment than they do about humans, because they drew the deer in front of the human.
>
> Another possibility can be seen if you make your eyes blurry it looks like there are two evil people after the deer. This shows that on the outside people can look nice, but when you delve deeper you can see what they're all about.

- After listening and viewing a news broadcast, have students write about their reactions.
- When introducing a difficult mathematics selection, ask students to read and record questions that need clarification. These questions then become the focus of class discussion.

Example:

I am having a hard time understanding what a function is. The explanation with x's and y's is hard to follow. It has to do with ordered pairs and graphs, but I don't know why the graphs on page 138 are different from the one at the top of page l39. Next question: Can the x value of a pair ever be the value of the function? Next question: Are all linear equations functions?

- If students are having trouble getting started with free-writes, encourage them with sentence starters:

Literature Examples

This chapter was _____ (use a descriptive word here—exciting, scary, sad, confusing, etc.) when . . . (tell what in the chapter made it that way).
This chapter made me feel . . .
I was confused when . . . This was confusing because . . .
_____ from the book reminded me of . . . in my life (in another book, etc.).
I could use the information I learned to . . .
I can really relate to . . . because . . .
I didn't like . . . because . . .
My favorite part was . . . because . . .

Mathematics Examples

General questions:

What are you thinking?
Explain so that a fifth-grader would understand it?
What does X stand for?
What does the equation say in plain English?
Could you draw a picture of that?
Why did you write that equation?
Tell why that last step makes sense?

When you are stuck:

Why are you stuck?
What makes this problem difficult?
What information do you need to get unstuck?
How can you get the needed information?

When you are finished:

What were you thinking about when you did step X?
How can you show that you did this correctly?
Could you have done this in a different way?

All Subject Areas Examples

Summarize what you read, saw, or heard. (I learned that . . .)
Ask a question about the material. (I wonder . . ./ Why or why not . . . ?)
Tell something you found interesting or surprising. (I was surprised that . . ./ It is interesting that . . .)
Other: Anything else related to the topic (Draw a representation, present a related fact or piece of information, make personal connections, etc.)

Learning Strategy

Double-Entry Reflective Journals

Double-entry reflective journals (Tovani, 2000) guide students to becoming more aware of what they are thinking while reading. Students divide their papers lengthwise, as if they are going to take two-column notes. On the left side of the paper, readers lift quotes, comments, or summary statements from the materials they are reading and then use the space to the right to record their thoughts. Tovani suggests using some of the following thinking prompts:

Direct quote or summary from source and page number	Thinking prompts: This reminds me of . . . I predict . . . I am confused because . . . I will help myself by . . . I think this means . . . I wonder . . .

Tovani recommends starting with one prompt at a time. Then slowly add others.

Introduction, Modeling, and Reflection

1. Select one prompt, such as *This reminds me of,* and write it on the top of the right-hand column.

2. Read a selection aloud. As you read, write down a quotation, a single word, or a summary statement on the left side of the page. Talk-aloud, demonstrating how the quote ignited connections with your own background or with other things that you have read. Briefly summarize these connections in the right-hand column. Continue modeling.

3. Ask students to work in pairs, constructing double-entry notes over the rest of the selection. In the following example, students read an article about prejudices during the 1920s.

Sacco and Venzetti accused of robbery, no clean evidence for this, were electrocuted	**This reminds me of . . .** *how immigrants are often not treated fairly in the courts today . . . still too much prejudice . . . too many African Americans and Hispanics are in prison. More African Americans are executed than Caucasians.*
Trial probably unfair, convicted because they were Italian immigrants; one of most controversial events in American history	**This reminds me of. . . .** *other groups who have been treated unfairly. I just read an article about immigrants from Haiti whose boat sunk as they were trying to come to the U.S.*
Attorney General Mitchell Palmer jailed thousands of people born overseas. "Those deported should be sent away in ships of stone with sails of lead."	**This reminds me of . . .** *U.S. would have sent them home anyway. Would we do the same if a boatload of white French immigrants landed on a U.S shore?*

4. Students use their quotes and reflections as part of a whole class discussion.

5. Once students feel comfortable with one thinking option, introduce another, following a similar instructional procedure. Take time for reflection. For example, you might choose selections that reflect challenges students might meet in a particular piece of writing.

In the next example, students read a difficult science selection and kept track of ideas that confused them. Asking students to note their confusions helps them not become so overwhelmed by difficult materials. In fact, the struggle to understand can actually be quite invigorating. "Are we going to let this author defeat us? No! The struggle to understand can actually be a lot of fun. Besides that, it is probably not our fault because many authors don't know how to write clearly. Let's give it a try." Then, ask students to write about what they did to "get unstuck." (The following example based on a textbook, comes from an advanced-placement biology class.)

"Protons, neutrons, and electrons are the most stable subatomic particles."	I am confused because . . . *I don't know what the author means by stable. The author seems to think I should already know this.* I will help myself by . . . *rereading the previous sections in this chapter and by reading further to see if the author explains it. He seems to think I should already know this and I don't. Maybe I can ask my lab partner about it. She always seems to know everything.*
"Atoms contain protons, neutrons, and electrons, all arranged in a definite manner."	I am confused because . . . *I don't know what is meant by definite. Does it mean unchanging? I think this might be the point of this section, but I am not getting it.* I will help myself by . . . *trying to figure out the table. It could have something to do with atomic number, but I don't really understand that either. I am going to ask about this in class.*

Encouraging students to struggle with their confusions helps them to read and comprehend actively and also guides them to become more active, metacognitive readers, less easily defeated by difficult material. Good readers always have questions. In this particular example, the teacher asked her students to read their assignments and do double-entry reflective journals, before she ever talked about the concepts in class. She found that students actually read their assignments and came to class prepared with questions about the key scientific concepts. She began her lectures by listing students' questions on a large chart, and then addressed these questions as part of her presentations.

6. Talk about how the prompt *This reminds me of. . .* fits CRISS[SM] philosophy. Discuss why relating reading to one's personal experiences is what comprehension is all about. "You don't really comprehend unless you make these personal links!" Or, if the prompt is *I am confused because,* talk about how great readers always have questions about what they are reading. "Expert readers always struggle to make sense of the message."

Support and Extensions

- Make a chart of the writing prompts introduced.
- Provide options for response as in the following assignment from a selection by Maya Angelou (Glencoe Literature, *The Reader's Choice,* Course 2, used by permission of the publisher, Glencoe/McGraw-Hill).

Each of us has the right and the responsibility to assess the roads which lie ahead, and those over which we have traveled, and if the future road looms ominous or unpromising, and the roads back uninviting, then we need to gather our resolve and, carrying only the necessary baggage, step off that road into another direction. If the new choice is also unpalatable, without embarrassment, we must be ready to change that as well.	**Thinking prompts:** **I wonder . . .** **This reminds me . . .** **I am confused because . . .**

Dialogue Journals

As readers, we talk to our friends about the books and articles we read. Reading literature naturally inspires talk. We want our classrooms to mirror real life, in which informal talk about reading occurs everywhere. One way to achieve this goal is through writing. After students write, ask them to trade logs, read their partner's entries and write comments in response. Peer response becomes very motivating. It makes learning more social, and writers get feedback right away. It is also a "legal way" of passing notes in school!

Introduction, Modeling, and Reflection

1. Ask students to select partners. Partners write entries related to the same selection. Provide a purpose, or have students do free-writes.
2. After students write, model a response. "Write about the ideas presented. Do NOT evaluate your partner's response." Talk about the language of response. Some starters might be:

   I agree . . .
   I disagree . . .
   In my opinion . . .
   I think . . .
   I understand what you mean when . . .

3. Have students pass their logs back and forth as they read. Challenge them to avoid talking about their entries. "Writing is your conversation." In this example, Jose and Brandon became journal buddies while reading *Wrinkle in Time*. Notice how predictions, feelings, and questions emerge as part of the process.

Brandon:

I think the kids are going to the town and get split up. Then one of them will find their father. The other two will probably have to fight the dark thing. And then they will almost get killed and Mrs. Whatsit will save them.

Jose:

I disagree with you when you say Mrs. Whatit will save them. I don't think she can. I think Mrs. Whatsit believes these kids will have to solve the problem themselves. She believes in them. Who do you think will find the father?

Brandon:

I think the Black Thing took over the father and disguised him as the guy with red eyes. Then I think Charles will get into the guy with red eyes's mind and find out if it is his father. Then I think the three kids will release their father from the black thing.

Jose:

I understand what you mean. But I don't agree with you. I think their father is held prisoner somewhere, but not in the guy with red eyes. I think the kids will have to break him out. I am worried that Charles might be a goner. Something seems to be taking him over. What do you think is going on?

4. Ask students to talk about journaling as a process. "Did writing about what you were reading help you gain more from your reading? Did you read more carefully because you knew you were going to write to your partner?"

Support and Extensions

- Dialogue entries can also be based on field trips, speakers, videos, lab activities, or about books students are reading for pleasure. If both partners have computers at home, they can e-mail their entries, then print out their dialogue. They could then use the classroom or laboratory computers to complete their correspondence. Consider e-mail partners from other school districts, states, or countries for your students.

- Include yourself in the conversations. Student-teacher dialogue journals provide a way to "talk" with your students about books they are reading or concerns and ideas they have about content. You also learn more about individual students in your classroom. Frequently, writing brings forth more personal ideas than does talking. Keep it manageable by writing to three or four students in your class each day. By the end of several weeks, you will have written at least once to each student.

Use your responses to focus students on important content and on analytic ideas. Notice how Marylin Nelson does this in her response to one of her student's entries.

Dear Miss Nelson,

I have just started reading a book called "The Ceremonies," by T. Klein. So far the book goes into a lot of detail and it is pretty hard to understand. I am going to continue reading it for the challenge. Have you heard of this author before? If so can you tell me anything about his writing?

Thanks,

Angie

Dear Angie,

I'm not familiar with "The Ceremonies" nor with T. Klein. What's the book about? Maybe once you get into the book, it won't seem so difficult. Sometimes writers take a while to get going. Is the book just wordy, or does the author use detail for a purpose?

Sincerely,

Miss Nelson

● Create "Blessed Books" wall posters. Have groups of students write their dialogue journal entries on flip chart paper. The entries can focus on books students are reading as a whole class, in small groups, or individually. Students record brief comments or ask questions about the book on the poster. Making book discussions public provides a way to "bless" books that students are reading or may want to read.

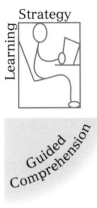

Strategy
Learning

Guided
Comprehension

Pre- and Post-Reading Entries

Pre- and post-reading entries provide a natural way for students to link their own background knowledge to content, to set purposes for reading, to note pre-reading misconceptions and to become more metacognitive.

Introduction, Modeling, and Reflection

1. Write key concepts from a reading selection on the board. Ask students to brainstorm in their logs about what they think the concepts mean. Then have them talk with a partner.
2. As a whole class, discuss the ideas and questions generated in their pre-reading discussions. After reading, students write again, adding new information and noting any misconceptions they might have had about the content before reading.

Social Studies Example

Topic: Creation of a Federal Law

Pre-Reading:

I think laws are created by either the president of the U.S. or senators or representatives. They write up what they want and then they all vote on it. If a representative starts the law, then I think just the House has to vote on it, plus the President has to agree. I think it is the same in the Senate. If most of the senators vote for a law and the President likes it, then it becomes a real law. I think the Supreme Court might have something to do with it because of the "balance of power" thing, but I'm not sure what they do.

Post-Reading:

I kind of had the right idea, except that what the Senators and Representatives write up is called a "bill." The bill has to be passed in both houses, and a lot of the time what they pass is different in each house, so they have to get together in a committee. The committee has both House and Senate members and they try to agree on one bill that is between the two different ones. If they can agree and pass the same bill in both houses, and the President signs it, then it becomes a law. The President can veto it if he doesn't like it, but then the houses can override the veto with a 2/3's vote in each house. The Supreme Court gets in there if someone thinks the new law is unconstitutional. If the Court thinks it is, too, then the Court can kill it.

Science Example

Topic: Glaciers

Pre-Reading:

Glaciers form where it is very cold, usually on mountain tops. They are really just lots of snow that does not melt during the summer time. They can be found in Alaska, Glacier National Park, and probably the Alps. They are dirty on the top with cracks where some explorers have fallen into them and died. I think someone died on Mt. Everest by falling into one of the cracks. I think some are really old like a million years ago during the ice age.

Post-Reading:

Some of my ideas were a little off. Glaciers are more than just snow, but they start as snow. When the snow gets really deep—100s of feet—it is so heavy that it packs down the bottom part and turns it into like ice. Because of the weight above, the ice flows forward—like when you step on a rubber ball and it squishes out beneath your shoe. This movement is really slow, about one foot a year, but still the glaciers changed the shape of the earth. Like they made mountain valleys and lakes. They also made hills and put a lot of gravel in the soil. The Great Lakes were made by glaciers. There are still glaciers today like I said, and they do have cracks called crevices. The last ice age was actually 11,000 years ago, not a million . . .

3. As an additional post-reading entry, ask students to write a process entry. "What did writing about your ideas before and after reading do for you as a learner?"

   Process Discussion Entry

   I felt more interested in reading about glaciers because I thought about it before I read. I was surprised I knew as much about them before reading the assignment. Writing helped me put down what I already knew. It made me more interested in reading because I wanted to know if I was right. Knowing that I was going to have to write when I finished reading made me read more carefully. I learned more.

4. Ask students to write about how the pre- and post-reading entries worked for them as learners. Use one of the following prompts.

   What CRISS℠ Principles did you employ with this journal activity?
   How did pre- and post-reading entries help you become more metacognitive, to transform information?
   Were you more interested in reading the selection after writing your pre-reading entry?
   Was your reading more purposeful?
   Did the reading either support or contradict anything you had written?
   Was the *post* entry easier or more difficult than the *pre* entry? Why?
   How could you improve the process to make it work better?

Support and Extensions

- Pre and post entries can also be used before and after viewing a video, listening to a speaker, doing a lab, or going on a field trip.
- Use pre- and post-reading entries with selections on the Internet. Students first preview for key ideas by viewing pictures, page titles, and subheadings and write a journal entry. After reading, they write again.

Remind students to note any errors or misconceptions made on their pre-reading entries. Partners could work together and write a post-reading entry which they record in their individual journals.

Observation Entries

Learning logs are vehicles for seeing more clearly and for developing and recording ideas. Learning logs inspire precise observations, which naturally lead into questions. As students write their observations, they discover meaning in what they see.

Introduction, Modeling, and Reflection

1. Ask students to look at an object in your classroom. On a blank transparency, model your written observations. As you carefully note each detail, talk aloud as you write down what you see. In this example, a science teacher had distributed fresh cut flowers to each cooperative team. The teacher modeled the following entry on the overhead:

Observation Entry

Right below the outside of the flower, the stem thickens into a little case or holder for supporting the flower. It looks almost like a crown. I see a ring of petals. The petals are in two layers. The lower petals are greener and look more stemlike than the upper petals. I wonder what use all of these petals have? Maybe they attract bees. Maybe these petals protect the flower in some way. Next, I see a ring of petal-like parts in the middle of the flower. There are four of these, and each tiny petal has two sharp parts. Are these the stamens or pistils?

2. Talk about how writing helps you to think about and to question what you have seen. How do observations automatically lead to questions for further explorations?

3. Have students choose an item to observe. Then have them write an observation entry and share.

4. Ask students, "When you had to write about the object, did you notice more than you realized?"

Support and Extensions

● Observation entries are a natural response for the visual arts. In the example below, a high school art teacher asked her students to write down their observations about African masks.

I think this mask must have belonged to the Ashantis of Ghana. I think the wood is mahogany. This wood feels so hard. It must have been difficult to carve. There are hundreds of beads stuck in the wood around the eyes, nose and mouth. The beads are arranged in colors. I wonder if the colors have any significance. There are also little stones and blue and beige beads. The beads might be turquoise. I am amazed at the little triangles of metal that surround the eyes and lead up to the forehead. It looks like bronze or maybe it is copper. The metal is organized into a geometric pattern. It probably means something too. This mask must have taken many days to make. I bet they used it for religious celebrations of some sort.

● A high school football coached asked his players to view a video from their last game. They wrote about their observations. "What advice would you give to the players? How might you make this play more effective?" Writing helped his players begin to see how they might win the next game.

Adaptations

You Ought to Be in Pictures (Buehl, 2001).

When looking at paintings, old photographs in family albums, or photos of historic events, we often imagine what life was like for the people captured in these images. What were the life events reflected in Mona Lisa's face? What stories lie behind photos of farm families abandoning their homes during the Great Depression?

Pictures call forth emotions, feelings, and responses that can communicate far beyond the written word. Frequently, photographs and other visuals embedded in text are ignored or, at best, receive cursory attention as readers rush to complete assignments. Yet, a few minutes spent walking through the visuals can bring readers into the text before they start to read. You Ought to Be in Pictures invites students to step inside an image and become a quiet observer, connecting conceptually and emotionally with people and events in the scene.

Select a photograph in your text or from another source that will evoke feelings and extend curriculum concepts. For example, when your student are about to read a chapter about the Great Depression, walk through the history textbook, noting photographs and other visuals. Identify photographs that capture key ideas and themes of the times. Take your students inside. As you step into the photograph, ask students to record their thoughts and feelings. Your guided imagery might go something like this:

> *Dorothea Lange, a photo journalist of the 1930s, teaches us to see the realities of the Depression. She took to the streets and photographed hundreds of migrant workers and Dust Bowl refugees streaming into California.*
>
> *This Dorothea Lange photo* (see below) *shows a family in a squatter's camp. During the Great Depression, people sifted through their belongings for the journey west. They packed into cars and wagons, moved out of their homes, and fled, looking for work. People who previously had homes became squatters. Highways became streams of people. Camps sprung up along the roads, filled with hungry children and with women wearing high-heeled shoes outside of their canvas homes.*

Source: Courtesy of Library of Congress.

Look carefully at this squatter family. Observe the mom, her children, their clothes, the tent, the car. Notice their downtrodden look, their facial expressions. Look at the mom's shoes and the way she sits. Has she always been poor? Describe what her life might have been like in the years before this photo. What do you think happened this day? Why are the children nestled around her? What do you see happening in the weeks and months ahead for this family? (As you talk, allow time for students to continue writing.)

Now imagine you are one of the people in this photograph. What are you thinking? How do you feel? Why are you living in this tent? What do you predict will happen to you tomorrow? (Then take your students into the future and ask them to write again.) *It is fifteen years later, and you are looking back at this photograph. You are sitting with a good friend. What are your memories of this day?*

Provide time for students to read portions of their entries aloud. Guided trips inside visuals tap into the heart, reaching emotions too often lost in lines of print. Students will leave this scene ready to read and learn more about these times.

Adapt "You Ought to Be in Pictures," using paintings and photographs such as those in science, literature, and social studies. Ask students to become witnesses to details in other visuals, which may or may not include people. For example, ask them to step inside photographs of deforested areas or to play along with wolf pups scampering along a stream.

Learning Strategy

Perspective Entries

In perspective entries, students can take on the roles of characters, animals, and famous people. Students might choose a literary character and write what that person is thinking and feeling. Or they could write from the perspective of a water drop moving through the water cycle.

Guided Comprehension

Introduction, Modeling, and Reflection

1. Select a person in history or current events or a character from a story. Talk briefly about the person's situation, then brainstorm how that person might feel or react, what decisions the person might make, or what actions that person might take.

2. Using student input, write the first few sentences of a short journal entry from the perspective of your selected person. For example, the wolf in *Little Red Riding Hood* might write. . . . .

   "My, my, my, but I am hungry, and so very, very tired. I just don't think I have the energy to chase a rabbit or ground hog today. What, oh, what am I to do? Oh, my, oh, my, my, my, here comes a tasty looking morsel. She is all dressed in red and looking very plump and juicy. Now, let me see, what should I do, do, do!!!. . ."

3. Next, have students select an appropriate person, animal, or thing from their course reading. Through discussion, focus them on three or four possible topics. Students might choose a famous person from history and develop entries giving clues about the person's life. Notice how the vocabulary and sentence structure changes as an eighth-grade student takes on the role of Merriweather Lewis.

July 27, 1771 Today Daddy died. Why, I don't know, but he did. Mummy will be so lonely.

April 4, 1788 Mom has remarried to a different man. He will be my new father, but I will always remember my real father.

Oct. 9, 1792 The President has asked me to be his private secretary. He is a good fellow with a kind heart. I will live with him at Monticello when he goes there to escape the torrid summer in Washington.

Oct. 13, 1793 After being with the President one year, he has been very kind to me. He has been the father I never had. He has even asked me to head the Voyage of Discovery that will take my travels through the Louisiana Purchase territory. That should be very interesting! I will leave soon to start this wonderful journey.

4. After students write, talk about how perspective entries worked for them as readers and writers. "Were you more interested in learning about your person? Were you able to connect emotionally? How did perspective entries help you transform and change information? How did you like this more informal writing? How do perspective entries compare with writing a traditional report on a famous person?"

Support and Extensions

- Use perspective entries as part of novel studies. Taking on the role of a character helps students empathize with a character's feelings and problems.

Example:

The Pearl - Kino's Perspective

What is going on here? I finally have a chance to get money and bring my family out of poverty. I know this pearl can bring me the money. I need to get my son educated and provide my wife with a real church wedding, but everyone tells me it is worth nothing. I think they are trying to take advantage of me. Do they think I am that stupid?"

- Students can also take on historical and science perspectives. The students took on the role of a kapok tree in Ecuador. The oil barons are coming to convert the rainforest to an oil field. The tree can keep a journal of observations and changes.

Example:

Entry 1:

I am so tall that I see for miles, stretching over the tops of all the trees. I am the tallest tree in Africa and South America. I grow beside the Napo River in Ecuador. The Huaorani villagers tell me I may be close to 200 years old. My limbs reach over a 100 feet high and my trunk is very wide—at least 15 feet across.

Entry 2:

Humans have been my friends for over 200 years. Right now, Amo and Enqueri are in their tree fort, which I shelter for them. None of the other children in their nearby Huaorani village know our secret. I always nestle my leaves close around them so they can't be seen in our hideout.

Entry 3:

I see a group of Huaorani elders meeting with members of the Shell Oil Company. The company wants to build a road into the rain forest so they can cut down trees and take the oil. I have seen trees fall all around me as they build this road. I think I will be next. There is no way the Huaorani can fight with an oil company.

Explanation and Process Entries

When students write explanations of ideas and concepts, they discover whether or not they really understand a concept. Moreover, writing helps students identify sequences and use the steps in a process. This is particularly true in process-oriented content areas such as mathematics, science, technology, and vocational education.

Introduction, Modeling, and Reflection

1. Talk about the importance of writing complete explanations so that someone who doesn't understand anything about the topic can carry out the task.
2. Begin by having the students write the steps involved in a simple process like tying shoe laces. Have them read out loud the process they have written while someone follows the directions. Make sure listeners don't do anything that isn't written in the directions. In most cases, the author will leave out critical steps like "pick up one lace with the right hand and the other with the left . . ."
3. Next, select a familiar process within your content, such as adding two decimal numbers or getting ready to use certain software in the computer. As a whole class, write an explanation. Have students check the explanation by carrying out the task.

Mathematics: Multiplying decimals

When you are multiplying two decimal numbers, the procedure is really quite simple. For example, remember when you multiplied two numbers like 32 × 105? It looked like this:

$$
\begin{array}{r}
105 \\
\times\ 32 \\
\hline
210 \\
3150 \\
\hline
3360
\end{array}
$$

Well, let's say the numbers you wanted to multiply were 1.05 and 3.2. You would do the multiplying exactly the same way, but there has to be a decimal in the answer. You can figure out where it goes in two ways. First, just look at the numbers. The first one is about 1 and the second one is around 3. If you multiply 1 × 3 you get 3, so in the decimal problem your answer would be just a little more than three or 3.360. Another way to do it is to count the numbers to the right of the decimal in the two numbers to be multiplied. There are two in the first number and one in the second. If you add them you get three, so that tells you there should be three numbers to the right of the decimal point in your answer, 3.360 again!

Art: Decorating eggs with wax and dyes

a. *Draw pattern lightly on egg with pencil.*
b. *Using "Kistka" (tool), apply wax to egg over penciled design (waxed area will remain white).*
c. *Place egg in yellow dye until the color looks right to you.*

d. *Put wax over areas you want to remain yellow, then place the egg in orange dye.*
e. *Put wax over areas you want to remain orange, then place in red dye.*
f. *Put wax over areas you want to remain red, then place in black dye.*
g. *Melt the wax off by holding the egg next to a candle flame until the wax melts, then wipe off with a tissue.*

4. Ask students, "How did the explanation/process entry help you to understand the concept or process. Did it help you with metacognition? Did you become a more active reader and listener?"

Support and Extensions

● Sue Harding asks her fourth graders to design their own math problems. She writes a number such as 9 on the chalkboard. Students have to derive a variety of problems that have this number as the answer. Then they explain the processes to solve the problem. Matthew's example follows:

$$5 + 4 = 9$$
$$(10 - 2) + 1 = 9$$
$$20 - 11 = 9$$
$$30 - 21 = 9$$
$$10 - 1 = 9$$

Then students choose one of the problems to write a story problem. Matthew writes:

Story problem for 9. I had 20 pumpkins all cut out with scary faces. On Halloween before I went trick or treating, I set out my 20 pumpkins on the porch. I went trick or treating for 2 hours. Then I went to a Halloween party for 3 hours. I was out for five hours total. When I went home 11 of my pumpkins with scary faces were gone. How many pumpkins do I have left. 20 − 11 = 9.

After students write, they meet in pairs and evaluate one another's problems. Do their creations contain the key elements of a story problem? The following checklist will assist them in their evaluation:

Problem-Solving Checklist for Writers

▶ Does the problem contain a clear question?
▶ Will the reader know what to do?
▶ Does the author present facts clearly?
▶ Does the author give you clues as to what operations you are supposed to use?

In the next example, high school mathematics students paired with fifth-grade buddies. As the high school students reviewed key mathematical processes, they wrote to fifth-graders, explaining the processes. The fifth-graders responded with comments about whether or not the explanations were clear. Writing for younger audiences provided the older students with an incentive to write clearly.

Dear Dawn,
    You are wondering how to solve this problem $3x + x = 12.04$. Well, there are three steps you have to take before you can get the answer. The first step is to add the like terms which are three x and just x. Don't forget there is a one in front of the plain x. If you add them right you get four x. Then you put an equal sign on the right side of the four x and put the 12.04 on the right side of the

equals. Then divide both the 4x and the 12.04 by a plain 4. Do not put the x by the dividing 4. When you are all done you should have gotten the answer 3.01. Here are the steps you should have taken.

$$3x + x = 12.04$$
$$4x = 12.04$$
$$\frac{4x}{4} = \frac{12.04}{4}$$
$$x = 3.01$$

I hope you can figure it out.

Your friend,

Brandy

Stacy Auck, a seventh grade mathematics teacher, asks students to write as they do mathematical computations. Writing helps them think through steps in problem-solving.

Problem: Last summer we went camping in Yosemite, and the first night we did a dumb thing: we left our food on the ground. A bear came along and ripped up one third of our total number of dried meals. The next day we ate four more of the meals and tied the food up in a tree. It didn't seem to help because one third of the meals we had left were ripped open by another bear. During our third day, we ate four more meals and that night, despite everything we did, one half of the remaining dried meals were ripped apart. We gave up, ate the four remaining dried meals, and headed home. Can you tell how many dried meals we started with?

Student's written and computation response:

To get your answer you have to start at the end. It says that half of the remaining meals were eaten by the bear to give the 4 eaten by the campers on the last day. So you have to multiply by 2 to undo the half.

$$4 \times 2 = 8$$

This gives you 8. Plus the 4 more meals they ate on the third day gives you 12.

$$8 + 4 = 12$$

Now if 1/3 of the number before this was ripped apart, that means that they have 2/3 of that number left. So, 2/3 is 12. So, 6 is half of the 2/3 that is left or 1/3.

$$12/2 = 6$$

Then you have to add 6 to 12 to get 18.

$$6 + 12 = 18$$

Let's double check. If you minus 1/3 (6) from 18 it gives you 12.

$$18 - 6 = 12$$

So that's right. Then, they ate 4 more meals to give them 22 meals.

$$18 + 4 = 22$$

The next step you do is the same as the last. 1/3 was ripped up of the number before this. You have to find out what half of 22 is because 22 is equal to 2/3.

$$22/2 = 11$$

And that's how much is left. The number is 11. So add 11 to 22 and it gives you 33.

$$22 + 11 = 33$$

That's your answer. They must have started with 33 dried meals.

▶ Management and Evaluation

We recommend reading the students' learning logs. Reading the logs gives us rich knowledge about our students and about their understanding of content. Their questions and confusions also guide our planning.

We find time to read some logs during the class period. As students write, we move around the class and read as many responses as we can. Sometimes, we collect five or six journals a day.

Whenever appropriate, respond to students. Ask students to leave you a space to write back. Our responses encourage them to take their logs more seriously. When responding, be careful with your red pen. Learning logs must remain a safe place to write. Comments should focus on what students are saying. Accept responses and nudge students on with your questions. This personal dialogue provides the individual attention so often missing with middle and high school students.

We don't grade the logs, but often give points for completion. Some students need "point" motivation to take their informal writing seriously.

▶ Summary

Our students have many opportunities to write informally during class. Learning logs take a variety of forms, depending upon the purposes of a particular lesson. Free-writes encourage students to become emotionally engaged in their reading, to generate their own questions, and to make predictions. Double-entry journals guide students to become more aware of their thinking while reading. Dialogue journals inspire instructional conversations about content and literature, while perspective entries encourage readers to examine characters and issues from multiple points of view. Pre- and post-reading journal entries assist readers with difficult content. Students record what they already know about the topic, develop their own purposes for reading and, afterwards, discover how much they have learned. When students write explanations, they internalize concepts and processes and self-evaluate their understanding. One cannot write about something that he or she doesn't understand.

Whenever we want our students to process content deeply, we have them write about it in their logs. Class and small-group discussions are far richer if students respond in their journals first. These quick writings ensure everyone becomes an active participant.

Research Conclusion	Reference
Students become better writers and more active learners when they write often.	Zinsser, 1988

CHAPTER 8

Formal Writing to Learn: Writing Reports and Essays

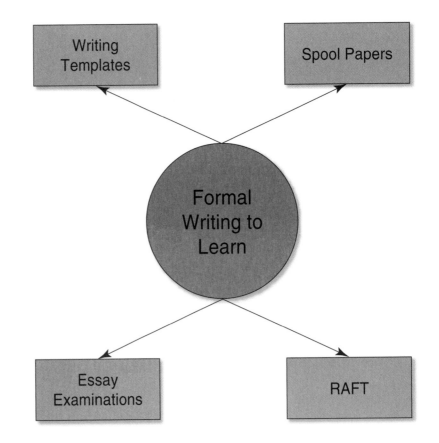

Writing Templates

Spool Papers

Formal Writing to Learn

Essay Examinations

RAFT

CRISS[SM] students benefit from a rich variety of writing experiences. In addition to the informal writings in learning logs, they should have more formal experiences which usually lead to completed pieces. This chapter focuses on strategies we find particularly effective in content area subjects.

Our students participate in process writing, in which instruction matches what writers do. They go through various overlapping and recurrent processes in producing a piece: pre-writing, drafting, revising, proofreading, and publishing. Due to space limitations, we decided not to include a chapter on process writing and Writing Workshop in this book. For rich descriptions about teaching writing, refer to the work of Lucy Calkins (1994), Tom Romano (1987, 1995), Donald Graves (1994), Nancy Atwell (1998) and Linda Rief (1992). In this manual, we describe strategies designed more specifically for the content areas, with the implicit understanding that students have opportunities to take their pieces through the writing process.*

We want students to learn how to be considerate writers. In fact, the discussion about considerate text in Chapter 2 applies to our own and our students' writing. Effective writers strive to be kind to their readers by leading them through their thinking, explaining their ideas fully. As writers, we don't want to mirror unfriendly textbook authors afflicted with the *mentioning* problem—those writers who simply list concepts without ever explaining them. We always assume that our readers know less than we do about the topic, and that our job is to teach by explaining with clear examples and details. We strive to make our verbs active, to vary sentence lengths, and to write simply without jargon and clutter. We also want our work to have a clear beginning, middle, and end, with transitional features guiding the reader from one idea to the next.

The content areas become the logical arena for teaching formal strategies such as writing reports and essays. We have already described some of these strategies in our discussions about how writing emerges from student notes derived from reading. For example, the organizational formats described in Chapters 5 and 6 evolve naturally into writing (maps, frames, problem-solution formats, two-column notes). Once students have organized information from their reading, they can readily use it for writing. For example, conclusion-support guides become a tool for persuasive writing. Problem-solution notes can easily become analytical papers; and main idea-detail notes contain the essential ingredients of a summary.

In addition to writing from these note-taking formats, we show students how to write using templates, spool papers, RAFT assignments, and multi-genre research papers. We also include in this chapter a section about negotiating essay examinations.

Strategy

Learning

Writing Templates

Writers consciously or unconsciously use a set of internal structures, or templates, in their writing. Templates exist for writing memos, business letters, and thank-you notes, as well as formats for writing persuasive pieces and that ambitious doctoral dissertation. Many students have no real grasp of the mental structures more advanced writers use intuitively.

---

*An additional strategy that works well in conjunction with the ideas presented throughout this CRISS[SM] manual and the CRISS[SM] philosophy about teaching and learning is Analytic Traits (Spandel and Stiggins, 1997). Analytic Traits defines the features of excellent writing (idea development, organization, voice, word choice, sentence fluency, and conventions), which students learn to use in drafting and revision. Unfortunately, a complete explanation of ways to incorporate Analytic Traits into your day-to-day teaching is outside the scope of this book.

Making these mental structures explicit through the use of templates helps students cope with a variety of writing tasks.

Writing templates provide skeleton formats for organizing key ideas and supportive details. Within these templates, transition words guide the structure of student writing. Template design varies from simple main idea—detail constructions to more complex structures such as comparative, problem-solution, and persuasive formats. Templates are particularly effective for assisting students with essay examinations. Once students understand how to compose a well-organized problem-solution paper, scaffolding the answer with a template isn't necessary.

Writing templates work particularly well for essay tests and for assisting struggling writers and younger students with more coherent writing.

Let's begin this discussion at the most basic level—simple paragraph writing.

Introduction, Modeling, and Reflection

1. Explain the structure of the paragraph template.
   ▶ Begins with a topic sentence that specifies a general statement or opinion.
   ▶ Follows with three to five sentences that provide examples to develop the topic or opinion.
   ▶ Uses transitions when needed to connect sentences. (See Blackline 24a and 24b.)
   ▶ Ends with a sentence that restates the topic or opinion.
   ▶ Incorporates a variety of sentences—long and short, simple and complex.
2. Give students an example of a template similar to the following essay examination template, and use it as a guide for writing a response together.

Science

Discuss how you think our city's solid waste management problem can be solved, and support your argument with three pieces of evidence.

Essay template: *I think recycling would be the best solution to our city's solid waste management problem. First, . . . Second, . . . Third, . . . So, . . .*

Completed essay: <u>*I think recycling would be the best solution to our city's solid waste management problem.*</u> *<u>First,</u> surveys have shown that paper takes up the most space in our landfill, and I think it would be fairly easy for schools and businesses to collect their paper for recycling instead of just throwing it away. <u>Second,</u> I called the paper mill in Jonestown, and they said they are already using some recycled paper and they could use more. <u>Third,</u> I called two grocery stores and they said that recycled paper products sell quite well. <u>So,</u> it seems to me that if it is easy to recycle paper, if the mill can use the recycled products to make new products, and if people buy those products, the best solution to our landfill problem must be recycling!*

3. Have students develop their own topics for a paragraph template.
4. Determine transitions or prompts that will indicate details/support and a conclusion.
5. Ask students to complete the paragraph and then edit their drafts.
6. Provide students opportunities to talk about how the template worked for them. "How did this template help or hinder your writing? Did the template teach you anything about how to structure your own writing?"

Support and Extensions

- Continue using paragraph templates as guides until students begin to develop their own plans for structuring their ideas.
- Incorporate "powers" with paragraph templates. The first sentence is the Power 1 statement in the template. It indicates the number of items to follow.

Democrats differ from Republicans in three ways (Power 1 sentence). First . . . Next . . . Finally . . . (Power 2 and 3 statements).

- Challenge students to develop their own paragraph templates from their conclusion-support notes or concept maps.
- Include a template essay question on a test. Convert the question to an opening statement, and guide content with sentence beginnings. The following example comes from a twelfth-grade government class.

The United States government is based on a system of checks and balances. This system maintains a balance of power among . . . Some of the checks and balances are . . . and . . . In summary, our forefathers' idea of checks and balances was developed to . . . because. . .

- Invite students to develop their own templates to structure different types of text such as analytic papers, laboratory research reports, or problem-cause-effect-solution papers.

Mathematics:

Dividing fractions requires several steps. First, . . . Next, . . . Then, . . . Finally, remember . . .

Dividing fractions requires several steps. First, you need to change any mixed numbers into improper fractions. Next, change the division sign to multiply and change the second fraction (the one you are dividing by) to its reciprocal (flip it upside-down). Then, multiply the two top numbers—that will be the top number of your answer. Multiply the two bottom numbers—that will be the new bottom number. Finally, remember to reduce the fraction to its lowest terms and change it to a mixed number if the top number is bigger than the bottom one.

Character analysis:

_____, a character from the classic novel _____ by _____, seems to have been a (an) (_adjective_) person. An example of this was when . . . Another example was . . . Finally, . . . This character, _____, always . . . [Note: use a line "___" when only a word or two needs to be added. Use three dots ". . ." when more text is needed.]

Huck Finn, <u>a character from the classic novel</u> The Adventures of Huckleberry Finn <u>by</u> Mark Twain, <u>seems to have been an</u> adventurous boy. <u>An example of this was when</u> he decided to run away from the widow's house where he was staying. <u>Another example was</u> when he and his friend Jim rode a homemade raft down the Mississippi River by themselves. <u>Finally,</u> Huck decided to adventure back to the widow's by himself. <u>This character,</u> Huck Finn, <u>always</u> dared to do exciting things.

Problem-cause-effect-solution paper:

A critical problem is . . . because . . . In addition, . . .

Several causes such as . . . and . . . explain why this problem occurred. These reasons show why . . . has become such a problem.

This problem has led to several important effects. First, . . . Second, . . . Finally, . . .

The problem could be solved in a number of ways. For example, . . . This would help solve the problem because . . . Another way to solve the problem is . . . This solution seems plausible because . . . A final solution is . . .

Scientific paper:

I. Introduction: Topic and Question

I conducted a research study on _____. This topic was important to investigate because . . . The hypothesis for my study was . . .

II. Methods and Procedures

In order to investigate this question, I followed these procedures. First, I . . . Second, . . . Third, . . . Finally, . . .

III. Results and Discussion

My main result was . . . In addition, I found . . .

These results show that . . . because . . .

Some questions I have about my research are . . .

Therefore, I plan to . . .

Learning Strategy

Spool Papers

While some students seem to develop ways to structure writing on their own, most will acquire report-writing skills more rapidly when they learn organizing structures. Nunnally (1991) compares these structures to learning how to ride a bike with training wheels. They help the fledgling writer hold an essay together. Once students have a sense of structure, they can get rid of the training wheels and go mountain biking. They begin to move away from the rigid form and apply principles of effective non-fiction writing in more innovative ways.

A spool paper provides an organizational system in the shape of a spool. It starts broad with an introductory paragraph containing a definite thesis, narrows to detailed supporting paragraphs, and widens again in a concluding paragraph. The spool paper may vary in structure, much like a real spool, depending upon its purpose. Some spool papers are short and concise, others long and involved.

You can structure students' spool papers as tightly as necessary. Ask them to start their papers with an introductory paragraph, beginning with a lead to draw the reader into the piece, followed by some additional introductory comments, and concluding with a thesis statement that previews the topics developed in the subsequent paragraphs, or body of the piece. The number of paragraphs and the presentation of ideas in the body paragraphs are directed by the thesis statement. Students then conclude their paper with a summary paragraph, which includes a restatement of main points.

SPOOL PAPER

The spool system is a standard method of organization for expository text. It forces the student to organize his/her writing through use of a thesis sentence that breaks the paper into a logically structured sequence with a definite conclusion.

LEAD

Build - up

BODY

wind - down

"CLINCHER"

Introductory Paragraph: This starts with a **lead** (question, interesting fact, quote, anecdote) to gain the reader's attention (Power 0). The last sentence in the introduction is the **thesis,** which is the controlling idea and contains the topics for each paragraph in the body (Power 1).

Body: This should contain at least two paragraphs. Each paragraph deals with one of the **topics** (Power 2's) in the thesis. Adequate **support** for each topic should be included (Power 3's & 4's). In a persuasive paper, the weakest reasons should come first; the strongest reason should be last.

Concluding Paragraph: This paragraph starts with a **restatement** of the thesis sentence (Power 1), followed by "clincher" sentences (Power 0's), giving the feeling of business completed. These may relate back to the lead.

In this example, Carol Santa's high school students had just completed *House on Mango Street,* by Sandra Ciscernos. Carol introduced students to spool papers with a sample paper, which students then analyzed according to the features of a spool paper.

Lead

"That's one boring book!" says Mark. "It's a chick book, not a book for guys." "Yeah, I agree. I couldn't get into it. Why did you make us read it anyway?" Sam announced. "You could of at least chosen one that had a story to it."

Introduction

Why hadn't these boys connected with House on Mango Street? I didn't expect such responses. After all, I love this book. They hadn't appreciated the author's spare, luminous prose. They hadn't walked in the character's footprints or even empathized with Esperanzo's rageful and poignant journey into womanhood. Had I made a mistake in selecting this book? For a moment, their complaints made me wonder. As I thought harder though, I realized I had made a good choice. I had my reasons. Sandra Cisneros writes magnificently, and I wanted my students to begin to read like a writer. **I wanted them to see how a writer crafts sentences, uses powerful verbs, and creates images.** I wanted

Thesis

them to use her work as their teacher.

Body

Sandra Cisneros writes eloquently and sparingly. She slices each sentence to the essence of meaning. She reminds me of Ernest Hemingway, who revised and revised each sentence to the bones. For example, notice the mother's words in the vignette, "Smart Cookie." "Shame is a bad thing, you know. It keeps you down. You want to know why I quit school? Because I didn't have nice clothes. No clothes, but I had brains." Her writing is clean. No clutter. Every word works. Notice how effectively she uses phrases and in this example, one word sentences. "She met him at a dance. Pretty too and young . . . And how was she to know she'd be the last one to see him alive. An accident you know. Hit-and-run." Some of her sentences are long; others short. Some are one word utterances. She clips every line to its core and uses a variety of sentences.

Sandra Cisneros surprises us with her choice of verbs. Note her verbs in these sentences: "Some days after dinner, guests and I will sit in front of a fire. Floorboards will squeak upstairs. The attic grumbles. Rats. They'll ask. Bums, I'll say, and I'll be happy." The verbs, *squeak* and *grumble,* add color and voice to her writing. Verbs capture the terror of Angel Vargas ". . . nobody looked up not once the day Angel Vargas learned to fly and dropped from the sky like a sugar donut, just like a falling star, and exploded down to earth without even an 'Oh.' " The reader can't escape from the horror painted by these words. An angel exploding and nobody cared! Her clean, precise language, particularly her use of verbs, creates haunting images.

Personification and similes permeate her writing. Attics grumble and squeak. Observe how she uses personification in describing her house on Mango Street. "It's small and red with tight steps in front and windows so small you'd think they were holding their breath. Bricks are crumbling in places, and the front door is so swollen you have to push hard to get in." The inanimate becomes animate. The house takes on human qualities. She uses similes like an artist's thin brush stroke. Notice how she paints the three sisters. "They came with the wind that blows in August, thin as a spider web and barely noticed. Three who did not seem to be related to anything but the moon. One with laughter like tin and one with eyes of a cat and one with hands like porcelain." I also like the way she uses unusual similes in her closing sentences in the vignette "Linoleum Roses." "She looks at all the things they own: the towels and the toaster, the alarm clock and the drapes. She likes looking at the walls, at how neatly their corners meet, the linoleum roses on the floor, the ceiling smooth as wedding cake." She animates her writing with personification and unusual images.

Sandra Cisneros teaches us about writing with her distinctive style. **She paints pictures with sparse, clean sentences. She chooses her verbs carefully so they aren't bland or boring, but precise, clean, and filled with voice. Finally, she teaches us about figures of speech.** We learn from phrases like, "Only a house quiet as snow, a space for myself to go, clean as paper before the poem." Thank you, Sandra—you teach us well.

Perhaps my dear students you now understand why I chose this book. Have I convinced you?

As the class analyzed the paper, they noted how the writer drew the audience into her piece with a lead—in this case, a dialogue between two students who had complained about reading the book. As part of this modeling she also talked about some different possibilities for leads such as Blackline 25. Following the lead, she included a few introductory remarks followed by a thesis statement or Power 1 sentence (bold) that lets the reader know about the content of the next several paragraphs. In this example, three ideas (Power 2's) are presented in the thesis, indicating that there will be a corresponding paragraph for each point presented. Notice that the paragraphs are then presented in the same order as specified in the thesis. Each paragraph is also highly-structured, with a clearly stated main idea (in italics) followed by sentences that elaborate on the main point. The concluding paragraph repeats the thesis (bold) and contains a few summary comments.

While the spool format is not particularly conducive to creative writing or personal responses to literature, it is an excellent tool for reports and other content writing. As a basic expository writing format, it helps students begin to internalize a sense of structure.

Writers learn how to explore different leads, to set up the thesis for their readers, to develop their ideas, and then to present a strong conclusion. It helps writers understand how to guide their audience through their writing. Once students have internalized this basic format, they should be encouraged to structure their writing less rigidly.

By writing spool papers, struggling readers also learn about main idea. The spool paper structure provides an excellent tool for teaching and assessing a student's understanding of concepts. And, it prepares students for the reading and writing tasks found on state language arts and reading assessments. If students can write a spool paper, they will not only be able to write a coherent response, they will also be able to understand how authors use main ideas and supporting details in materials they read.

To help students plan a spool paper, encourage them to draft their ideas in a power outline. Encourage the use of transition words and phrases to connect their power ideas.

You may want to use the following instructional sequence to introduce your students to spool papers:

Guided Comprehension

Introduction, Modeling, and Reflection

1. Your explanation and modeling might go something like this: "What comes to mind when you hear the word *spool?* Were you thinking of a spool of thread or perhaps the big phone cable spools that some people use for picnic tables? Although spools come in lots of sizes and shapes, they are all used to organize and transport stuff—from threads to cables. The size and shape of the spool is determined by its purpose. In a similar way, the spool paper is a template used to organize and communicate ideas. The size and design of the spool paper depend on the purpose of the writing."

   "The spool paper generally consists of at least four paragraphs, but has no upper limit. The first paragraph is called the *introductory* paragraph. It explains what the paper will be about. The rest of the paragraphs, except for the last one, provide all the details and support. We call this part of the spool paper the *body*. The last paragraph of the spool is called the *concluding* paragraph. It summarizes the main ideas presented in the paper."

2. Present the spool paper planning sheet on the overhead (Blackline 26). Explain that the outline is a format for planning a paper that clearly develops several main points. Some students may find the power structure helpful.

26
Blackline

Name: _____   Date: _____

Spool Paper Planning Sheet

Introductory Paragraph
Lead
Thesis statement (Power 1):
List the Power 2 ideas:
2a
2b
2c

Body
2a. Topic sentence
   3. Detail sentence
   3. Detail sentence
   3. Detail sentence
2b. Topic sentence
   3. Detail sentence
   3. Detail sentence
   3. Detail sentence
2c. Topic sentence
   3. Detail sentence
   3. Detail sentence
   3. Detail sentence

Concluding Paragraph
Restate the thesis using different words (Power 1):
Wind-down/conclusion

304 CRISS™ Manual   © Kendall/Hunt Publishing Company

3. Select a familiar topic, and discuss the audience and purpose of the piece. Brainstorm ideas related to the topic. Narrow to two or three issues. (If you have two points in your thesis, this will be a four-paragraph paper. A three-point thesis will result in a paper at least five paragraphs long.)

4. Collectively, develop a lead or introductory statement (Power 0). A lead might be a question, an interesting fact, a quotation, or a dialogue that will catch the reader's attention (Blackline 25). Include a thesis statement as the last sentence in the introduction. You can mark the ideas in the thesis statement as Power 1 ideas. Explain that a thesis is a controlling idea that contains the main ideas developed in the paper. Then brainstorm details that develop the main points in each of the paragraphs, and write the paragraphs together.

5. Finally, draft a conclusion and restate the main points of the thesis.

6. Through class discussion, develop an editing checklist or rubric and demonstrate how to use it with the class paper.

An editing checklist might look like this:
- ▶ Does the lead make you want to read the rest of the paper?
- ▶ Does the first paragraph contain a thesis statement? (Have students read and circle or put 2's by the points in the thesis.)
- ▶ Does the second paragraph explain the first point in the thesis statement?
- ▶ Does the third paragraph explain the second point in the thesis?
- ▶ Do each of the paragraphs contain a main idea statement? (Have teams underline the main idea sentence in each.)
- ▶ Do each of the paragraphs contain Power 3 and 4 ideas to develop the main idea? (Have students selectively underline these ideas.)

7. Hold process discussions. "Did the spool paper format help you organize your writing? Or, did you find it too constraining? Did the checklist help you analyze your own paper? How might the spool paper work for you in writing a report? How might you modify the spool paper format to better meet your own needs?"

Support and Extensions

- ● Divide the class into small groups or pairs. Provide a topic related to the content being studied, or ask each group to come up with a topic. Have each team draft a spool paper. Then have teams trade drafts and edit one another's papers.
- ● Have students write a "how-to" paper on how to write a spool paper. Ask students to evaluate their work using the spool paper editing checklist.

Example:
> "Oh, I can't believe it. I just got another "D" on a report I wrote."
> "Do you know what you did wrong?"
> "No, I'm not really sure. The teacher said it was pretty poorly organized. I am not really sure how to write reports. All we did the last two years is write creative stories and poetry. I am pretty good at that."

Well, I think I have just the thing to help you out. It is called the Spool Paper. It will help you write reports, and it is actually quite simple. **The spool paper consists of just three parts—an introduction, a body and a conclusion.**

We call the first paragraph of the spool paper the introduction. This paragraph begins with several sentences, which are designed to grab your attention. They might be questions or a quote. We label this part a "lead." After the lead, you will need a thesis sentence. This sentence tells what the paper will be about. Usually, several sub-topics will be listed or suggested in the thesis.

Following the introduction is the body. The body consists of two or more paragraphs that support the thesis. Each body paragraph will contain information about one of the sub-topics mentioned in the thesis. Usually that sub-topic is written in the first sentence of the paragraph. The other sentences provide details and examples.

The last paragraph of the spool paper is called the conclusion. The first sentence of this paragraph restates the thesis, but in different words. Several more sentences follow. They are called the "wind down" and should be similar to the lead in the introductory paragraph. These sentences tie the paper together, so the reader isn't left hanging.

Once you understand the three components of the spool paper—introduction, body, and conclusion—writing a report becomes easy. Now, wouldn't it be nice if you had this conversation with your parents:

"Boy, I can't believe it! I just got an 'A' on this paper I wrote for Biology."
"That's wonderful. How did you do it?"
"I wrote the paper in a spool format."

● Use spool papers as a format for essay tests.

The Essay Examination

Think back to those dreaded essay tests in your high school English class or college history course—cold sweat, those butterflies in your stomach, rushing against time, not remembering the stuff well enough to actually explain it, being the last one to turn in the test. Or were you one of those irritating kids who always finished on time and scored high, while the rest of us struggled? Unfortunately, the authors of this book don't fit in this second category. Yet, we might have, if just one teacher had taught us how to take essay tests. Instead, our teachers assumed too much, and no one ever taught us what do. Taking essay tests was part of the underground curriculum no one talked about. Imagine how our testing lives might have been different.

Some students negotiate essay tests confidently; most do not. Most begin writing without reading the question carefully, without planning the response, and without having any clear plan about how to organize their ideas quickly. They stop, start, and begin again only to find they have spent far too much time and have to rush through the rest of the test. Or they simply admit defeat and leave the question blank. To compound the torture, essay examinations have become more important, as written responses are now included on state and national assessments.

Teaching students how to read a question and set up an answer will make a dramatic difference in how well they perform on essay examinations. Many of the CRISS[SM] strategies we have discussed work in concert to improve test performance.

Have students follow these steps:

▶ Step 1. Read the question with particular attention to the verb and key words.
▶ Step 2. Focus the answer by recasting the question as the topic sentence in the response.
▶ Step 3. Determine the type of organizational format required to answer the question and brainstorm information into that format.
▶ Step 4. Write the response using information from the notes.
▶ Step 5. Reread the question and the answer to make sure all parts have been addressed.

Briefly structuring an answer helps students to recall information and develop coherence. Think about which organizational format works best for brainstorming. If the question requires analyzation or evaluation of an issue, brainstorm using a conclusion-support framework. If the question requires the analysis of a problem, use a problem-solution format to recall possible answers to the question. In other situations, the question might simply require an explanation with a listing of several different ideas. Then the writer might use a power outline to organize, and the answer could follow a spool format.

Introduction, Modeling, and Reflection

1. Read through the question. Underline the verb and key words, particularly those that note number or the order of ideas. Talk about how verbs give important clues about the answer: evaluate, compare, contrast, describe, explain, criticize.
2. Rewrite the question, making it the topic sentence of the essay.
3. Make a decision about what format to use to organize the answer. Use sample questions to determine the possibilities. The following examples will help students "walk" through the process:

Example: Science

Step 1. Read the question. Note each part of the question that needs to be answered. Underline the verb and key words, particularly those that note number or the order of ideas.

Question: Should the U.S. government <u>have access</u> to logging wilderness areas in the Rocky Mountains? <u>Present both points of view</u> followed by <u>your own conclusion</u>.

Step 2. Develop a topic sentence:

"There are different points of view about whether or not the U.S. government should have access to logging wilderness areas in the Rocky Mountains."

Step 3. Select an organizing framework and brainstorm the answer.

Conclusion-Support Notes

Conclusion	Support
Government should have access to logging wilderness areas	1. Logging industry needs support 2. Trees grow back quickly 3. Wilderness areas have the best timber 4. Environmentalists have too much power
Government should *not* have access to logging wilderness areas	1. Only a few places are left with virgin forests 2. Logging will destroy these forests forever 3. Protection of endangered species—spotted owl, grizzly bear 4. Great for recreation—hiking, fishing, camping
My conclusion:	

Step 4. Write your answer.
Step 5. Reread the question and your answer to make sure your response addresses all parts.

Example: Social Studies

Step 1. Read the question. Underline the verb and key words, particularly those that note number or the order of ideas.

Question: What were the <u>three major factors</u> occurring during the 1920s that <u>led</u> to the <u>economic collapse</u> of the Great Depression?

Step 2. Develop a topic sentence:

"Three major factors during the 1920s led to the economic collapse of the Great Depression."

Step 3. Select an organizing framework and brainstorm the answer.

Power Notes

1.   Three factors that led to economic collapse
2. Farmers had a difficult time
3. Over-production
3. High costs of materials and machinery
3. Land costs high
3. Low prices for farm goods
2. Banks unstable
3. Couldn't get enough farm loans
3. Banks closed
2. Mass production
3. Workers replaced by machines
3. Wages low
3. Corporations didn't pass profits on to workers

Step 4. Write a response using the spool format.

Step 5. Reread the test question and your response to make sure all parts of the question have been addressed.

---

4. Talk about what makes essay questions so difficult to answer. Having open discussions will help students realize that they have plenty of company. Lots of people find essay tests torturous! Start the discussion with some leading questions: *Why is it hard to get started? How do you calm your nerves? Why does changing the question into your thesis statement help focus your answer? Why does taking time to figure out an organizing pattern for brainstorming help you recall what you know about the topic and help you structure your answer? How might the procedure just described for "doing essay tests" help you feel more confident about taking tests?*

Support and Extensions

● Teach the format for essay questions used on state and national assessments. In some states, like Florida, students read a selection, to which they are then allowed to refer as they write a short or extended answer to an essay question. They need to use information from the selection to answer the question. Show students how to convert key words from the question for developing their first sentence and how to go back into the reading selection and find supportive evidence. Model how to do selective underlining and marginal note taking. Students can then use this information directly in their response or convert it to an appropriate organizing format such as power notes or conclusion-support.

- Have students develop essay questions as an on-going component of studying. After they take two-column notes or develop a concept map, have them design an essay test question that will tap higher order ideas. Ask them to practice answering their questions orally and in written form. As part of reflective conferences, talk about essay questions that make sense for a particular content topic. Encourage students to figure out what essay questions make sense for the material they are learning and then practice answering them. If they can answer their own questions, they will be prepared for questions the teacher might ask.
- Have students practice writing and answering questions as part of small groups.

Learning Strategy

RAFT

We want our students to write about content, but we find that much of their writing is carelessly constructed, brief, and boring. Our assignments may be part of the problem.

The most common assignment, particularly in the content areas, produces a bland essay written for the omnipotent expert, who already knows everything. Why should students feel compelled to teach an all-knowing, critical audience? There's little motivation to compose with vivid voice, imagination, and detail when writing for the "teacher." In addition, many of our content assignments lack focus and are too broad in scope for students to wrap their pens around. RAFT assignments shift students out of their familiar roles and inspire them to write for different audiences using formats other than the essay. RAFT encourages them to infuse their work with more voice and imagination.

RAFT, originally conceived by Nancy Vandevanter (1982) as part of the Montana Writing Project, clarifies the design of assignments. RAFT, an acronym for **R**ole, **A**udience, **F**ormat, and **T**opic, defines the decisions students must make before they start writing. It helps them consider who they are as writers, for whom they are writing, the most appropriate format for the piece, and the tone they want to take with the expected content. Untangling and labeling these components help students build a better metacognitive awareness of what writers do before they write. Writers don't just pick up a pen and go at it. They do a bit of planning first. Students also begin to understand that writing has possibilities beyond the classroom. RAFT, like other CRISS[SM] strategies, serves to de-mystify what might be an amorphous, complex process by clarifying its components. RAFT also incorporates strong verbs to focus and energize the piece. A RAFT assignment doesn't ask students to *write*, but to *plead, convince, or complain.*

Examples:

R. **R**ole of writer: Who are you? a soldier, Abraham Lincoln, a slave, a mathematical operation? (See Blackline 27 for other possibilities.)

A. **A**udience: To whom is this written? a mother, Congress, an integer? (See Blackline 27 for other possibilities.)

F. **F**ormat: What form will it take? a letter, speech, obituary, conversation, memo, journal? (See Blackline 27 for other possibilities.)

T. **T**opic + strong verb: *Persuade* a soldier to spare your life; *demand* equal pay for equal work; *plead* for a halt to coal mining in our valley. (See Blackline 27 for additional strong verbs.)

RAFT gives students more control over their own writing assignments. Allowing students to define their own role, format, and audience when explaining a specific topic preserves some freedom of choice. The results make lively reading.

Guided Comprehension

Introduction, Modeling, and Reflection

1. Explain that all writers must consider four components of every written piece: role of the writer, audience, format, and topic.
2. Brainstorm writing topics from a previous or current unit of study. Select several topics from those presented.
3. Write RAFT on the board, and list possible roles, audiences, formats, and strong verbs that are appropriate for each topic. (Blackline 27.) Make sure students are familiar with the formats. They may need to research or collect samples of obituaries, resumes, etc.

   Explain to students "RAFT assignments are written from a viewpoint other than that of a student to an audience other than the teacher in a form other than the standard essay. Seldom do we use the word *write* in our assignments, but rather choose to incorporate strong verbs such as *plead, convince,* and *clarify,* which focus the assignment by setting the tone of the response."
4. Provide students with examples similar to those presented here.

Science

A biology student uses a travelogue to explain the function of red blood cells in the circulatory system.

Student example:

R. Blood cell.

A. Human body.

F. Travelogue.

T. Topic + strong verb: Explain the function of blood cells as they travel through the human body.

Hello, Human Body. I am one of your very own red blood cells. I want to tell you a few things about myself, and then talk about how I travel through the highways in your body.

I am a cell in your blood. I carry oxygen. I am quite small. If you were to line me up in a row of l50 red blood cells, we would be only 1 millimeter long. That is about as wide as your pencil lines. I am round with thick edges and a thin center. I have 25 trillion red blood cell buddies all traveling around in your vessels. That's enough about me. Now on with my travels. I am like a delivery man. I help with the blood's job of being a pickup and delivery service, but I have lots of fun sliding around in your vessels. The oxygen gas coming into your lungs is picked up by me as I pass through the capillaries in the lungs. The lung is my favorite part of the trip. I splash around in the lungs while my hemoglobin picks up oxygen. I perform the job of pickup and delivery so well.

Now I am on my journey again to the heart. I am making the pulmonary trip from the lungs to the heart. Now I am inside the heart. It is very slippery riding up and down and around curves and out of valves. Finally, I leave the left ventricle and begin the journey carrying my oxygen to the cells. The blood vessel is a wet-and-wild place to be. We slide down branches of the vessel, similar to climbing up the highest branch on a tree until we find just the right capillary, which is like a twig. Finally, my buddies and I squeeze single file into these tiny capillaries where we unload our oxygen. We then get back together again in veins and work ourselves back to the heart. The heart pumps us through the pulmonary system to the lungs where our journey begins again. Off to deliver more oxygen to tired cells.

Mathematics

The following is a letter that persuades the audience of the importance of a geometric form.

R. point
A. teacher
F. letter
T. convince your teacher that you have an important function

Dear Mrs. Havens,

I am Pete the point. I am a point of an endless number of points in space. I want to ask you if you will teach your students about us points and how every single geometric figure is made of us. It is very important to me, because it seems that many people think of the point as a small part of geometry since it is so little. Though we are little, we are one of the most important factors of our world of geometry. Without me and all other points there would be no other geometric figures. We are their building blocks. Though all lines are drawn with one solid mark, in reality a line is an endless set of points going in opposite directions. A sphere is a figure with all points at an equal distance from a center point like me.

So please tell your students all about us points. It troubles me when many think of us as unimportant specks in space. Please spread the reality of our importance to the students you teach. My partners and I would greatly appreciate it. Thank you.

A Point,
Pete

---

5. Have students write one of the generated assignments.
6. Ask students, "How did your writing change when you composed for audiences other than the teacher? How might RAFT help you plan your own assignments? Did RAFT make writing more fun? Could you put yourself into the piece more? Could you start living your character's life, fuse into the action, place yourself in the scene?"

Support and Extensions

- As part of a unit study, ask students to develop topics for writing and create their own RAFT assignments. Take the pieces through the steps in the writing process. Post their completed works on bulletin boards, or publish them in a class magazine. Have a Writer's Celebration during which everyone reads his or her piece aloud.
- If an assignment is to be based on a book or video, students should know their roles and the audience before reading or viewing.
- Challenge your students to write a multi-genre research paper (Romano, 1995). Rather than the rigid spool paper, ask them to come up with other formats. One cooperative team of four students chose to do their research project on the Civil War, using a newspaper format. They wrote reports from the battlefield, songs, obituaries, and "Dear Lizzie" columns. In effect, they combined a series of RAFT assignments into one publication.
- Multi-genre reports also work well as individual assignments. After reading *To Kill A Mockingbird,* a sophomore wrote a factual piece about some of the main historical events that occurred during the time of the book, a poem about prejudice, and a journal from Jem's perspective (one of the characters). She also included some of her own illustrations.
- After discussing a topic, have students come up with their own RAFT assignments.

◗ Summary

Our students deserve the opportunity to write constantly in our classes. Writing is what we do to learn, to understand, to explore ideas. The strategies described in this chapter provide scaffolding to help fledgling writers move ahead on their own. Given the scope of this book, we had to limit our discussion to a handful of strategies—strategies which we have found to be particularly useful in content classrooms. We invite you to learn more. If you haven't read the work of Tom Romano, Donald Graves, and Nancy Atwell, indulge yourself. You are in for a treat.

Writing templates and spool papers are designed to help students begin to internalize structure in their writing, to carry their audiences forward, as they move from one idea to another in a logical progression. Warning! These approaches are transitory, used only as long as students need them. Spool papers and writing templates can be overdone! Once students have internalized a sense of structure and know how to teach their readers about what they know, the rigidity of these formats becomes too confining. Know when to remove the training wheels.

Bring the underlying curriculum to the forefront. Take the mystery out of the dreaded essay test by teaching students how to approach it. Don't leave this important skill to chance, particularly in these days of high stakes assessments. Show students how to analyze questions, plan their responses, and write logically.

With RAFT and multi-genre reports, writers discover more flexible dimensions of writing. These innovative assignments encourage students to discover their own voices, using unconventional formats to present their ideas. Writing experts tell us that students need opportunities to choose their own topics. School writing, they say, should mirror the work of real writers; it should be on topics of personal value for real audiences. As we think of ourselves as writers, we understand the validity of this argument. Yet, content teachers want their students to write about their material. Allowing students to choose their own role, format, and audience to explain a topic preserves some freedom of choice even when the content is necessarily limited. As a result, content writing also becomes livelier and more fun to read.

We invite you to try some of the ideas described in this chapter. Writing touches the heart of learning by penetrating the external shell of memorized facts and superficial understanding. When we can explain concepts to ourselves and to others, we can claim new knowledge as our own.

Research Conclusion	Reference
Most students acquire report-writing skills more rapidly when taught organizing structures.	Nunnally, 1991

CHAPTER

9

Vocabulary

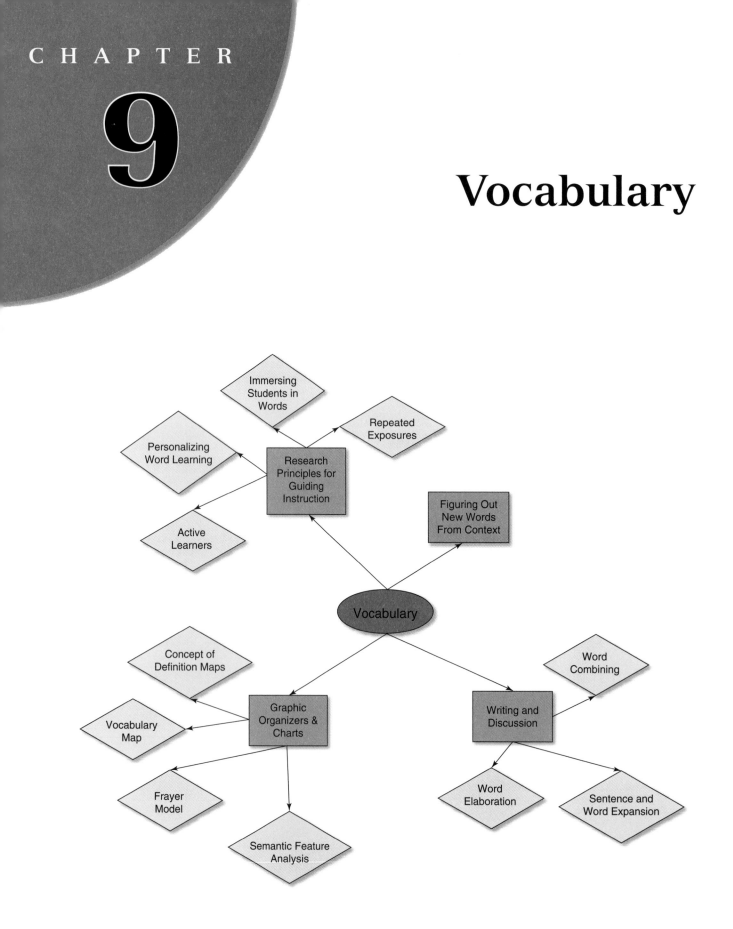

Words communicate content. If students do not know the vocabulary particular to a content area, they will have difficulty understanding and learning the course information. Vocabulary knowledge plays an instrumental role in understanding text (Nagy and Scott, 2000). The richer your vocabulary, the richer your comprehension. In fact, some say that vocabulary knowledge is the single most important factor in reading comprehension (Laflamme, 1997).

As teachers, we all know the importance of teaching vocabulary. In fact, many content classes—particularly science and mathematics—are, in effect, studies in vocabulary. Bill Holiday notes that some high school chemistry texts contain 3,000 content specific words unfamiliar to high school students. This staggering number of words exceeds the vocabulary taught in most foreign language classes! While some of these words are not necessary for the conceptual understanding of chemistry, these figures clearly demonstrate how important it is to deliver the best possible vocabulary instruction to students. Let's once more examine how research can guide our practice.

◗ Research Principles for Guiding Instruction

In a comprehensive review of vocabulary instruction, Camille Blachowicz and Peter Fisher (2000) offer strategies from four major research areas to guide instruction: students as active learners, personalizing word learning, immersing students in words, and learning through repeated exposure. Let's briefly examine each of these principles.

Students As Active Learners. Engaging students as active learners is hardly a new idea for us. But how do we incorporate this concept in our vocabulary instruction? Blachowicz and Fisher describe several lines of research that provide some answers to this question. For example, they find considerable research support for strategies that help students actively focus on the relationships among words. In most of these studies, students use vocabulary terms in conversations and writing and then expand definitions through a variety of elaborations. Researchers have found far less support for more traditional learning methods such as memorizing definitions and figuring out words in context.

It makes sense that research consistently supports situations in which students construct interrelationships among words and ideas (e.g., Semantic Feature Analysis, Concept of Definition Map). Understanding words within a rich semantic context helps students build meaning and allows them to become actively engaged. However, the success of these strategies depends upon students—not teachers—making the meaning. When the teacher organizes words into semantically related groups, students learn less effectively than when generating the relationships themselves. Stahl, Burdge, Macnuga, & Stecykk (1992) found no benefit of teaching words in semantically related sets to fourth-graders. Yet other researchers found beneficial effects when investigating instructional procedures where students actively made connections among words. As we've emphasized throughout: when teachers do all the work, students remain passive recipients. They don't make connections, and they don't learn.

What about looking up words in a dictionary? Take a moment to think about your own student career. Remember the list-on-Monday-test-on-Friday scenario? We got a vocabulary list on Monday, looked up the words in the dictionary and copied definitions on Wednesday, then memorized them for a test on Friday. The following week we received another list and followed the same routine. Very few vocabulary words stuck beyond the Friday test.

Blachowicz, Fisher, and a host of other researchers claim that we don't learn much by looking up words in a dictionary and memorizing definitions (Nagy and

Scott, 2001). In a series of studies, Bos and Anders (1989, 1990, 1992) compared learning definitions to a variety of more engaging strategies in which students expanded upon the definitions of words and examined their interrelatedness. Students exploring new words through interactive techniques performed better than students who simply memorized definitions. Knowing a word means being able to do things with it—use it spontaneously in conversations and in writing. Understanding a word requires more than memorizing its definition; besides, memorizing definitions is passive and deadly boring!

But what about context? We all use written and oral context as an aid in learning new words. Do readers learn new words by analyzing how they are used in written context? The answer is both yes and no. Research on learning words from context indicates that readers don't learn much about a word from any single encounter. Meeting an unknown word in context may give readers a vague familiarity with the word, but it requires more to make it part of a working vocabulary. Asking students to focus on how words are used in context is an important first step, not an end in itself. Once students have a vague idea of a word from context, we have to enhance their learning by encouraging them to use the word in a variety of active ways.

Personalizing Word Learning.   When students personalize word learning either by selecting their own words to learn or by using mnemonic strategies, their active engagement in learning increases. So, too, does their learning success. Nobody likes being told what to do; we want choices.

Studies by Blachowicz and Fisher (2000) indicate that students seem to be more actively engaged when allowed to select their own vocabulary words. Studies with fourth- and seventh-graders (Fisher, Blachowicz and Smith, 1991; Fisher and Danielsen, 1998, in Blachowicz and Fisher, 2000) showed that students learned words more effectively and remembered the meanings of the words they chose longer than words chosen by the teacher. The effect of student choice becomes even more pronounced when the teacher first models how to select words that are important for understanding the text. For example, Dole, Sloan, and Trathen (1995) found that 10th graders who were taught a process for selecting important words as part of their literature groups learned better than students who selected words without any instruction.

The work on personalizing word lists makes sense given students are more likely to be interested, and therefore actively engaged, in learning words they select themselves. Even though this research took place with literature content, it can be extended to other content areas. What happens in the content classroom when students have less choice about the specific words and concepts to learn? When using a textbook, we must make sure students know the author's clues to important vocabulary (e.g., bold or colored print), and guide them in our pre-reading activities and in our discussions to focus on the important words. Then, we must figure out ways to provide students some latitude in selecting words to learn in depth. This approach makes sense. Perhaps, we should do some research to validate our hunches.

We can also personalize word learning by giving students opportunities to develop their own elaborating strategies. For example, Blachowicz and Fisher (2000) review several research studies that support the use of images (Carr and Mazur-Stewart, 1988) and the acting out of meanings (Duffelmeyer, 1980). Again, students were given choices about how they constructed their word images and about ways to act out new words. Combining choice with active processing fits with current brain research (Jensen, 1998), and it makes good sense.

The research on personalizing strategies also fits well with CRISS[SM] principles and philosophy. We want to teach students a variety of ways to engage themselves in word learning. Once they feel confident using several different strategies, they need opportunities to choose from their repertoire of strategies. Again, it's all about showing students how, and then turning them loose to make their own informed choices about how they learn best.

Immersing Students in Words. We all know that incidental word learning occurs as part of listening and reading. Blachowicz and Fisher (2000) summarize studies about listening, family literacy, and word learning from context. Results from these studies confirm that environments rich in literacy experiences encourage vocabulary learning. In classrooms where students have opportunities to become immersed in reading and writing, qualitative data support the positive effects on the development of students' vocabulary.

Learning through Repeated Exposure. As noted earlier, learning a new word involves more than one trial, and it requires more than memorizing a definition. We have to use it multiple times and in different ways (e.g., vocabulary mapping, adding contextual information, writing and speaking) before a word becomes part of our working vocabulary.

These four principles provide a framework for the vocabulary strategies described in the next portion of this chapter. Keep in mind it is better to learn a few words well than many words superficially. This premise creates extra challenges in content areas such as mathematics, science, and social studies, which contain an overwhelming number of new concepts. We must think hard about the vocabulary our students really need to understand, and assist them in selecting the most important words for deep learning. They need to know how to sift the important words from the jargon.

Consider the following questions before planning instruction:

What do I want my students to remember ten years from now?
How much prior knowledge do students have about a word or concept?
Do I need to pre-teach a vocabulary word before students read?
Are there words that I can help students group together to enhance meaning?
How can I help students incorporate a word into their speech and writing?
How can I engage students in repeated exposures to a word and still keep their interest?

Figuring out New Words from Context

Strategy
Learning

We intentionally begin our discussion of instructional strategies with ways to help students become more skilled at figuring out new words from context. Usually they pay little attention to context, passing over the many clues authors provide. We need to hone our students' abilities to figure out new words in context and then show them ways to deepen their understanding of the word through elaboration. Using context alone is not enough.

Start by helping students understand the contributions as well as the limitations of context to word learning. Sometimes authors are explicit with synonyms, bold print, clear examples, and direct definitions. In other instances, they merely suggest some vague relationships or attributes.

Introduction, Modeling, and Reflection

1. Familiarize students with the types of information context can provide. Choose a reading selection rich in different kinds of clues.
2. Make wall charts with examples found in the reading selection. As students read on their own, have them add examples to the charts. Categorize by the type of clue.

Types of Clues (The contextual clue is in italics.)

Definition or synonym: Definition and synonym clues are the easiest.

The patient suffered from **amnesia** or *loss of memory.*
A **dilemma** is a situation that requires *a choice between two equally unfavorable options.*
The water ran quickly through the **gully**, *a deep ditch,* then slowed as the land became level.

Properties or characteristics: This type of clue is a little more difficult. You are given only the properties or characteristics of the word.

A **friend** is someone you *like and trust*—someone who *understands and helps you.*
The **cypress** has *scale-like leaves* and *round, woody cones.*
The **pike** lives in *fresh water* in the Northern hemisphere. It has a *long snout* and can grow to over *four feet* in length.

Examples and/or non-examples: This type of clue is even more challenging. You have to figure out what critical characteristics the examples have in common or what critical characteristics the non-examples are missing in order to have some idea of what the word means.

Domestic animals like *cats, dogs,* and *cows* can live comfortably on a farm.
Several kinds of **marsupials** live in Australia, for example *kangaroos, koalas,* and *wombats.*
Squares, rectangles, and *rhombuses* are **quadrilaterals,** but *triangles* and *circles* are not.

3. Once students have a basic understanding of the different ways authors go about clarifying words through context, guide them with the following questions:

Is the word in bold print?
What contextual clues does the author provide?
Are there other aids, such as pictures, illustrations, graphics, or marginal notes?

4. Ask your students, "How did identifying the author's clues help you with a word's meaning? Do you have a better understanding of the word?"

Support and Extensions

● Photocopy selections with key concepts underlined. Instruct students to underline contextual information that explains the concepts. Then have students create their own definitions derived from the contextual information. On note cards, expand definitions using pictures, synonyms, examples, and non-examples.

● Using the following chart, ask students to skim through their reading assignment and record unfamiliar words. Remind them to attend to headings, italics, bold print, and other visual information. They then should record the page number and predict the definition from context. After reading, they check the definition in a dictionary. Finally, have students write the word in an original sentence.

Word w/sentence in which it occurs	Page	Definition from context	Dictionary definition	Original sentence

❱ Graphic Organizers and Charts

Word maps and charts help students expand word meanings and discover relationships between vocabulary terms. They also help students develop elaborated definitions, rather than simple, one- or two-word descriptions. In addition, they provide students with a way to learn vocabulary independently.

Concept of Definition Maps

It seems logical to begin vocabulary instruction with the qualities of a definition. Too many students have a narrow conception of what the meaning of a word encompasses. Most conceive definitions as simplistic, imprecise statements lacking elaboration and personal comment. Schwartz and Raphael (1985, 1988) designed an instructional approach for teaching students a broader concept of a definition, one that encourages them to integrate their own knowledge. Once students understand the qualities of a definition, they apply this general knowledge to expand their own vocabularies and to master unfamiliar concepts. Schwartz and Raphael recommend using a Concept of Definition Map to help students visualize the components of a definition.

Introduction, Modeling, and Reflection

1. Use a Concept of Definition Map to help students visualize the components of a definition (Blackline 28). The map includes three relationships essential to a rich definition: "What is it?" (Category) "What is it like?" (Properties), and "What are some examples?" (Illustrations).

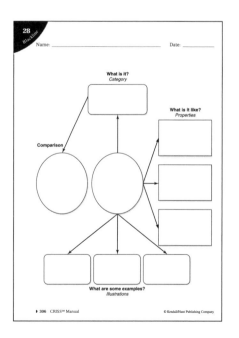

2. Begin instruction by explaining to students that in order to understand new vocabulary, they need to know what makes up a word's definition. Go over the three questions that make up a definition.

3. Model the process using a familiar concept. Show them the map and describe its parts. For example, ask students about a favorite pet, such as a type of

dog—a *terrier.* Write the word *terrier* in the center box. Above terrier (in the top box) write a word that describes the category of animal under which *terrier* fits-*dog.* On the right side, list the properties of the terrier, answering "What is it like?" In these boxes, you might write: *wiry hair, vary in size, bred to hunt small animals.* The bottom boxes are for examples of terriers. In these boxes, you could write: *Cairn Terrier, West Highland Terrier,* and *Jack Russell Terrier.*

Concept of Definition Map—Terrier

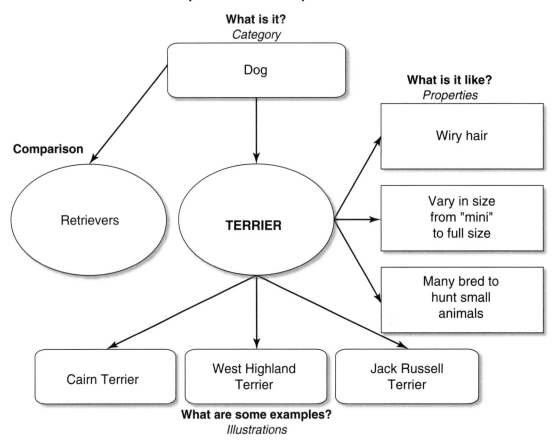

4. Sometimes, when thinking about properties, it is helpful to have a comparison item. In this case, a comparison could be *retrievers,* another type of dog. Write this to the left of terriers in a box connected to the top box-dog.
5. Once students have completed the Concept of Definition Map, ask them to write a definition using the information on the map.

   One of my favorite types of dogs is the terrier. The terrier breed is different from the popular retriever breed in several ways. First, terriers have coarse, wiry hair quite different from the smooth or silky retriever coat. Unlike the larger retriever breed, terriers come in all sizes, from a five pound Yorkshire terrier to an eighty pound Pit Bull terrier. They were bred to be tireless while chasing small animals like rats, rabbits, and badgers. Three of the smaller types of terriers are the Cairn terrier, the West Highland terrier, and the Jack Russell terrier.

6. Talk about why expanded definitions are so much better than those typically found in a dictionary. "Do you have a better understanding of the word? How does expanding a definition help you really know it?"

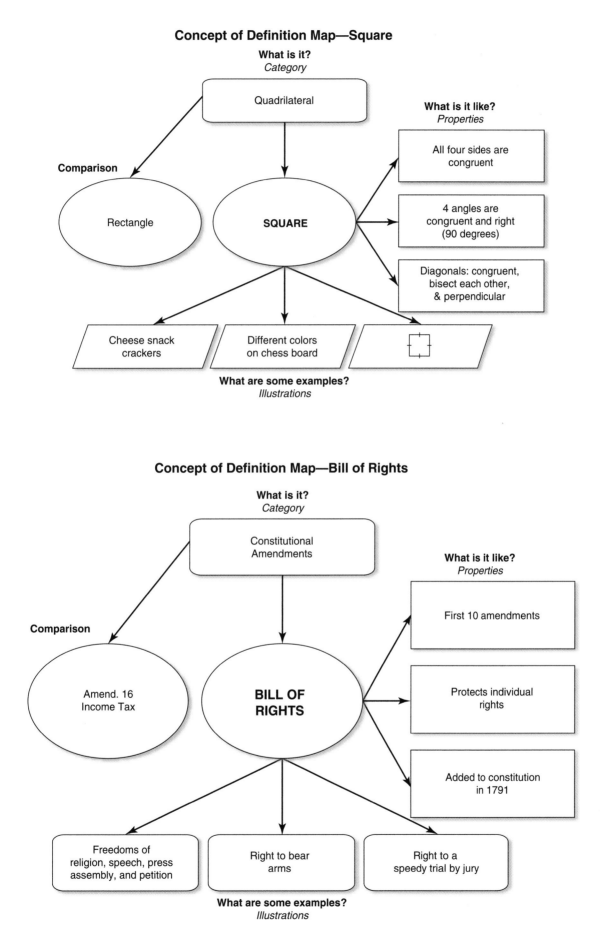

Concept of Definition Map—Square

What is it?
Category

Quadrilateral

Comparison

Rectangle

SQUARE

What is it like?
Properties

All four sides are congruent

4 angles are congruent and right (90 degrees)

Diagonals: congruent, bisect each other, & perpendicular

Cheese snack crackers

Different colors on chess board

What are some examples?
Illustrations

Concept of Definition Map—Bill of Rights

What is it?
Category

Constitutional Amendments

Comparison

Amend. 16 Income Tax

BILL OF RIGHTS

What is it like?
Properties

First 10 amendments

Protects individual rights

Added to constitution in 1791

Freedoms of religion, speech, press assembly, and petition

Right to bear arms

Right to a speedy trial by jury

What are some examples?
Illustrations

Support and Extensions

● As part of the pre-reading discussion, ask students to brainstorm what they already know, using the Concept of Definition Map. Next, have them skim the selection and list unfamiliar concepts or terms. (You can add to this list, too.) After students read, have them work in pairs to fill in additional information. Students then present their maps for discussion.

In the following example, the teacher modified categories of information on the Concept of Definition Map, then had the students brainstorm what they knew about jazz before reading an article. This information is indicated in bold and non-italicized print. After reading, the students expanded their definition. The new information is recorded in italics.

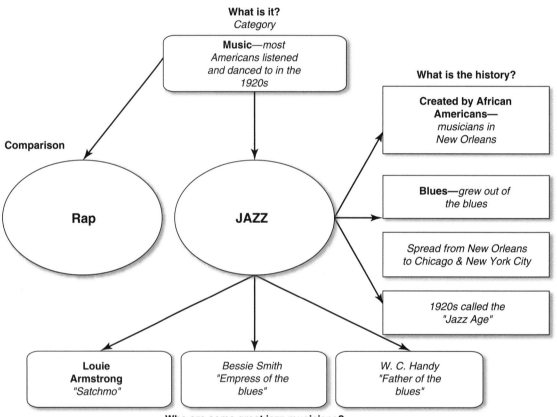

Concept of Definition Map—Jazz

What is it?
Category

Music—*most Americans listened and danced to in the 1920s*

What is the history?

Created by African Americans—*musicians in New Orleans*

Blues—*grew out of the blues*

Spread from New Orleans to Chicago & New York City

1920s called the "Jazz Age"

Comparison

Rap

JAZZ

Louie Armstrong *"Satchmo"*

Bessie Smith "Empress of the blues"

W. C. Handy "Father of the blues"

Who are some great jazz musicians?

● Students can use their map as a guide for note taking from discussions and content texts. For example, a sixth-grade class defined concepts from a social studies unit on state government. One of the terms was *lobbyist*. The students read and took notes on several articles. They organized their notes on a Concept of Definition Map and then wove their ideas into a definition. One student's example follows:

Person who works at the capital

what is it like?
what do they do?

Lobbyist

tries to influence legislators to vote for or against certain bills

NRA guns

Plum Creek Timber

Greenpeace – environment

Can't go into chamber must register

EXAMPLES

A lobbyist is a person who tries to influence lawmakers to vote for or against specific legislation. Some lobbyists are paid by a company or business like the Burlington Northern Railroad or Plum Creek Timber. Others work for special interest groups like the teachers' union, Greenpeace, or the National Rifle Association. They all have to register at the Capitol before they can try to influence legislators. This year there were 542 lobbyists registered. They cannot work in the chamber, so they work by visiting with legislators in their offices or in the lobby. Many provide written information to the legislators. Sometimes they provide the senators and representatives with drafts of bills they would like to see enacted. They are not allowed to influence legislators by giving them money.

- Students use blank maps to evaluate one another's written definitions. For example, after the students wrote definitions of *lobbyist,* they traded papers and filled in the blank concept maps. They looked in the definitions for information about categories, properties, and examples. By using the blank maps as editorial tools, they could easily tell whether the definition was complete or in need of revision.
- Assign students to develop Concept of Definition Maps for key terms as a way to study and review for tests.
- Encourage students to modify or create their own Concept of Definition Maps. In the example on page 202, sixth graders were studying the Commonwealth of Nations. They decided that these were the important things to know about the concept: a definition, the facts, reasons for its existence, and examples of countries comprising the commonwealth. Students took notes from their social studies text and then used their notes to write an explanation.

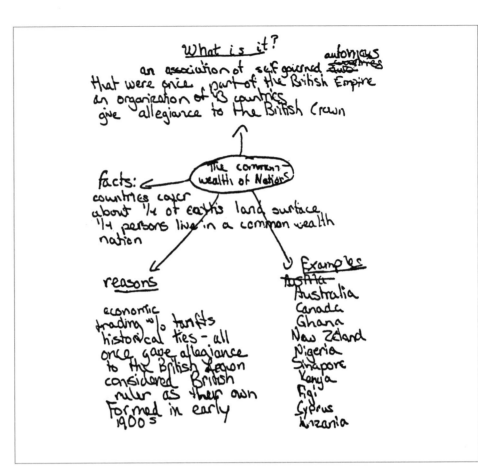

What is it?

an association of self governed ~~states~~ autonomous ~~countries~~
that were once part of the British Empire
an organization of 43 countries
give allegiance to the British Crown

The common-wealth of Nations

facts:
countries cover
about 1/4 of earth's land surface
1/4 persons live in a common wealth
nation

reasons

economic
trading w/o tariffs
historical ties - all
once gave allegiance
to the British ~~Legion~~
considered British
ruler as their own
formed in early
1900 s

Examples
~~Austria~~
Australia
Canada
Ghana
New Zeland
Nigeria
Singapore
Kenya
Fiji
Cyprus
Tanzania

The Commonwealth of Nations

The Commonwealth of Nations is an
organization of countries who mutually benefit
through trade agreements. It is an organization
of 43 self-governing, autonomous (independent in
government; having the right of self-government)
countries that were once part of the British
Empire. The Commonwealth of Nations was
formed in the early 1900's. In addition to their
shared history of once giving allegiance to
the British Crown, the member countries share
trading without tariffs. The member countries
cover about 1/4 of the earth's land surface. One
of every four persons on earth lives in a
Commonwealth nation. The organization includes
Australia, Canada, Ghana, New Zealand, Nigeria,
Singapore, Kenya, Fiji, Cyprus, and Tanzania among
its 43 members. Because of its size, the
Commonwealth of Nations impacts world
economics.

- Modify maps for taking notes on biographies. In one class, fifth graders reading biographies of American heroes developed maps defining the unique qualities of these historical figures. Their maps served as pre-writing material for brief reports.

Concept of Definition Map—Thomas Edison

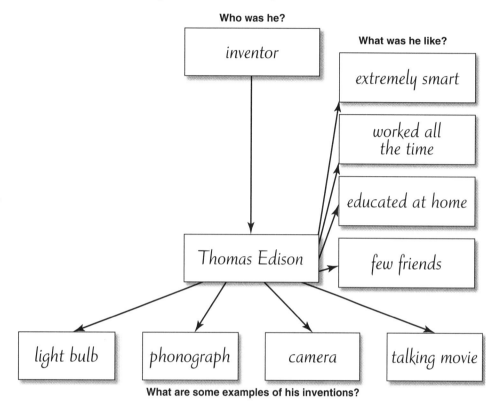

Sample report:

Thomas Edison was a famous inventor. He thought of all sorts of things. He invented the light bulb and made a talking movie. He also invented a phonograph and camera. He must have been very smart. He was such a hard worker that he didn't have many friends. He also didn't make friends at school. He must have been kind of lonely.

- The examples we have shown so far have been nouns, but the Concept of Definition Map can be modified slightly to fit with other parts of speech. In the example on page 204, students were asked to expand upon unknown words they self-selected while reading a novel.

Concept of Definition Map—Fastidious

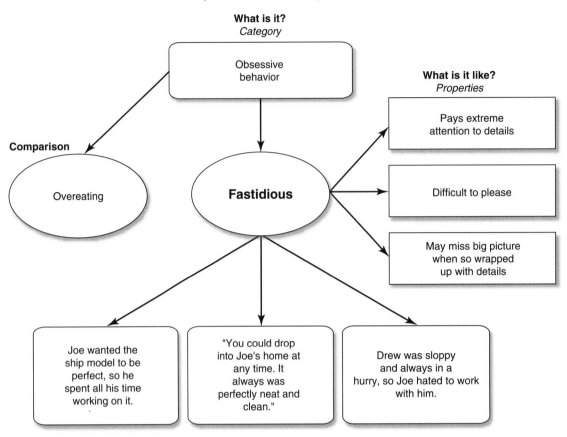

What is it?
Category

Obsessive
behavior

Comparison

Overeating

Fastidious

What is it like?
Properties

Pays extreme
attention to details

Difficult to please

May miss big picture
when so wrapped
up with details

Joe wanted the
ship model to be
perfect, so he
spent all his time
working on it.

"You could drop
into Joe's home at
any time. It
always was
perfectly neat and
clean."

Drew was sloppy
and always in a
hurry, so Joe hated to work
with him.

What are some examples from the story of Joe's fastidious behavior?

Learning Strategy

Vocabulary Map

Another version is a Vocabulary Map where students elaborate on concepts by recording definitions, sentences, synonyms, and pictures.

Guided Comprehension

Introduction, Modeling, and Reflection

1. Explain to students developing vocabulary maps provides another way to elaborate on important concepts.

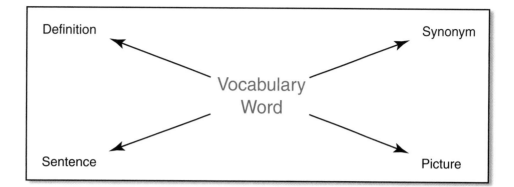

2. Model with a familiar word. List the word in the center of the page and surround it with the following information: the definition (in their own words), a synonym, a picture illustrating the word or statement, and an original sentence containing the word.

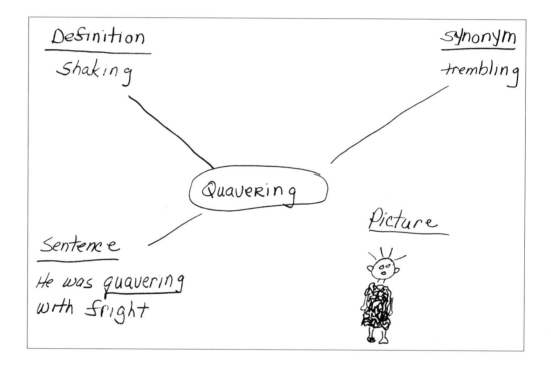

3. Pair students, and have them develop several vocabulary maps together. Then ask them to present their word maps to the class.

4. Talk about how expanding definitions helps students attain a better metacognitive awareness about how well they know a concept. "If you can't map a word, what does that tell you about how well you understand the word? Why does mapping a word lead to long term retention of the concept?"

Support and Extensions

● The vocabulary map also works extremely well for learning vocabulary in a second language, as in this Norwegian example.

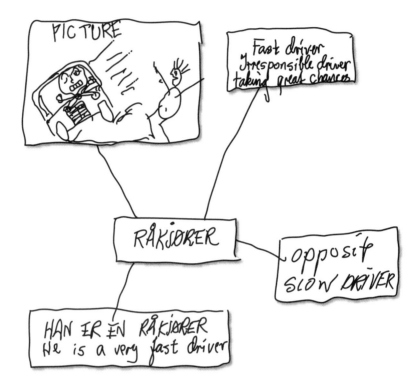

● Students studying mythology in a ninth grade class also expanded words with pictures, definitions, and sentences. In addition, they linked the words to their roots in mythology.

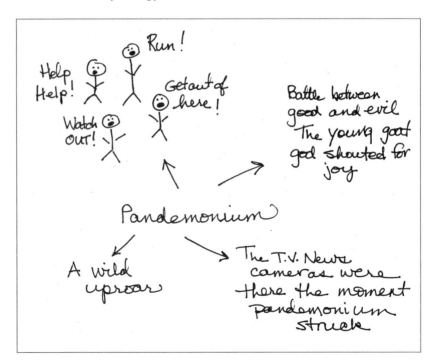

● Catherine Rosenbaum (2001) developed a word-mapping sequence for middle-school students that incorporated examining how a word is used in context. Students identified an unknown word in a reading assignment, wrote it on their map, recorded what they thought it meant based on its context, found the word in the dictionary and wrote a brief definition, added synonyms and antonyms to their maps, and then wrote the word in an original sentence. Her students successfully used this mapping sequence to teach difficult words to their peers.

Modified Vocabulary Map

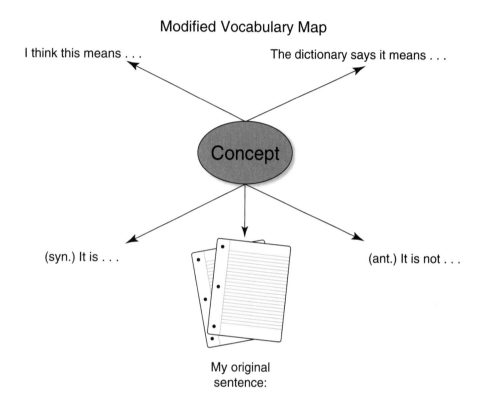

I think this means . . .

The dictionary says it means . . .

Concept

(syn.) It is . . .

(ant.) It is not . . .

My original
sentence:

● Encourage students to expand definitions using vocabulary flash cards. Challenge them to include pictures, synonyms, antonyms, and original sentences as in the following example.

Vocabulary Flash Cards

Side one: illustration
word divided into syllables (colored)

Side two: definition
synonym & antonym
original sentence

i·con·o·clast

ICONOCLAST

Definition: A person who attacks popular ideas or traditions (sometimes religious ideas)

Synonym: attacker, overthrower, rebel
Antonym: follower, conformist, brown-noser

Sentence: We feared the **iconoclast** might be elected to an important state office and eliminate the programs we all believe in.

Once students have seen a variety of adaptions, ask them to design their own. In the following example, sixth graders from Grand Bay, Alabama (Jane Simms and Ann Taylor's class), explained their designs.

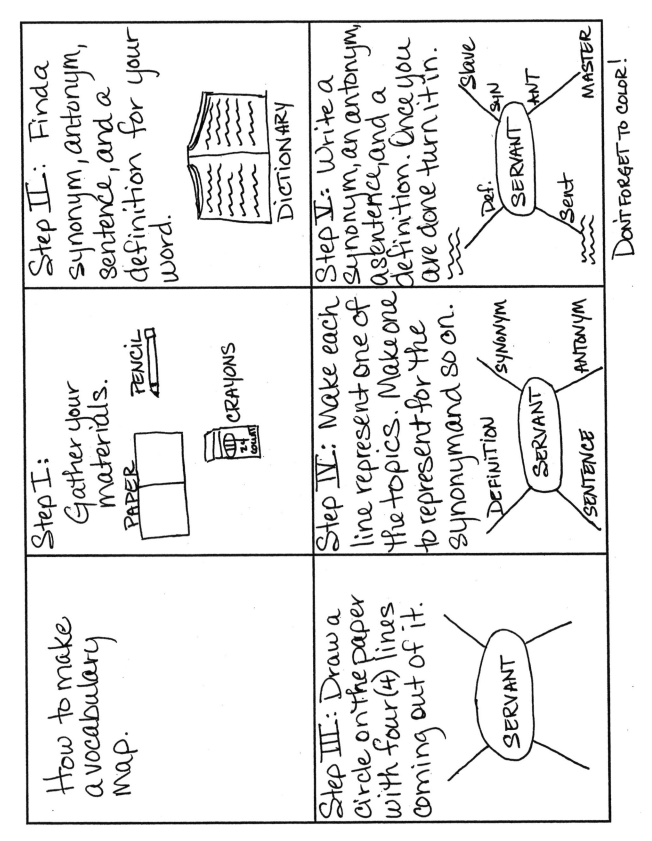

How to make a vocabulary Map.

Step I: Gather your materials.

PAPER
PENCIL
CRAYONS

Step II: Find a synonym, antonym, sentence, and a definition for your word.

DICTIONARY

Step III: Draw a circle on the paper with four (4) lines coming out of it.

SERVANT

Step IV: Make each line represent one of the topics. Make one to represent the synonym and so on.

DEFINITION
SYNONYM
SERVANT
SENTENCE
ANTONYM

Step V: Write a synonym, an antonym, a sentence, and a definition. Once you are done turn it in.

Def.
Slave
SIN
SERVANT
ANT
Sent
MASTER

Don't forget to color!

● For another variation, have students create a flip book (directions below) to hold all vocabulary words from a unit of study along with appropriate word maps and charts.

Directions:

1. Stack three sheets of paper so the short edges are 3/4–1″ apart (3 sheets = 12 words, 4 sheets = 18 words). Use colored paper!
2. Fold up from the bottom to create a book with six tabs visible, all the same size.
3. Turn and staple at the top fold.
4. Ask students to cut two slits in each of the four middle pages. Leave the cover intact. This should give them three equal columns with 12 flips in the middle to write vocabulary words.
5. Ask students to write the topic or unit title on the top cover page.
6. On each tab, they should write one of the vocabulary terms so it is visible when the book is closed. Above the word on the tab they should do a vocabulary map.
7. Ask students to write original sentences which combine several of the words or have them write a summary paragraph on the full page at the back of the flip book.
8. Students can then use their flip books to self-test or to buddy up with a partner to share ideas and review.

Frayer Model

Think about how we learn a new concept. Initially, we have a superficial understanding, perhaps a one- or two-word definition. As we meet the concept over a period of time, we start to understand it more deeply. We begin to know its essential and non-essential characteristics and to understand examples that illustrate it. We follow the process of deepening understanding described in the Frayer Model of concept development (Frayer, Fredrecik, and Kausmeither, 1969 in Buehl, 2001).

The Frayer Model is a visual organizer that contains four sections: essential characteristics, non-essential characteristics, examples, and non-examples (Blackline 29).

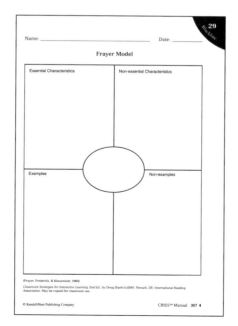

This model helps us differentiate the characteristics that define the concept and those only marginally associated with it. Let's try it with the concept "metacognition." What does it mean to be metacognitive? What are the essential characteristics? Non-essential characteristics? What are some examples of being metacognitive? Non-examples?

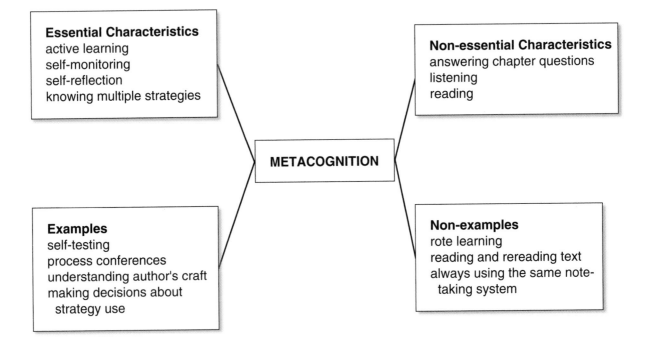

Essential Characteristics
active learning
self-monitoring
self-reflection
knowing multiple strategies

Non-essential Characteristics
answering chapter questions
listening
reading

METACOGNITION

Examples
self-testing
process conferences
understanding author's craft
making decisions about
  strategy use

Non-examples
rote learning
reading and rereading text
always using the same note-
  taking system

Introduction, Modeling, and Reflection

1. Review the Frayer Model format. Have students fold a paper in four sections and label it with the four categories, or use Blackline 29.
2. Introduce an important concept from your content area, and write it in the center of the Frayer Model. Working in pairs or small groups, ask students to generate examples and non-examples of the concept. Then create a class list of examples and non-examples and record them on your Frayer model. Students may add to their individual model from the class list.
3. Examine the list of examples. Ask which essential characteristics the examples have in common. Make a list of these common features, checking back to make sure that these illustrate the concept, and write the features in the Frayer Model.
4. Ask students to read or listen for new information about the concept and record it on the model.
5. After students have completed the reading, go back to the original model and ask them to confirm or reject information previously generated as a class. Check for misconceptions and shift items to different sections of the model. After reading and learning more about a concept, students will find that some of their essential features may be more appropriately listed as non-essential.

In the following example, American history students used a Frayer Model to extend their knowledge of Progressivism. Students discussed what they already knew about Progressivism, then revised their maps after completing the reading. Using the Frayer Model as a pre-reading activity, the teacher guided students in setting goals for their reading and provided them with a way to organize their notes and check their understanding of a key concept.

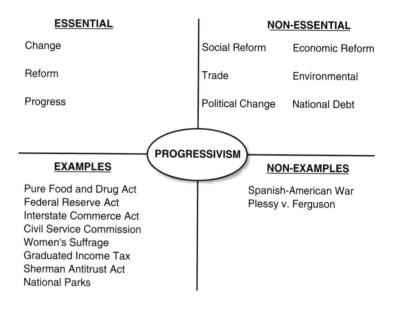

6. Ask students, "Why does analyzing a concept using examples and non-examples help in clarifying concepts? How did it help to organize your thinking?"

Support and Extensions

● Ask students to list the major concepts in a unit and then work in pairs to complete a Frayer Model over one or two concepts. Make sure all concepts are covered by at least one group. They can present their models to the class, and you can post their work around the room as a class review.

● Use this model as an assessment for important concepts. List three or four key concepts from a unit. Have students use a Frayer Model to elaborate on the concepts.

● Information on the Model can be used as a study guide or a writing tool.

● Some teachers find it unnecessary to use the non-essential characteristics of the Frayer Model. They have simplified it to include: essential characteristics, examples and non-examples.

Learning Strategy

Semantic Feature Analysis

Semantic Feature Analysis (Johnson and Pearson, 1984; Rupley, Logan & Nichols, 2002) is a procedure that links key vocabulary to major ideas from a content selection. It is a graphic display that focuses on the features that distinguish words in a particular category. Using a matrix grid, students analyze the distinguishing features of concepts according to key characteristics.

Semantic Feature Analysis (SFA) is well-grounded in research (Anders and Bos, 1986). Students use background knowledge, become actively involved in relating ideas and, with practice, can learn to use the procedure independently. More importantly, the strategy leads to improved learning, particularly for students who have reading difficulties.

Introduction, Modeling, and Reflection

1. Place a blank SFA grid on the overhead. Model, using a familiar category such as computer software (Blackline 30).

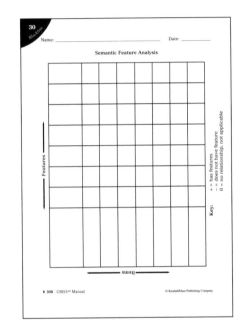

2. Solicit examples (Microsoft Word, Access, Excel, Inspiration, etc.) and write them in the spaces on the vertical column. For the horizontal column, ask students to think about characteristics or attributes of software (spread sheets, word processing, photo editing) and write these in the horizontal spaces.
3. Model how to code the examples and the attributes. Discuss relationships between the features and the terms. Plus (+) represents a positive relationship and minus (−) represents a negative relationship. Zero (0) indicates no relationship.

Semantic Feature Analysis—Computer Software

Terms	Features						
Software Application	Spread Sheet	Word Processing	Graphic Design	E-Mail	Database	Internet Browser	Photo Editor
Word™	–	+	+	–	–	–	–
Access™	+	–	–	–	+	–	–
Netscape™	–	–	–	–	–	+	–
Excel™	+	–	–	–	–	–	–
Inspiration™	–	–	+	–	–	–	–
Word Perfect™	–	+	+	–	–	–	–
Photo Shop™	–	–	–	–	–	–	+
Publisher™	–	+	+	–	–	–	–
Paint Shop™	–	–	+	–	–	–	+
Outlook™	–	–	–	+	+	–	–

4. Have students substantiate their decisions for the various codes (+, −, 0).
5. Ask students, "How might you organize other concepts using SFA? How does analyzing concepts by attributes help deepen your understanding?"

Support and Extensions

● Use SFA as a pre-reading activity. After students read, have them revise the codes and modify existing features. Encourage them to include additional features and terms on the matrix. In the example on page 214, students worked in groups using the SFA matrix to analyze the characteristics of Progressivism. After students read, they listed the different acts passed during this era and then compared them. Students didn't always agree, and found they had to refine the matrix by adding some additional characteristics.

Semantic Feature Analysis—Progressivism

Name Date	Social Reform	Political Reform	Economic Change	Industrial	National Debt	Environmental	Health
Pure Food and Drug Act							
Federal Reserve Act							
Interstate Commerce Act							
Civil Service Commission							
Women's Suffrage							
Graduated Income Tax							
Sherman Antitrust Act							
National Parks							

- After students have read a novel, list the main characters in the vertical column and personality features (sensitive, evil, manipulative) in the horizontal column. As part of team discussions, use the matrix to analyze characters. Teams can then present their matrices as part of a whole-class discussion.
- Students can readily use the information organized in the matrix to write about the topic.
- Use the matrix as a review for a test. Also consider using SFA matrices as an alternative way to assess.

Active Processing Through Writing and Discussion

Effective vocabulary instruction encourages students to discuss and demonstrate meanings. The instructional strategies in this section focus on ways to expand definitions of words through reading, writing, and talking.

Learning Strategy

Word Elaboration

Vocabulary is truly learned when it can be used naturally in speaking, listening, and writing. Word Elaboration involves four steps: talking, listening, writing, and reading.

Guided Comprehension

Introduction, Modeling, and Reflection

1. Select eight to ten words that relate to a single topic or concept students have studied. Write these words on the board or overhead.
2. Begin discussing the topic with the class. In your model discussion, include words with context clues.

Example:

Vocabulary words: *square, rhombus, rectangle, parallelogram*

Student 1: I learned that a *square* is a four-sided geometric figure. All four sides are equal.

Student 2: What you say is true, but a *rhombus* also has four sides of equal measure. What's the difference?

Student 1: That's right. The difference is that the *square* has to have all four angles with the same measure—90 degrees. That is not required for a *rhombus*.

Student 2: You know that's kind of like the *parallelogram* and the *rectangle*. The *rectangle* has to have four right angles but the *parallelogram* doesn't have to.

Student 1: The *square* is a special *rectangle* with all sides equal, and the *rhombus* is a special *parallelogram* with all sides equal.

Notice that each person offers new information about the terms when speaking. Not all of the words have to be used in one sentence

3. Pair students. Partners hold a conversation using as many words as they can figure out from contextual clues. Each student keeps track of the words his or her partner uses correctly.
4. Using the vocabulary words, each student writes a summary or brief paper on the topic.
5. Ask students, "What does this strategy do to help you really understand and learn new concepts? How is it based on CRISS[SM] principles of learning?"

Support and Extensions

- Use Word Elaboration as a review of key vocabulary for a test or for foreign language practice.
- After students have read an assignment, have them list one or two key concepts from their reading and the vocabulary related to the concept. Follow through with the steps outlined above.
- Have students carry on their discussions via e-mail. Have them save and turn in the whole conversation.

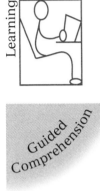

Sentence and Word Expansion

Expansion is a brainstorming procedure that helps students elaborate on concepts and terms. Students can then use the expanded vocabulary in their speech and writing. Word expansion works well as a revision procedure for incorporating more precise vocabulary in writing. It can also help students untangle difficult readings.

Introduction, Modeling, and Reflection

1. Take a concept from a book and use it in a simple sentence.
    Plants photosynthesize.

2. Develop a series of questions that make sense for the particular concept. Then answer the questions.

    What kind? green trees, flowering plants, grass
    When? daytime, summer, when sun is out, in artificial light
    Where? chloroplasts, leaves, chlorophyll
    What is necessary? sunlight, water, carbon dioxide, temperature
    What is formed? glucose, oxygen
    Why? to change light energy to chemical energy

3. Then ask students to expand the original sentence.

    Revision: *Trees and flowering plants photosynthesize in the daytime. The chlorophyll in the chloroplasts located in the leaves combines with light, water, and carbon dioxide to form glucose and oxygen. The end result is that light energy is changed into chemical energy.*

Support and Extensions

- Expansion activities work well at the single word level, particularly when the expanded word is dull and overused. When a fourth-grade teacher noticed that her students constantly used the word *said* in written dialogue, she decided to have a contest to get rid of the monotony. She divided her class into four teams and had each team find alternatives to *said*. Each team kept track of their words on a large sheet of paper. Each time a student thought of a new word for *said* or came across one in their reading or conversation, they wrote it on the chart. The group that came up with the most words won.

Replacement Words For Said . . .		
asked	snorted	questioned
exclaimed	continued	guessed
replied	laughed	begged
muttered	yawned	grunted
yelled	screamed	suggested
explained	called	promised
groaned	screeched	demanded
whined	comforted	grumbled
wailed	squealed	mumbled
whispered	gulped	complained
cried	chuckled	begged
growled	gasped	commanded
boasted	requested	murmured
threatened	answered	refused
moaned	pleaded	decided
sighed		gasped
giggled		

● You can do a similar activity with other worn-out words such as *walk*.

stroll	parade	stumble	glide
slouch	strut	hobble	slink
waddle	bound	shuffle	tiptoe
march	dash	stride	tramp
meander	tiptoe	stalk	slither
ramble	limp	pace	charge

● Have students use a thesaurus to brainstorm $1, $10 and $100 words. List old worn-out words in the dollar column.

$1	$10	$100
big	huge	gigantic massive stupendous
nice	friendly caring	sensitive genuine
sad	unhappy upset	depressed despondent

This activity works best in cooperative teams. Give each group a copy of a thesaurus and a large sheet of flip chart paper. Display words as a resource for writing.

A middle-school social studies teacher used the reverse form of word expansion to help her students untangle the meaning of the *Gettysburg Address*. She copied the *Gettysburg Address* on a transparency. Then she took students through the document line by line. They replaced complicated vocabulary with simpler, everyday language.

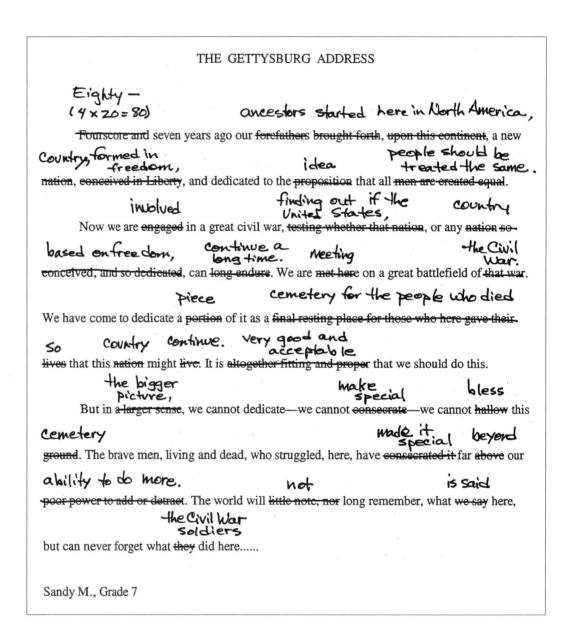

THE GETTYSBURG ADDRESS

Eighty —
(4 x 20 = 80)   ancestors started here in North America,
~~Fourscore and~~ seven years ago our ~~forefathers brought forth, upon this continent~~, a new

country, formed in
freedom,   idea   people should be
                                                         treated the same.
~~nation, conceived in Liberty~~, and dedicated to the ~~proposition~~ that all ~~men are created equal~~.

                involved   finding out if the
                                United States,   country

Now we are ~~engaged~~ in a great civil war, ~~testing whether that nation~~, or any ~~nation so~~

based on freedom,   continue a   meeting   the Civil
                     long time.   War.
~~conceived, and so dedicated~~, can ~~long endure~~. We are ~~met here~~ on a great battlefield of ~~that war~~.

                piece   cemetery for the people who died

We have come to dedicate a ~~portion~~ of it as a ~~final resting place for those who here gave their~~

So   country   continue.   very good and
                             acceptable
~~lives~~ that this ~~nation~~ might ~~live~~. It is ~~altogether fitting and proper~~ that we should do this.

        the bigger
        picture,   make
                                      special   bless
But in a ~~larger sense~~, we cannot dedicate—we cannot ~~consecrate~~—we cannot ~~hallow~~ this

cemetery   made it beyond
                                            special
~~ground~~. The brave men, living and dead, who struggled, here, have ~~consecrated it~~ far ~~above~~ our

ability to do more.   not   is said
~~poor power to add or detract~~. The world will ~~little note, nor~~ long remember, what ~~we say~~ here,

        the Civil War
        soldiers
but can never forget what ~~they~~ did here......

Sandy M., Grade 7

After brainstorming the students rewrote the *Gettysburg Address,* using the replacement words.

Student Revision:

Eighty-seven years ago our ancestors started here in North America, a new country, formed in freedom, and dedicated to the idea that all people should be treated the same.

Now we are involved in a great civil war, finding out if the United States, or any country based on freedom, can continue a long time. We are meeting on a great battlefield of the Civil War. We have come to dedicate a piece of it as a cemetery for the people who died so that this country might continue. It is very good and acceptable that we should do this.

But in the bigger picture, we cannot dedicate—we cannot make special—we cannot bless this cemetery. The brave men, living and dead, who struggled, here, have made it special far beyond our ability to do more. The world will not remember very long, what is said here, but can never forget what the Civil War soldiers did here. . .

Sandy M.
Grade 7

● A problem solving strategy in mathematics is rewriting a word problem into simpler language and/or form.

Original problem: *Find three positive, even, consecutive integers such that the product of the two smallest integers is equal to two-thirds the product of the two largest integers.*

Rewritten problem: *Find three even numbers, all positive. They must be in a row, like 2–4–6 or 10–12–14. When you multiply the two smallest numbers, your answer should be the same as multiplying two-thirds times the answer you get when you multiply the two largest numbers.*

Strategy

Learning

Word Combining

With Word Combining, students combine new words into original sentences and short paragraphs. Use it to reinforce vocabulary previously introduced. Students must have some familiarity with the words in order to use them successfully in their writing.

Guided Comprehension

Introduction, Modeling, and Reflection

1. List three to five words on the board. The words should be somewhat related conceptually.
2. Review the words in a class discussion.
3. On the board, write one or two sentences using the words.
4. Model how to write sentences that include contextual clues that explain the words and, if possible, show how the words relate to each other, as in the following mathematics and social studies examples.

Mathematics—geometry unit on circles

Vocabulary words: circle, center, diameter, radius, circumference

The *diameter* of a *circle,* which is twice the length of the circle's *radius,* is the distance across the *circle* and through its *center.* The *circumference,* or distance around a *circle,* is about three times the length of the *diameter* and about six times the length of the *radius.*

Social Studies—Civil War

Vocabulary words: civilian, bounty, draft, habeas corpus

By 1863, the Union gave *civilians,* those who had not joined the army, up to $300 in *bounties* or payments to join the Union forces. Because of the shortage of volunteers, the government passed a *draft* law requiring men between the ages of 20 and 45 to serve. To stop riots that broke out in protest of the *draft,* Lincoln suspended *habeas corpus,* the right to have a hearing before going to jail.

5. Ask students, "How does Word Combining help you to think metacognitively about your understanding of important concepts? How did this strategy help you become more actively involved in learning?"

Support and Extensions

● Incorporate Word Combining with lectures. After lecturing from five to ten minutes, list key ideas from your lecture on the board. Using their learning logs, students quickly combine the words into a sentence or two. Take time to share, then move on.

● Use Word Combining to review main idea–detail notes. Use the key words on the left, and have students combine them into one or two sentences.

● Ask students to do Word Combining as a way to determine their background knowledge about key concepts in a forthcoming reading assignment or lecture. Provide five or six words, and ask students to use at least two in each sentence. Even if they are not sure about the meanings of all the words, they should try to predict the way they relate to one another. As they read, they can decide whether their sentences are correct. If not, they should revise them.

▶ Summary

Vocabulary knowledge is essential for content learning. We have stressed various ways to help students learn content vocabulary, including Contextual Analysis, Concept of Definition Maps, Vocabulary Maps, Frayer Model, Semantic Feature Analysis, Word Elaboration, Sentence and Word Expansion, and Word Combining. Underlying each of these methods is an understanding of the theoretical notions that guide our teaching. These include careful word selection, activating students' background knowledge, involving students as active learners, immersing students in words, and learning through repeated exposure and elaboration. In the end, we want our students to be flexible and competent with a variety of procedures so they intuitively know the best approach for a particular learning situation.

Research Conclusion	Reference
Vocabulary knowledge plays key role in text comprehension.	Nagy and Scott, 2000
Vocabulary knowledge increases when students (not teachers) make connections between vocabulary terms.	Blachowicz and Fisher, 2000
Vocabulary knowledge increases when students select their own vocabulary words.	Blachowicz and Fisher, 2000
Vocabulary knowledge increases when students create their own images and actions to represent word meanings.	Blachowicz and Fisher, 2000
Vocabulary knowledge increases when students use new vocabulary terms in multiple ways (writing, talking, organizing, graphics, etc.).	Blachowicz and Fisher, 2000

10

Assessment

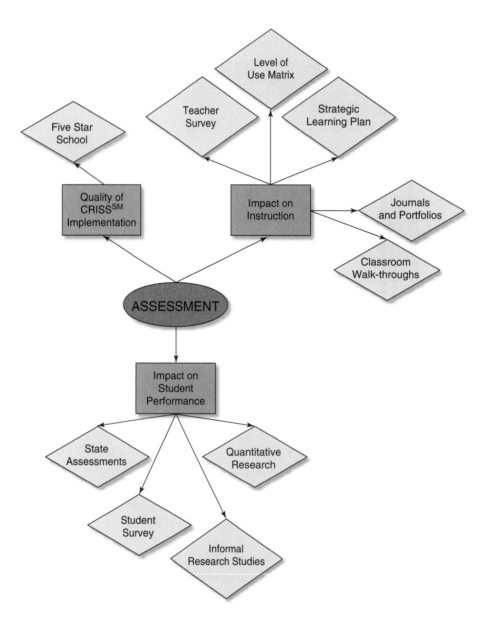

We are asked many questions about ways to incorporate CRISS[SM] into a district's assessment plan. For example, how do I know if CRISS[SM] is helping students achieve better in the content areas or on state assessments? Are students involved in Project CRISS[SM] able to read and learn from their classroom materials better than those who have not been involved? Have teachers changed the way they teach because of Project CRISS[SM]? How can we best evaluate whether or not CRISS[SM] has been effectively implemented in a district?

Before answering these questions, we need to clarify several issues. First, we have intentionally not developed a CRISS[SM] standardized test. Building such a test is beyond the scope and mission of CRISS[SM]. Students already spend considerable time, in many cases too much time, taking state and national tests in school, and we have no intention of adding to a student's or district's testing burden. Second, most districts already have an extensive plan for student assessment, which means that the logical approach is to figure out ways to include CRISS[SM] as part of the district's overall assessment plan rather than as a separate evaluation. Therefore, the design of this chapter is to help you think through ways to evaluate CRISS[SM] within your own school context.

Before even considering issues of student or teacher change, the first area to examine is the depth of the Project CRISS[SM] implementation within a school. Has the implementation been broad-based, or have only a few teachers participated? If only three or four teachers in a school have attended a 12- to 18-hour CRISS[SM] workshop, you can't really look beyond the specific effects in a few individual classrooms. To expect changes within a broader school or district setting would not be reasonable. One way to examine the depth of a CRISS[SM] implementation is to evaluate it in terms of an ideal benchmark.

Our gold standard of implementation is the CRISS[SM] Five Star School. Schools reaching this standard have used the project for several years and have progressively embedded the program within multiple layers of their school setting. Analyzing your level of implementation provides a useful road-map for making future decisions about how your school might progress toward becoming a CRISS[SM] Five Star School.

▶ Quality of Project CRISS[SM] Implementation

Take a moment to review Blacklines 31a–d, Project CRISS[SM] Five Star School Evaluation and Plan. This form pulls together all the features of a Five Star School and provides space wherein schools can assess their level of implementation and plan for future growth.

In the Five Star School, the principal and other key administrators and at least 75 percent of the faculty have attended a Project CRISS[SM] Level I workshop (See Blacklines 31a–d). The Five Star School has a designated on-site CRISS[SM] Facilitator/Certified Trainer (a teacher or administrator) who works with faculty and administrators to ensure continual implementation. The CRISS[SM] Facilitator plans Level I workshops for teachers and support staff, including classroom aids, substitute teachers, and student teachers who have not yet participated in the project. He or she also facilitates follow-up sessions during or after school in which teachers have opportunities to share ideas and learn more about the program. The Facilitator works in classrooms with teachers, conducts model lessons, and oversees the writing of an in-house newsletter of CRISS[SM] ideas. This person also helps plan annual CRISS[SM] for Parents workshops. The Facilitator oversees the collection of teacher and student data. In addition, the Facilitator encourages teachers to conduct their own classroom research and to share what they have learned with other faculty. He or she often organizes college classes as a way for teachers to earn extra credit for attending Level I workshops and follow-up sessions. In general, the Facilitator/Trainer becomes the in-house knowledge broker, who circulates professional articles, conducts workshops, encourages teacher collaboration, and generates a professional energy within a school. Professional energy is really what CRISS^{SM} is about.

In a Five Star School, all of the administrators have attended a Project CRISS^{SM} Level I workshop and many of the follow-up sessions. They encourage teachers to incorporate CRISS^{SM} principles and strategies in lesson plans and classroom practices. CRISS^{SM} becomes integral to being instructional leaders. They focus on the key components of CRISS^{SM} as part of the classroom walk-through process (described later in this chapter). Because of their deep understanding of CRISS^{SM} principles and instructional strategies, they know when teachers implement the project successfully and how to support them. Administrators also use CRISS^{SM} strategies in the daily operation of the school, integrating the strategies into meetings with staff, parents, and the community. They work closely with their CRISS^{SM} facilitator to create opportunities for teachers to come together as a learning community. They support and perhaps even participate in CRISS^{SM} parent workshops.

Use the Five Star School Evaluation Plan to determine where your school lies on the path to Five Star School status. The important consideration here is that Five Star Schools have a far greater chance of making a positive impact on student performance than schools in which only a handful of teachers participate or schools where administrators are not knowledgeable about CRISS^{SM} and the impact it has on student success. If your school has not yet met the criteria for a Five Star School, how might you move it in this direction? What steps need to be taken? Use the criteria summarized on Blacklines 31a–d for planning your next steps. If your school is only at the beginning stages of implementation, you can't expect the same level of teacher growth and student achievement as those schools that more closely align to the Five Star criteria.

▶ Impact of Project CRISS^{SM} on Teacher Instruction

Project CRISS^{SM} is a staff development program designed for improving instruction; it makes sense to assess teacher instruction and then move to examining potential effects on students. Start this process by posing questions: What are some ways you and other teacher participants in Project CRISS^{SM} can evaluate your own lessons? What changes have you made in your teaching practices in light of CRISS^{SM} theory and strategies? Good teaching requires strategic planning that is well-thought out. Tools useful for guiding your self-assessment are the Teacher Training Survey, the Level of Use Matrix, and the CRISS^{SM} Strategic Learning Plan. In addition, you may want to keep a journal and a portfolio of student examples.

Teacher Training Survey.   Think about these fundamental questions: How has the project changed you and your colleagues' views of teaching? Do you think differently about what it means to teach because of your participation in the program? At the end of our workshop, we ask teachers to begin a process of self-reflection by completing a Teacher Training Survey. Did your responses change as a result of attending the CRISS^{SM} workshop?

This survey, Blackines 32a and 32b, asks participants to consider the key features of the project immediately before and after participating in the workshop. For some, this survey serves as a positive confirmation, since many teachers already use some of the CRISS^{SM} strategies in their teaching. The survey also serves to remind teachers of key principles and strategies they might explore.

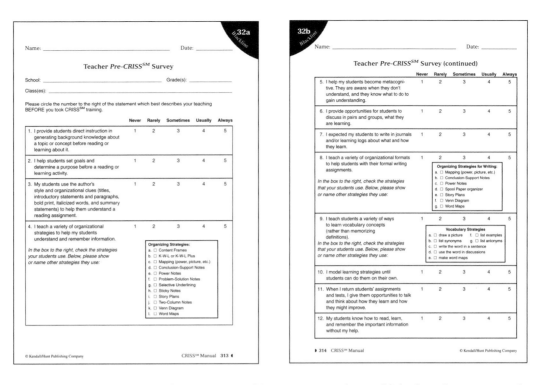

In any case, the survey provides an opportunity to think about how you teach. Most of us don't take time to think about why we teach in a certain way. We just do it! By taking time for self-examination, we begin to see why some lessons work better than others. Usually, our more effective lessons embody CRISS^{SM} strategies and principles more than the less effective ones. Such reflection spurs us to use CRISS^{SM} even more as we make changes in our teaching. We begin to "live" CRISS^{SM} principles and philosophy. The survey provides us with this metacognitive opportunity.

Use this survey periodically. Refer to it again three or four months after completing the workshop. What strategies have you added to your teaching repertoire over the last several months? How do your responses on the survey compare to those completed before and directly after taking the CRISS^{SM} workshop. Has your teaching changed? Are there strategies listed on the survey you haven't tried yet that might fit within your future teaching plans? Are there others you want to know more about?

Results from this survey are useful for planning follow-up sessions. After several months of implementing the project, participants can fill out the survey again. The CRISS^{SM} Facilitator can tabulate the results to find out the strategies used most and least frequently by teachers. Use this information to determine which strategies to explore at support sessions. Administering the survey at the beginning of a follow-up session provides a review of Project CRISS^{SM}, initiates professional conversations, and helps to formulate ideas for the next follow-up sessions.

Level of Use Matrix. This matrix, (Blacklines 33a–e), can be used as a self-assessment tool to monitor implementation. Notice the left-hand column contains the main components of Project CRISS^{SM}, and the next three columns contain descriptions of implementation levels ranging from ideal to unacceptable. The behaviors in the ideal column portray components in terms of student ownership and knowledge. The teacher has succeeded in turning principle and strategy knowledge over to the students. Now, move to the "acceptable" column. As you glance down this column, notice that the difference between ideal and acceptable has to do with teacher control. The behaviors classified as acceptable remain in the hands of the teacher. The teacher is doing the work; not the student. Remember, teacher control is not all bad. We have to take some control in the beginning as we model and demonstrate strategies or when material is particularly challenging. Control only becomes a problem if we never release power to the students even when they could do the work themselves. When the teacher continues to provide all explanations, connections, and transformations, **we** do the meaning making, **not** the student. Thus, we move back and forth from the ideal to the acceptable, depending upon the difficulty of the material and where students are in their understanding of strategy use. Yet, we always strive for the ideal. OUR MOTTO: **Successful teachers make themselves progressively unnecessary.**

Next, skim through the behaviors described in the "unacceptable" column. All of these descriptors serve as reminders about things to watch out for in our own teaching. Except in the rarest of circumstances, we don't want to land here.

CRISS[SM] **Strategic Learning Plan.** We also recommend self-assessment based on an overall model for teaching that we call a CRISS[SM] Strategic Learning Plan. While the plan can take a variety of forms, as seen on Blacklines 34 and 35, it usually includes (1) content standards addressed, (2) learning goals, (3) methods of student assessment, (4) strategic instruction, and (5) identification of CRISS[SM] philosophy components. Organizing instruction around a plan provides us with a more holistic way to think about our teaching. We have included several different formats as blacklines. Feel free to use and modify them as you wish. To see how this plan works, select a format and use it to analyze one of your own lessons. See the example below:

CRISS[SM] STRATEGIC LEARNING PLAN - *For Teachers*

Topic/selection and Standards: *"The Restless Decade" (No standards - teacher lesson)*

Objective: *Teachers will learn how to group strategies together into a Learning Plan, and they will become familiar with and able to introduce to students the following strategies:* **Mind Streaming, Concept of Definition Map, Picture Mapping,** *and* **Sentence and Word Expansion.**

Assessment (objective & performance): *(1) Teachers will develop a Learning Plan which incorporates at least one of the above strategies, (2) Teachers will successfully deliver the lesson to their students, and (3) They will reflect on the quality of the lesson using the questions on the reverse side of this Learning Plan form.*

Learning Plan	Strategies & How Applied to Content	CRISS Principles & Philosophy						
		BK	**AI**	**D**	**W**	**O**	**M**	**M&E**
BEFORE *Prepare*	**Mind Streaming:** Topic: The 1920s. Students work in pairs–one minute brainstorming for each partner. Share with whole group when done	✔	✔	✔			✔	
DURING *Be Involved*	**Concept of Definition Map:** Model with one of the mind-streamed words. Have participants individually complete modified Concept of Definition Map on "1920s" – *theme* (top), *features of 20s* (side), and *examples of behavior* (bottom).		✔		✔	✔	✔	✔
AFTER *Organize*	**Picture Map:** Model with Picture Map of CRISS[SM]. Create groups of 3 to 4 students. Within group, members share theme ideas and choose one. Complete Picture Map on decade using selection and group's background knowledge. Make sure images support overriding theme. Share maps with whole group. Debrief with process conference	✔	✔	✔		✔	✔	✔
POST *Use, Apply*	**Sentence Expansion:** Explain & share examples in manual. Brainstorm more sophisticated replacement words & elaboration for "The woman..." sentence based on the 20s selection. Teachers write expanded sentences and share.	✔	✔	✔	✔		✔	✔

Key to CRISS[SM]*P & P:*   **BK** = Background Knowledge   **W** = Writing   **M&E** = Modeling & Explanation
AI = Active Involvement   **O** = Organization
D = Discussion   **M** = Metacognition

For sake of illustration, look at the Learning Plan on Blacklines 34a and 34b. Blackline 34b begins with a question about aligning the lesson with content standards. In many states, teachers are required to note in their lesson plans how a particular lesson fits state standards. If your state doesn't have this requirement, ignore this part of the plan.

Next, did your lesson teach students about something important for them to learn, and were these same understandings evaluated? Our assessments must match essential content. Unfortunately, we all can recall teachers who tested for trivial information, not for what was truly important to learn. Moreover, many also tested us on information they had not targeted for us to learn. As students, we felt disrespected, tricked, and helpless. To keep this from happening, we must begin our lessons by first determining the essential understandings and then making these learning goals apparent to the students so they know what they are supposed to understand. Finally, we must follow through by testing them on the same targeted information. When students know what they are expected to learn and know these processes and content will be assessed, they gain confidence and a sense of control over their learning.

The next part of the lesson plan poses questions about modeling and guided practice. Lessons typically flounder because of insufficient modeling. As you think through a lesson, did you model enough for students to feel competent to take off on their own? If not, what could you have done differently?

Next, what instructional strategies did you use to help students understand the big ideas of the lesson or unit? Did these strategies help students use their background knowledge? Did students have opportunities to talk about what they already knew about a topic? Did they know what they were going to learn from the lesson? Did you help them set clear purposes and targets for learning? Did students have ample opportunities to talk, read, write, and transform information in meaningful ways through different organizational formats? Did they self-monitor so they knew whether they understood the essential content of your lesson?

Afterwards, did you give students sufficient time to discuss process? Did they talk about the learning strategies that helped them understand and assess their learning?

In short, Project CRISS[SM] can help with strategic lesson plan design and provide a way for you to examine your own teaching. Include several learning plans along with your reflections and student samples in your teaching portfolio. Chapter 12 contains a more detailed explanation of the CRISS[SM] Strategic Learning Plan along with two examples.

Teacher Journals and Portfolios. A teaching journal can be an important data source. Too often, we forget not only what we have taught, but the details of our instruction. We gain valuable insights about our own teaching when we take time to think and write about our lessons. Teaching Journals become invaluable tools. They create a place for analyzing the success of a particular lesson, for keeping track of new ideas, for thinking about specific students, and for making plans about future lessons.

Another important data source is a teaching portfolio that might contain learning plans, student examples, and your Journal. Keeping a collection of student work can be an excellent resource for you and is useful for sharing ideas with colleagues either informally or as part of organized follow-up sessions. A teaching portfolio also comes in handy to showcase your work as part of formal teaching evaluations.

Administrative Support: Classroom Walk-throughs. While these various tools for teacher evaluation (survey, Level of Use Matrix, CRISS[SM] Strategic Learning Plans, journals, and portfolios) provide us with ways to examine our own practice, having others observe our lessons can also be helpful. In particular, we recommend that principals and other supervisors have opportunities to see how CRISS[SM] is working in classrooms. This not only helps principals and supervisors gain expertise, but their presence also supports us in becoming more effective.

Project CRISS[SM] has a separate Administrator's Handbook and workshop for administrators. But we will take a moment here to describe some ways that administrators can support CRISS[SM] teachers. The first step, of course, is for administrators to have attended a Level I Workshop and to have participated in a number of follow-up sessions. Once they feel fairly well-versed in the project, they can provide valuable feedback.

We recommend classroom walk-throughs, where principals along with the curriculum specialist (reading coordinator) visit classrooms for short observations to note learning behaviors of students. Brief, frequent visits are better than infrequent, longer visits. Short observations lower teacher apprehension, make it feasible for administrators to fit visitations into their busy schedules, and provide opportunities for observing patterns of CRISS[SM] behaviors. With such continual access to the classroom, administrators become more effective instructional leaders, offering support and determining staff needs.

To help with these walk-throughs, we have included a sample observation sheet (Blackline 36) used by several high school administrators in Florida. Notice how it guides the observer to attend to the level of student engagement, to notice if the lesson aligns with district/state curriculum, and to note any use of CRISS[SM] philosophy and strategies. In addition, the observer is asked to "walk the walls" or attend to any displays of student work.

36 Blackline

Name: _____ Date: _____

School: _____ Teacher: _____

Subject: _____ Grade: _____ Date: _____

Walk-through Observation Sheet

Level of Student Engagement Count number of non-engaged students	
Alignment with District/State Curriculum (Level of Understanding) • Determine assignment or lesson • Materials (single/multiple source/multi-leveled/authentic) • Ask students the content and the purpose of the lesson	
Strategic Use of the CRISS[SM] Philosophy and Strategies • Key Elements of Learning • Four Instructional Steps • CRISS[SM] Strategies/Graphic Organizers (Refer to CRISS[SM]-at-a-Glance)	
Display of Student Work • Walk the walls	
Lesson Plans (Strategic integration of the CRISS[SM] philosophy and strategies?)	
Nature of Assessment	
Safe Learning Environment • Emotionally Safe • Physically Safe	
Other Comments	

Four Instructional Steps	**Key Elements of Learning**
• Introduction • Modeling • Guided Practice • Independent Application	• Background Knowledge (BK) • Defining Purpose (DP) • Understanding the Author's Craft (AC) • Active Involvement (AI) • Discussion (D) • Writing (W) • Reorganizing Information (RI) • Metacognition (M)

Valdez 8/02

© Kendall/Hunt Publishing Company

Over a number of visits, these observations generate a series of snapshots or portraits of student learning in a particular classroom. Administrators can readily use these portraits as a basis for discussions with teachers about effective implementation and for planning follow-up. Even more important, the administrator progressively gains more expertise about the variety of ways CRISS^{SM} can be implemented in the classroom. The brief walk-throughs help them become more effective curriculum leaders, coaches, and change agents. They also provide administrators with a viable way to increase their visibility and credibility. (The CRISS^{SM} Administrator's Workshop provides more details about walk-throughs as well as other information to ensure project effectiveness.)

In sum, CRISS^{SM} offers teachers and administrators a variety of options for analyzing CRISS^{SM} implementation in their schools and classrooms. Use those that seem most helpful to you.

▶ Impact of Project CRISS^{SM} on Student Performance

Our major goal with Project CRISS^{SM} is to improve student performance. Are students learning more effectively, and are they more self-confident as learners because of their participation in the project?

In this section, we offer a variety of suggestions for collecting student data. These suggestions range from evaluating CRISS^{SM}, based on your state assessment program to evidence from student surveys and informal research studies as part of implementation. Finally, we will briefly describe some of the more formal quantitative research information we have collected as part of our on-going evaluation of the project.

State Assessments. Some districts have examined the effects of Project CRISS^{SM} on standardized and state assessments. This only makes sense with schools in which a majority of the teachers have participated in the project and have met the criteria for a Five Star School.

For example, Meadowlawn Middle School in St. Petersburg, Florida adopted Project CRISS^{SM} as a part of their school improvement plan. CRISS^{SM} was the only major staff development program adopted by this school over a four-year period, so teachers and administrators felt any changes in student performance could be largely attributed to the project. Over eighty percent of their teachers, including the principal took the Level I training. The school had its own district-level trainer who worked with the principal to ensure continual implementation and follow-up. During this time period, the district used the same achievement test, the California Test of Basic Skills, and for several years tracked the same students. Prior to CRISS^{SM} implementation, the average reading scores of Meadowlawn students were considerably lower than the district average.

The gap between their students' reading scores and those of the district began to shrink. By the time these sixth-graders graduated from the middle school, their achievement test scores had moved from the 40th percentile to the 55th percentile on the assessment. Even more important, many teachers reported that students were doing better in school. School counselors also noted a reduction in truancy and behavior problems.

Other districts have made comparisons on state tests among schools that have adopted CRISS^{SM} and those that have not participated in the project. These comparisons, however, are often confounded by other factors that make it difficult to tease out students' gains in achievement based on Project CRISS^{SM} from gains derived from other effects. It is critical in these comparative studies that students are evaluated over a period of years with the same assessment measure. Nevertheless, the examples just described illustrate ways that districts have incorporated the assessment of CRISS[SM] into their district's assessment plans. Consider ways you might include an assessment of Project CRISS[SM] as part of your district's plan.

Student Surveys: Learning Strategies Inventory. The Learning Strategies Inventory (LSI—Blackline 37) is a quick way to gather data about students' strategy use. Administer the inventory to students before teachers participate in a CRISS[SM] workshop, and then administer it again several months afterwards. In most cases, students respond quite differently, reflecting far greater use and more knowledge about learning strategies on the post inventory (LSI). Teachers often administer this inventory several times during the year to monitor strategy use over time, as in the following example from Kalispell, Montana.

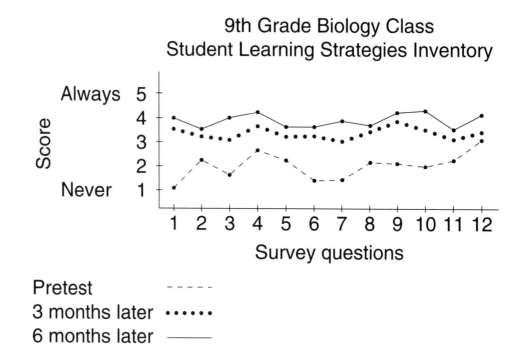

9th Grade Biology Class
Student Learning Strategies Inventory

Pretest   - - - - -
3 months later   • • • • • •
6 months later   ————

Teachers also use the data diagnostically. Students who continually do poorly in school answer items on the LSI quite differently than students who do well. These data show that even after teachers have incorporated many CRISS[SM] strategies in their classrooms, students who struggle academically still don't know how to apply the strategies on their own and revert to less effective methods. An analysis of individual batteries provides insights about a student's individual needs. Information from this survey becomes invaluable for instructional planning.

We also use this survey to collect comparison data on students in participating and non-participating CRISS[SM] classrooms. Again, the responses differ markedly between these groups. Students participating in CRISS[SM] classrooms show far more strategy use than those in non-CRISS[SM] classrooms. Consider using this inventory as part of your assessment program.

Informal Research Studies. Many CRISS[SM] teachers conduct informal research studies in their classrooms. This is an excellent way to convince both teachers and their students that application of CRISS[SM] theory and strategies makes a difference. Because we feel so strongly about teacher research, we have devoted a chapter in this book to it. For more in depth information plus several sample studies, please look at Chapter 11.

Quantitative Research.   Over the years, we have collected considerable quantitative research data regarding the effects of CRISS^{SM} on student learning, and we invite districts to participate in our national data collection efforts. The evaluation replicates the design we used for validation by the National Diffusion Network (NDN) of the U.S. Department of Education. The process provides districts with a way to investigate the success of the project in their schools. The challenge is that the design requires experimental and control schools, which often creates difficulties for districts interested in a broad implementation.

The evaluation involves at least two classrooms from grades 4, 6, 8 and 11. Not all of the levels are required to participate, but two classes at each grade level should be evaluated. One of the classes is the experimental group (uses CRISS^{SM}) and the other is the control group. The teachers of the experimental classrooms must be CRISS^{SM} trained and must keep a journal of the strategies they introduce in their classrooms. The control teachers will not have participated in a CRISS^{SM} workshop.

The evaluation involves two consecutive class days in the fall and two days in the spring (20–40 minutes each day). During the first class period, students at each of the grade levels read age-appropriate selections (4 to 8 pages in length) on a science or history topic. The students read and study the material any way they want. The next day, they take a free-recall test, in which they write down everything they can remember from the selection, answer questions on a multiple choice test, and respond to a short answer question. The same reading selections and tests are given in the spring. After the spring test, we ask students to write about how they learned the information in the selection. All scoring of data is done by an independent evaluator.

With successful implementation, districts find that students in the CRISS^{SM} classes learn and remember more from the reading selections than students who have not participated in the project. In addition, an analysis of the written responses on strategy use indicates that CRISS^{SM} students have a far richer repertoire of learning strategies than students in the control classrooms. (See the CRISS^{SM} web site for a summary of the most recent data and for a copy of the original National Diffusion Network validation report.)

If your district wants to participate as a data collection site, please contact the CRISS^{SM} office.

▶ Summary

In conclusion, CRISS^{SM} offers districts a variety of assessment options designed to fit within the assessment goals of a single classroom, a school, or a district. Evaluation choices depend upon the level of implementation and commitment. If schools within a system fit the Five Star criteria, consider a more in-depth, multi-faceted evaluation procedure. Begin by evaluating the level of implementation in your district or school. How does your school fit the Five Star criteria?

If you or only a few teachers in your school implement the project, it does not make sense to do a broad-based evaluation. Examine effects based on how well students are implementing the strategies within your own classroom. Consider using the Learning Strategies Inventory and doing some qualitative research similar to that conducted by Sandra Bradford or Sue Dailey described in Chapter 11, "A Story of Teachers and Students as Researchers." Design some of your own teacher research studies. Are students performing better on your classroom tests compared to last year? What happens to student performance when your students employ a rich assortment of strategies as part of a unit of study? Can students talk and write about their own strategy use? Such informal evaluations tend to be far more meaningful to you and your students than the more formal standardized assessments.

If your school has been using CRISS^{SM} over several years and meets the criteria for a Five Star School, look for changes beyond the individual classroom. Have there been changes in student performance on state assessments? Look for changes in teaching (Teacher Inventory, evidence collected from "walk-throughs," classroom research) and changes in students' knowledge about learning and studying (Learning Strategies Inventory). Consider also the possibility of collecting some qualitative data under the guidance of the National CRISS^{SM} office. Design an approach to assessment that best fits within your school's or district's overall assessment plan.

Research Conclusion	Reference
With successful implementation, districts have found that students in CRISS[SM] classes learn and remember more from a reading selection than students who do not participate in the project.	www.projectcriss.com

Project CRISS^SM: A Story of Teachers and Students as Researchers

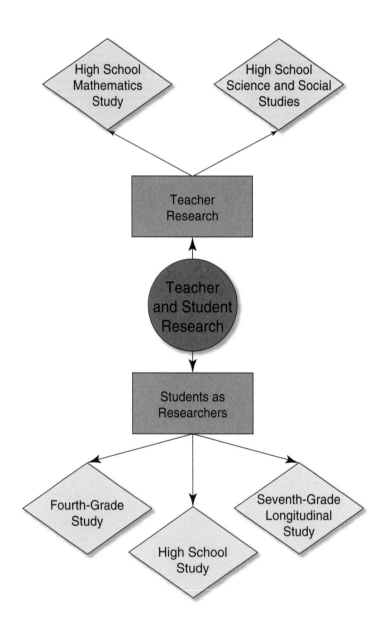

Project CRISS^{SM} is an unending story of teacher research. From the very beginning, we have been teacher researchers. It all started when Carol Santa landed in Kalispell in the early 80s, and she and a group of high school teachers began investigating questions about learning. Our group began examining questions by conducting informal studies in practically every content area. We spent time during lunch, during planning periods, and after school talking about what we were learning and sharing our informal data. We wrote about our research in brief newsletters, which we distributed to the rest of the high school faculty. Soon other teachers became involved. Through this work, we slowly and systematically began to build a base of knowledge, which formed the foundation of Project CRISS^{SM}.

Probably even more important than our growing understanding of how students learn was our emerging understanding of the power of teacher research. We were learning what it meant to be a teacher researcher. We had taken on a research approach that became a process of self-examination, growth, and continuing change. It is this research attitude that changed us as teaching professionals and has become the driving force in the evolution of Project CRISS^{SM}.

Proponents of teacher research argue it is the surest way to achieve school improvement and lasting change in education. We could not agree more. Some of this research literature focuses on the effectiveness of teacher research as a way to create new products such as curriculum, designing a new staff plan or, in our case, the revision of a CRISS^{SM} manual. While we agree the products and new understandings are an important result of teacher research, we see an even greater value in the **process** of researching.

During the past 20 years of working with Project CRISS^{SM}, we have been involved with literally hundreds of teacher researchers who have used informal experiments in their classrooms. Over these years, it became apparent it is not enough to simply share the fruits of discovery. Although some teacher researchers continue to be enthusiastic, energetic, and inspiring, others become stagnant because they haven't taken on the attitude of a researcher. For example, they might discover in a research study that two-column notes is an effective learning strategy, which they then blindly use for every chapter in their science book without continual examination. Those who become stagnant fail to engage themselves *and* their students in a continual process of inquiry. Successful CRISS^{SM} teachers continue to *live the process*. Teacher research becomes a way of teaching, of never really finding the right answer, but continually seeking ways of doing our job even better. It involves maintaining a research attitude that encourages constant examination, growth, and continuing change as opposed to finding the right solution to a problem. Teacher research promotes a dynamic approach to the teaching professional as opposed to maintenance of the status quo. Looking back on these years, we now know the real power of Project CRISS^{SM} lies in its potential for fostering a research attitude among teachers and students.

▶ Teacher Research: The Beginnings

We began the development of Project CRISS^{SM} by setting up simple, short-term experiments in the classroom. We did this in a natural way, where teachers used one of their class sections as an experimental group and another as a control, thus regulating teacher variability and allowing teachers and their students to determine for themselves the effectiveness of the variable studied. Teachers used regular classroom tests, typically short-answer quizzes, to assess the impact of manipulations, and tested hypotheses with simple t tests. After completing a study, teachers involved their students in discussing test conditions and had students talk and write about how the experimental strategies worked for them.

High School Mathematics Study

One of our first studies focused on pre-reading strategies. Cheryl Plettner, a math teacher, felt her students expected her to explain things to them and, consequently, she did most of the talking in her classes. Her goal was to generate more student involvement. She also hoped to increase the motivation of her students to read their math assignments. Cheryl decided to investigate whether or not it would be helpful to have her students briefly review the material and generate questions that might arise about the topic *before* whole group discussion.

In one of her three math classes, Cheryl had students pre-read their assignments in order to identify the concepts they did not understand and to formulate one or two questions concerning these problem concepts. Then she had students meet in pairs and talk about their questions. After these paired discussions, Cheryl listed all of the questions on the board. Students read carefully and purposefully as they searched for the answers to their questions. All of this occurred before Cheryl explained any of the concepts. It appeared that students were more engaged in the material with this approach. A brief quiz the following day confirmed what Cheryl had suspected; the pre-reading group outperformed the control group. She then shared the data with her classes, and found the results initiated some lively discussion about why one class did better on the quiz than the other. Cheryl and her students began to understand the value of pre-reading strategies.

High School Science and Social Studies

Don Neu, a biology teacher, investigated the effects of pre- and post-reading journal entries. Before students read a selection, he asked them to write about several key concepts. After they had read, students checked their pre-reading entries for misconceptions and wrote revised post-reading journal entries. One week later, Don administered a quiz on the concepts students had written about in their journals. More students in the experimental group exhibited an understanding of these concepts than did students in a control group. Again, both the students and the teacher were able to see the value of the experimental strategy.

In another series of experiments, history and science teachers examined the effect of two-column notes over their reading assignments. They each taught two different sections of the same class with one class as the experimental group and the other the control. They taught their experimental group students how to analyze their text, develop two-column notes, and study from their notes. The experimental biology and history classes that had been introduced to the text analysis and notetaking procedures did far better on chapter tests than did the control group students. At the conclusion of the studies, the teachers showed students the results and facilitated a discussion about why the different results occurred.

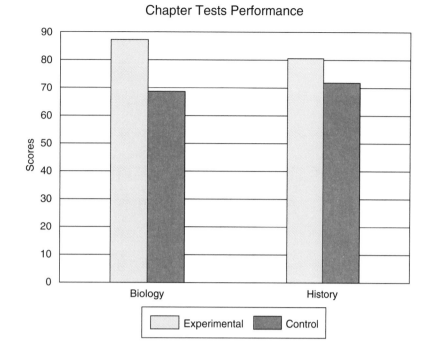

Chapter Tests Performance

In another study, Jim Scalf, a history teacher, proved to his students that studying from their notes was essential. He gave students in one class five minutes to test themselves using their two-column study guides. In the control class, students used the five minutes for studying; however, the teacher did not provide specific instructions to use their two-column notes, even though they were available. Most chose not to use them. Students who self-tested using the study guide format did better on the chapter examinations than those who did not use the study guide. Jim presented the data to convince the students to make better use of their two-column notes.

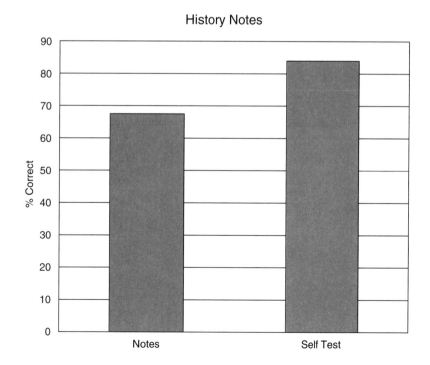

History Notes

An important aspect of these research efforts is the process conference. After completing a study, teachers and their students wrote about and discussed the research project. Students were encouraged to share their reactions. When asked to describe their study processes, students often became aware of them for the first time.

These examples show how research provides teachers and students answers to specific questions; more importantly, they demonstrate a researching attitude of continual examination and reflection. Teaching becomes a process of ongoing research.

▶ Students as Researchers of Their Own Learning

Involving students in the process of classroom research provides the same positive effect for students as it does for teachers. Students are empowered to ask questions about how they learn and to assume ownership of the learning process. As active participants in classroom research, students learn more. For both students and teachers, shifting the focus of learning from *content* to *process* promotes more involvement and builds life-long learning skills.

For example, teachers know how important background knowledge, organization, discussion, metacognition, and writing are to learning; but do their students understand these principles and how they operate within themselves? Sandra Bradford, a fourth grade teacher, Jennifer Watson, a high school English teacher, and Sue Dailey, a seventh grade social studies teacher, decided to address these issues directly by having students investigate their own learning.

Fourth-Grade Study

Sandra Bradford conducted her week-long study within the ongoing social studies curriculum. She divided a chapter from her social studies text into four sections. On Monday, the class collected baseline data by simply reading the first section of the chapter without doing any organizing strategies. On each of the following three days, using one of three comprehension strategies, students read a section of the text in order to evaluate the various strategies. On Tuesday, they used an adaptation of Ogle's (1986) K-W-L procedure, in which they brainstormed about the topic, categorized information, and generated questions before beginning to read. On Wednesday, the students organized the material using a power outline. On Thursday, they constructed concept maps on the material. For each of the readings, the students took a short quiz, graphed their individual tests results, and wrote personal reactions in learning logs. Sandra then asked her students to examine their own learning results and determine which of the strategies worked best for each individual. As predicted, strategies worked differently for different people. An example of one student's graph and journal is presented on the following page:

Student Graph

Handwritten student notes:

Monday was No help

→ indent

mrs. Bradford told us to read the pages and do the questions. I started and got a 23% I did not like it at all all. I like it when She reads it with us.

Brain Storming KWL

On Tuesday we did it by our self.(again) It was OK. I got 96%

Wed. Outlining

On Wednesday I got a 100%. She taught us how outline and showed us how to do it,

Thurs. Mapping

I felt good about mapping. I got a 95% on it. It is fun, cause she showed us how and you read a sentence and put down the important stuff.

Fri.

I liked Mapping the best I like it because it is fun and it takes a lot of thinking.

Sandra's study is a superb example of helping students begin to "own" strategies. Students did research on themselves and shared their results with one another. Practicing strategies and data collection and talking about learning helped students come to their own conclusions.

High School Study

Jennifer Watson and Carol Santa (1995) did a similar series of studies with sophomore language arts students. As part of a unit on writing scientific papers, students examined their own performance and came to conclusions about which study strategies worked best for them.

We began by teaching students about principles of learning, presenting the principles and philosophy portion of the CRISS℠ workshop to our students. Then students read a series of five articles, providing them with background information for the next class novel, *To Kill a Mockingbird,* as well as material for the investigation of study strategies. All of the selections were approximately 1 1/2 pages long. The investigation included five learning procedures—one for each article. Each procedure involved the students reading an article and using different study methods. They then put aside the article and any notes they might have taken and tested themselves by writing down on a blank sheet of paper information recalled from the article. They scored their own work by counting the number of ideas recalled and charting them on a graph. In this way, they could compare their performance across the different strategies. They also discussed and wrote about each strategy based on what they knew about learning principles, considering the value of each strategy in activating background knowledge, facilitating organization, and improving metacognitive skills. Next, they summarized their results in a scientific paper and evaluated their papers according to a revision sheet. The experiment lasted for about two weeks. A sample of the scientific paper and the revision sheet is shown on pages 240 and 241.

Sample of a Student's Scientific Paper

Researching My Own Learning

Introduction. For many years, researchers have been trying to find the most effective study methods. They have found that background knowledge, organizing, active learning, and metacognition are useful and effective study and learning methods. Metacognition is being aware of which information you know and which information you don't know. Based on my experiences with studying and preparing for tests and quizzes, using organizing strategies helps me learn best.

Methods and procedures. Our class read five articles about the years during the depression, each time using one or more methods of studying. We graphed the number of facts that we remembered for each article, so we could visually see which methods worked the best for each one of us.

On day one, we read an article about Eleanor Roosevelt. We only read this article once and then tested ourselves. We graphed the results of how much we could remember. This experiment was our control experiment.

For the next procedure, we read an article about Franklin Roosevelt. First, our class brainstormed for existing knowledge on this subject. Then, we skimmed through the article and again we brainstormed facts that we had just read. Lastly, we read through the article and tested ourselves to see how much we could remember. Then we graphed the results on our graph.

For the next study, we had an article on the Great Depression. First, we brainstormed for background knowledge and skimmed through the article. Next, we read the article, underlining the major points. Then we wrote study questions from the underlined phrases. Last, we wrote down the number of facts we remembered and graphed them.

Our next strategy involved brainstorming about what we knew about Black Americans during the Depression. We read the article, underlined, and then did a concept map. As before, we wrote down the facts and graphed our results

For the last study, we read an article about the author of *To Kill A Mockingbird,* Harper Lee. First, we skimmed the article, then we reread it and underlined key words and phrases. From the underlined information we made a concept map and then discussed the information with a partner. Again, we wrote down the facts we remembered and graphed the results.

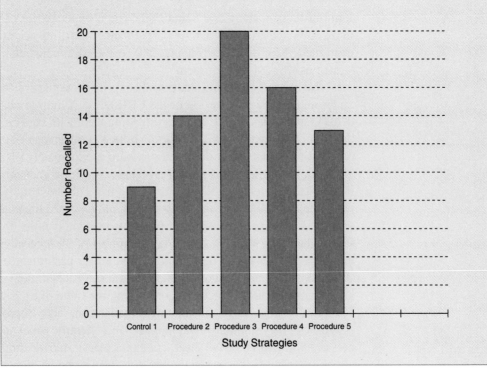

Results and discussion. As I mentioned previously, after using different study methods, we took a blank sheet of paper and wrote down everything we remembered. Then we counted up the number of facts and graphed our results in a notebook. My results are as follows:

I remembered the most facts about the Great Depression article. I think the reason I did the best was because I knew some thing about the Depression before I read the article. Another reason why I believe I did better on this article is because we wrote out our study questions for it, and that organization technique helped me remember facts better.

The article I did the worst on (except for the control–procedure one), was the one about Harper Lee. During this experiment we made a concept map for organization. I think it made the information harder for me to remember because the concept map was too cluttered and disorganized. I also didn't know anything about Harper Lee before reading the article. I also like working alone better than when working with a partner.

By performing these experiments and being able to visually see the results, I discovered that having background knowledge on the subject helped me remember more facts. Another thing that helped me was to have my information organized by using two-column notes or another organizational technique. In the future, I will try to brainstorm all of the facts I previously know about the subject to get my brain thinking on the right path. I will also try to be more organized with my studying and always be an active listener.

Revision Sheet for Student Use in Writing a Scientific Paper

Writer _____   Points possible:
                                        Rough draft editing sheet (25)   _____
                                          Final draft (125)   _____
                                          Total points   _____

Introduction (25 points)
1. Thesis statement
2. Theory
    Background knowledge _____
    Metgacognition _____
    Active learning _____
    Relate ideas to self _____
    Glimpse of upcoming study _____   Points _____

Methods and materials (25 points)
    Clear presentation of four conditions   Points _____

Results and discussion (25 points)
1. Graph _____
2. Explanation of results _____
3. Discussion of why results occurred _____   Points _____

Implications (25 points)
    Explanation of how results might influence future learning   Points _____

Conventions (25 points)
1. Spelling
2. Punctuation
3. Sentences
    Fragments
    Run-ons
4. Grammar   Points _____

Having our students investigate and write about their own learning helped them to internalize personal learning systems. Most found they recalled more when they had opportunities to organize information and to discuss what they were learning with other students. Students experimented with a variety of strategies, kept track of their performances, analyzed their results, and then wrote scientific papers presenting their data. As with Sandra Bradford's fourth-grade study, students responded differently to different strategies. These self-explorations both at the elementary and at the high school level helped students discover for themselves effective strategies for a variety of different situations and provided a way to evaluate whether or not CRISS℠ has become part of students' learning lives. Even more important, students became researchers; they became problem-solvers as they tested out their own theories of learning.

Seventh-Grade Longitudinal Study

Sue Dailey, one of our national trainers, provides another model of teacher research through a longitudinal study in which she followed a group of students from Grade 7 into high school. She wondered if her students could employ CRISS℠ strategies and theory not only while in her seventh-grade classroom, but as they progressed through school.

Sue taught a variety of CRISS℠ strategies to the students in her seventh-grade Montana history class. During this teaching, she also stressed theory as students discussed when and why to use certain techniques. But did they really get it? She decided to hit this question head-on while her students were studying about early pioneers who traveled to the Northwest on the Oregon Trail. She asked them to respond to a series of questions as they progressed through the unit.

She began by dividing her class into small groups of three and four students. Students kept all their work in folders and responded to questions in their learning logs. After discussing the question in their groups and performing a specific task, they wrote in their logs.

Pre-Reading Question 1.   *What are you going to do to activate your background knowledge before reading?*

Most groups decided to organize their discussions using an adaptation of the K-W-L strategy. As they talked about what they *knew* and what they *wanted to learn* about the Oregon Trail, one person in each group took notes, which students then used as a guide for their own journal responses.

My group decided to find out the definitions of the vocabulary words because we want to understand what the words are when we read the chapter later on. We decided to read the introduction because we thought it would help to set us up for what we are going to read and learn. Then we put our ideas on a K-W-L sheet.

What do I know?	What do I want to learn.
Covered wagons very little in Montana a lot of people got sick doing it to find gold - mad rush pioneers was after trapping was famous	who went where they came from - about their lives. where they traveled. what was it like in a wagon. why they went there

Sue didn't stop here. She wanted them to think hard about their particular strategy choices and to begin analyzing their own thinking.

Pre-Reading Question 2. *"Why were your pre-reading strategies helpful? Talk about this question in your group and then write about your own thinking."*

After their group discussion, they again wrote in their journals.

> *Doing these things before we read helped me to gain some background knowledge. If you know a little bit about what you're going to read, you can understand it a little better. Also, knowing the vocabulary words, I think will help me understand what I'm reading. If you know the vocabulary and how the facts fit together you can remember longer and understand what you're reading.*

Next, the groups made decisions about strategies for processing the information during reading.

Sue asked, *"How are you going to read actively and begin organizing the information? Just reading it through once isn't enough! Talk about this in your groups and develop a reading plan!"*

After each group spent some time discussing these issues, they responded to the next question in their journals:

During Reading Question 3. *What active strategies did your group decide to use and why did you choose them?*

> *My group decided to underline and take marginal notes while we read. We thought that it would help to underline but some things are kind of confusing and you don't know for sure what to underline, but you understand what it means, so you just have to jot down the facts on the side.*

After students in each group made their "strategy" decisions, they used them to complete their homework. The next day, they talked in their groups about their learning from the assignment and how well a particular strategy worked for them. They concluded by reflecting about their thinking in their journals:

During Reading Question 4. *How did your DURING strategy help you understand the material? Why is this a good one for you?*

> *We discussed what we underlined. This helped me understand the material because I had to think about what I read, so it is stuck in my head more. This is a good strategy for me because it's easy to re-read over for a test or when I need quick information.*

Next, Sue reminded her students about the importance of processing and transforming information so knowledge becomes personally meaningful. *"You have to do more with information than just read or read and underline. You have to change it, to transform it so it becomes your own. How will you do that?"* Sue challenged each group to come up with transforming or organizing strategies.

The groups decided how to organize the information to make it personally meaningful. Groups selected different ways to do this. One group chose to do a timeline:

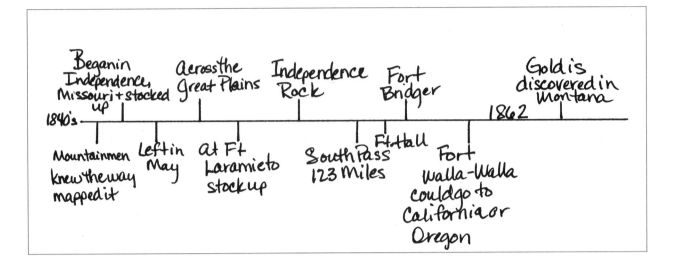

Another group chose to do a concept map:

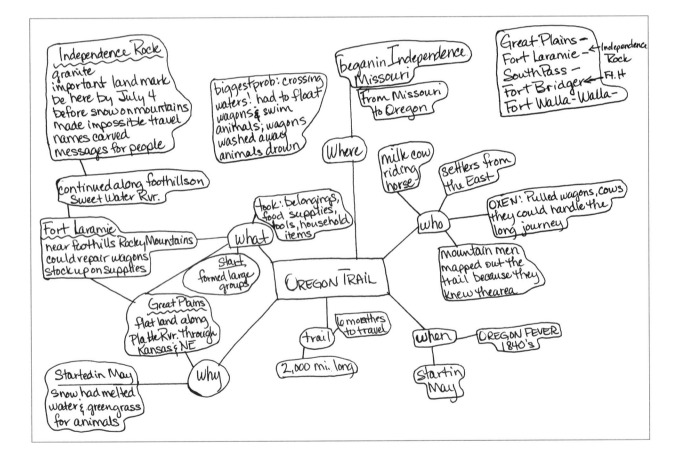

A third group did a picture map:

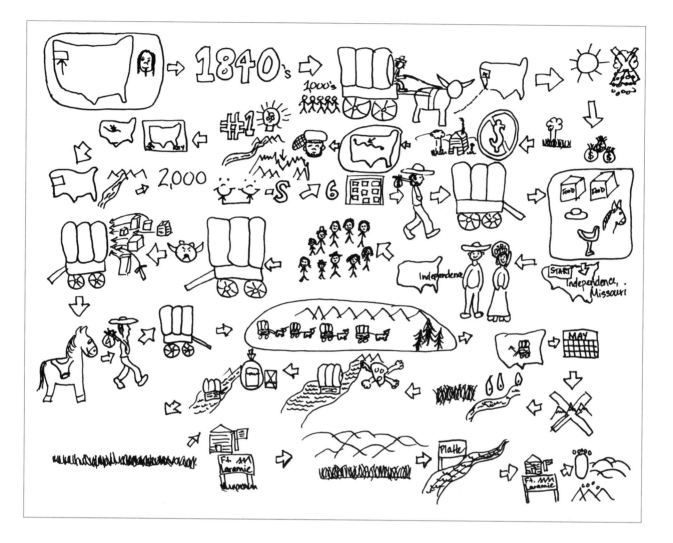

Upon completing their transforming strategies and talking about the information, students responded to Sue's next question:

After Reading Question 5. *Explain how you processed the information in your group.*

> *My group made concept maps to process the information. This really helps me to understand because while I am drawing, the information goes into my memory and stays there because I am drawing the facts the way I see them which helps me to remember them.*

Next, Sue asked the students to think about how they would study for a test. *"How are you going to study for your test? What do you have to do to make sure you understand and know the information? The only way you really know if you understand is to check your own comprehension. So, how are you going to do this? I want each group to come up with a way to self-test."*

After the groups discussed these questions, they came up with a plan. Most decided to convert their transformation strategies—concept maps, picture notes, timelines—into main idea-detail notes for self-testing. Each group developed key questions they thought might be on the test, which then became the focus of a whole class discussion.

After students developed their plans for studying, they once more wrote about their ideas in their journal.

Now we are going to take two-column notes to organize the data the way I understand it so I can quiz myself.

Oregon Trail — Lucy

1. When & Why did the Oregon trail start?	1. The first wagon train left in 1843. People wanted to go to Oregon to farm, because of climate and free land.
2. How did they prepare for the journey?	2. They met in Independence, Missouri with all their wagons. They put food staples in their wagons & left in groups. 2,000 miles
3. When did the wagons leave & why?	3. Left in May because there was plenty of water & green grass. Took 6 months.
4. Where did they go first?	4. across the great plains to Fort Laramie where they stocked

---

The next day, Sue led a discussion, reviewing major concepts about the Oregon Trail. Sue told them about items that would definitely be on the test so they could add them to their self-testing plans. Sue doesn't believe in surprises. Everyone has the right to do well! When the students felt ready, she gave them the test. After finishing, students responded to one final question in their journals.

After Reading Question 6. *Think about all of the strategies you used to learn about the Oregon Trail. Where do you think real learning takes place?*

With all the strategies that I used, I think they really helped me. I think these strategies don't really help unless you know what your purpose for doing all this work is for. You could just copy right out of the text and hand in your work and when test time comes you'd be clueless. I did as much as I could to learn metacognitively about the Oregon Trail. The strategy that helps me most with all these strategies is a picture map or a concept map. I understand the Oregon Trail very well now. I also think two-column notes and self-testing helped me a lot, too.

Sue continued to do similar lesson sequences with her students throughout their seventh-grade year. Yet, she wondered whether or not they would continue to live and breathe CRISS[SM] as they progressed through school. She decided to find out by writing to this group of students when they were eighth graders and then again as sophomores.

Eighth-grade example:

Dear Mrs. Dailey,

How's school going this year? It's doing pretty good here. I want to thank you for helping me with these skills last year. They have already helped me with eighth grade and I know they will help me even into college. I have found myself using any kind of map to help process science and social studies information. I also use two-column notes. These help me get the most important information to stick in my head by reading it a few times. Yes, two-column notes are expected from us. Thanks to you I know and understand how to do them and use them. I can also tell when I'm understanding information better than I could before. When I hit a "clunk," I reread the sentence or paragraph to see if I missed something or go to an adult or older brother. These things have helped me tons in my short eighth grade experience. Thanks again. I hope to see you around and I'll try to visit as often as I can.

Sincerely,

Becky

Sue wrote to them again as sophomores.

Dear Blue Team Sophomores!

Surprise! I haven't forgotten you. I am still teaching 7th graders lots of CRISS^{SM} Strategies and am still doing CRISS^{SM} workshops for teachers. I want to learn how students continue to use CRISS^{SM} strategies as they go through the grades. I am interested in the following things:

1. Are you a metacognitive learner? Do you know when you come to something in your reading that you don't understand and do you use fix-up strategies? Do your teachers encourage you to really learn the material by using lots of discussion, writing, and active learning strategies?

2. What CRISS^{SM} strategies are you encouraged or required to use by your teachers? This could include Power Thinking and Outlining, K-W-L Sheets, concept mapping summarizing, two-column notes, spool papers, RAFT, discussion, journaling, etc.

3. What CRISS^{SM} strategies do you use independently?

Thank you for taking the time to do this for me. I still miss you. The year you were here was still my best ever!

Sincerely,

Mrs. Dailey

Here is an example of one of her student's responses:

Dear Mrs. Dailey,

Hi, how are you? Your letter was quite a surprise. Yes, I do feel that I am a metacognitive learner. I can usually tell pretty quickly when I do and don't understand something. This has been a very important skill this year. The responsibility to make sure I'm on track and understanding the material has been shifted almost completely to my shoulders.

The only techniques I've been encouraged to use in most classes are two-column notes and discussion. Of course in English we still use all the techniques.

In general, I use discussion and journaling on my own. I still need to put things in my own words either verbally or by writing them out.

I hope this helps you out. It's nice to know you're keeping track of us.

Sincerely,

Julian

Sue's longitudinal study provided her clear evidence that her students had incorporated CRISS^{SM} theory and strategies as part of their learning lives. Her research methodology became a lesson in itself about how to lead students through a process of internalizing ways of learning. Including discussion and writing about learning as part of content instruction gives students an opportunity to begin *living* strategies. Students don't really *get it* unless *strategy processing* occurs as part of assignments over a time. Talking and writing about learning became a daily, year-long, multiple-year event.

▶ Summary

These examples demonstrate different ways effective CRISS^{SM} teachers use research as part of their day-to-day teaching. Key to their discoveries is their researching attitude. While the results of these studies have served to build the knowledge base of CRISS^{SM}, the outcome is not as important as the process of continuing examination. It is the on-going clinical process of exploring how to teach and how students learn. Teachers and students who engage in research about learning come to trust their own abilities to construct knowledge and improve their practice. Therefore, we must continually challenge ourselves and our students to become better clinicians of teaching and learning.

CHAPTER 12

The CRISS^{SM} Strategic Learning Plan

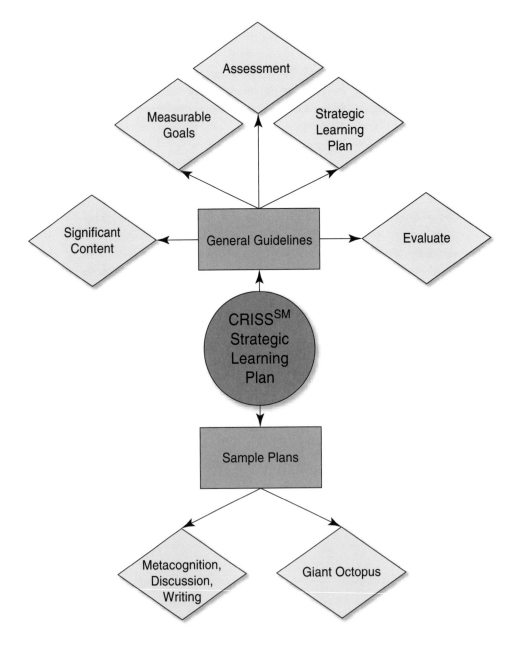

The *CRISS^{SM} Strategic Learning Plan (CSLP)* is a general instructional model for teaching and learning that integrates the various strategies in this text into a logical instructional flow. Basically, the CSLP involves everything the reader does before, during, and after reading to learn content information. As we discussed in Chapter 1, CRISS^{SM} provides the philosophical framework for planning instruction and ensuring student learning. The CSLP is a way for teachers to verify they have included the basic principles of learning within their lessons and for students to plan confidently for successful comprehension and learning.

▶ General Guidelines

Before we share two CRISS^{SM} Strategic Learning Plans found in the *CRISS^{SM} for Students: It's a Brain Thing ~ Learning How to Learn!* materials, we want to review some general guidelines for planning successful lessons.

- ▶ Choose significant content.
- ▶ Set clear and measurable goals.
- ▶ Plan assessment.
- ▶ Develop a CRISS^{SM} Strategic Learning Plan.
- ▶ Evaluate, evaluate, evaluate!

Choose Significant Content

Grant Wiggins and Jay McTighe (1998) cite a body of evidence which indicates that students spend the bulk of their time merely "covering" topics in a curriculum without really understanding the important concepts. For classroom instruction to be truly meaningful, we need to start by selecting and evaluating the content we want to teach. Use the following questions:

- ▶ Does the content really merit study?
- ▶ Is the content significant?
- ▶ Am I stressing the big ideas—the central organizing ideas of a content domain, rather than superficial details?
- ▶ Does the content relate to state and local curriculum guidelines?

Set Clear and Measurable Goals

For students to be metacognitive about their learning and to assess your students' performance effectively, make sure the purpose of your lesson is clear and the learning goals reachable. Evaluate your goals by responding to the following questions:

- ▶ Are my goals understandable and reachable by all students?
- ▶ Do I have a variety of resources for the students to use that will enable them to reach the content and learning goals?
- ▶ Will students be able to use these goals to monitor their comprehension?
- ▶ How will they know they have successfully reached these goals?

Plan Assessment

Wiggins and McTighe (1998) recommend a *backward* lesson plan design as the most effective way to achieve success with a learning plan. Before planning instruction, think about how you can evaluate your students' learning. Use the "Photo Album" approach. Don't just have one snapshot of how students have learned, but plan multiple assessments—throughout the learning plan, not just at the end—and plan a *variety* of assessments, both performance and objective. Evaluate your assessment plan with the following questions:

- ▶ Have I included a variety of evaluation tools (performance assessments, objective tests, writing prompts, etc.)?
- ▶ Are my tools actually assessing the goals and objectives I set?
- ▶ Am I assessing throughout the lesson?
- ▶ Are my assessments a learning experience for my students?

Develop a CRISS℠ Strategic Learning Plan

When developing a CSLP, we think in terms of this general four-step plan:

1. First, we **prepare** our students before the learning "experience" (reading, watching a video, going on a field trip, doing a lab, listening to a speaker, etc.). Usually, this includes bringing out the students' background knowledge and directing them to the purpose for learning.
2. Next, we want our students to **be actively involved** with the content as they are reading, listening, viewing, or doing. For example, writing questions or comments on sticky notes while reading or recording two-column notes while listening can help a student pay attention. These metacognition tools help students identify whether they are "getting it." If not, they can re-read, ask questions, or use any of the other metacognition strategies they have learned.
3. After students have read, etc., we want them to **organize** the information so it can be practiced and reviewed for learning and for more in-depth understanding. CRISS℠ provides a variety of organizing tools and formats, which students can apply to transform this newly acquired information.
4. Finally, we want our students to **use, adapt, evaluate,** and **apply** the information they have learned. This can be done through writing, discussing, organizing, or through a variety of practical applications.

Evaluate your CSLP with the following questions:

- ▶ What background knowledge will my students need before starting this lesson?
- ▶ What strategies will my students use to learn the information and to reach the intended goals?
- ▶ Where are they with this strategy knowledge?
- ▶ Do I need to introduce the strategies or just model them?
- ▶ How will I insure students are actively involved in their learning?
- ▶ How can I help them be metacognitive?
- ▶ Have I included a variety of individual, paired, and group activities?

Evaluate, Evaluate, Evaluate!

Assessment provides the only way we can improve our instruction and our students' learning. We need to assess the effectiveness of our lessons as we teach and again at the completion of a lesson. Of course, *we* must evaluate the effectiveness of our CSLP, but we also need to have our *students* evaluate the plan's effectiveness in terms of their learning. Evaluate by using the following questions.

Ask yourself:

- ▶ Did the assessments adequately measure the desired objectives?
- ▶ What could I do to improve this Learning Plan?
- ▶ Did my Learning Plan move students toward increased independence?

Ask your students:

- ▶ How did you organize the information?
- ▶ Did you assess your learning progress?
- ▶ What strategies worked best for you and why?
- ▶ Did you evaluate your understanding throughout this lesson?
- ▶ What could you do next time to improve your understanding?
- ▶ How can you apply what you have learned to your own life?

▶ Two CRISS℠ Strategic Learning Plans

With these guidelines in place, let's look at two CRISS℠ Strategic Learning Plans found in the *CRISS℠ for Students* materials. The first will be a plan designed by a teacher to help her students understand one of the major principles of learning— *metacognition.* The second CSLP demonstrates how to develop a lesson plan based on content—a chapter in the trade book, *Tough Terminators,* by Sneed B. Collard III. In this second CSLP, you will see how the teacher integrates the instruction of strategies with the instruction of content.

Both lessons will be introduced to you by teachers. You will hear, through their voices, how they developed the lessons, and at the end of each "think-aloud" piece, you will see their completed CSLP. In the first chapter of this book, we indicated the format of the CSLP can vary, and *should* vary, to accommodate the needs of each school or district. The CSLPs included in this chapter do not look the same, but both include all of the components mentioned in the preceding section of this chapter.

First CRISS℠ Strategic Learning Plan— *Metacognition, Discussion, Writing*

Meet the teacher: Hi, I am Ms. Dempster, a seventh-grade mathematics teacher working at a middle school. I am part of a middle school team. This year, we decided that early in the year each of the team members would be responsible for teaching one of the CRISS℠ principles for improved learning. In developing this lesson on metacognition, I was fortunate to be able to brainstorm with my other team members. We used the guidelines set up at the beginning of this chapter to help us get started.

Choose Significant Content.   Because we have taken the Level I Project CRISS℠ workshop, we know how important it is for students to be metacognitive. I feel this is especially true in mathematics, because my students would be much better problem solvers if they were able to discover exactly where their comprehension failed. I think this knowledge for the students would also help me to be a better teacher. Usually, they just tell me, "I don't get it!" When I ask for specifics, I get a blank stare. As I teach metacognition, I will include writing and discussion as strategies that will help them become more metacognitive.

This content relates both to our district standards, which emphasize problem solving in mathematics and mathematical communication (writing and discussion), and to the NCTM National Standards (2000) of Problem Solving (especially #4, "monitor and reflect on the process of mathematical problem solving"), Reasoning and Proof (#4, "select and use various types of reasoning and methods of proof"), Communication (all parts), and Connections (#3, "recognize and apply mathematics in contexts outside of mathematics").

Set Clear and Measurable Goals.   I want my students to learn what metacognition is and how to use it to help them learn mathematics. In addition, I want them to see how writing about mathematics and discussing mathematics with a partner or team can help them to become better problem solvers and better readers of mathematical materials (our text book and other math resources I provide in our class). My team members will be supporting what I do in math class in their classes. So students will have practice using metacognition, writing, and discussion in all of their classes.

In completing my CRISS^{SM} Strategic Learning Plan, I will rely on two major resources—the *CRISS^{SM} for Students* materials and a little booklet on metacognition that our reading teacher gave me. She picked it up at a reading conference. It was developed by Project MERIT in Philadelphia.

Plan Assessment.   I want my assessment to contain multiple pieces, so I can truly evaluate whether my students understand metacognition. I plan to use the objective question and written prompt provided in the *CRISS^{SM} for Students* book (see Exhibit 1); but I also want to know if my students are using metacognition to help them in mathematics; so I will continually evaluate their use of discussion and writing while they are completing their mathematics homework assignments. I can do this by walking around the classroom, listening to their discussions, and by having them put their math writing on their homework papers, which they turn in. Finally, I want to determine if they transfer knowledge about metacognition learned in my class to their other classes. I will have them bring in one sample of metacognitive work (perhaps a journal entry or sticky-note questions) from another class.

Develop a Strategic Plan.   Because I have the *CRISS^{SM} for Students* book, I will basically follow the 4-Step Strategic Learning Plan provided in the book (see Exhibit 2—an excerpt from the student manual, *CRISS^{SM} for Students: It's a Brain Thing ~ Learning How to Learn!*) to create my own CSLP (see Exhibit 3).

Evaluate, Evaluate, Evaluate!   For my personal evaluation, I plan to review each part of my CSLP as I am implementing it and also after I have completed the implementation. I will write down my reflections on sticky notes and attach them to my lesson plan, so when I do the plan again next year, I will know how I can improve upon this year's lesson. For the student part of my CSLP evaluation, I will use the last two writing prompts in the *CRISS^{SM} for Students* materials (see Exhibit 4), and I will also have a process conference with my students, so I can hear their reactions to this lesson and so they can hear how other students in the class are using metacognition.

Second CRISS^{SM} Strategic Learning Plan—
North Pacific Giant Octopus

Meet the teacher: Hi, I am Mrs. Furlong, and I teach reading in the high school. This year, I decided to use *CRISS^{SM} for Students*: *It's a Brain Thing ~ Learning How to Learn!* with my ninth graders. My goal is to help my students become more strategic in their learning. This CRISS^{SM} book introduces and models a variety of strategies, which are packaged into learning plans. Some of the learning plans deal with the CRISS^{SM} principles, but the one I want to share with you relates to a chapter in *Tough Terminators,* by Sneed B. Collard III. This trade book, which is part of the *CRISS^{SM} for Students* package, introduces twelve predators. For each predator, the author provides information on what the animal (or plant) looks like, what it eats, how it hunts, where it lives, and its interaction with man.

Through the various content and principle lessons, I hope my students will develop a toolbox of comprehension strategies to help them better understand and retain course information. I am very excited about this new book, for I know it will help my students become independent learners.

Let me walk you through my planning for the chapter in *Tough Terminators* called "North Pacific Giant Octopus."

Choose Significant Content.
I preview the content of this chapter, and then the planning begins. I think about content standards that align, and they are as follows:

> ▶ Students will select and use pre-reading strategies that are appropriate to the text, such as discussion, making predictions, brainstorming, generating questions, and previewing to anticipate content, purpose, and organization of a reading selection.
>
> ▶ Students will apply a variety of response strategies, including rereading, note taking, and summarizing.
>
> ▶ Students will write fluently for a variety of occasions, audiences, and purposes, making appropriate choices regarding style, tone, level of detail, and organization.

Because many of my students have problems attacking the content selections they encounter in their other classes, I know the principles and strategies they will be using with this chapter in the *Tough Terminators* will be worthwhile for them.

Set Clear and Measurable Goals.
I know how important it is for my students to know the purposes of the lesson. They will not just be learning about a predator, the North Pacific giant octopus, and why it is a skilled hunter, but they will also be learning and incorporating comprehension strategies. I will ask them to think about these strategies and determine not only what strategies worked best for them, but how they can use these strategies in other classes.

If an administrator walked through my classroom and bent down to ask one of my students what he or she was learning, it would be gratifying to hear the student respond, "I am learning about the octopus in this chapter, and I am also learning and using effective comprehension strategies that will make me a better learner." Wow, wouldn't that be a perfect response!

Plan Assessment.   My next step is to create assessments which will evaluate if my students reach the goals. I will build a rubric that includes performance tasks, as well as written assessments. I know how important it is to form my assessments before planning for the instructional components.

The multiple-choice and short response questions found in *CRISS*[SM] *for Students* will help me assess the knowledge my students have gained about the octopus. The homework assignment, a learning log where students are asked to reflect upon their learning processes, will help me monitor their progress in becoming strategic learners.

Assessment Rubric

	Very Good	Fair	Poor
Participation in completing the Anticipation Guide	2	1	0
Participation in Read-and-Say-Something	2	1	0
Two-Column Main Idea Detail Notes	2	1	0
RAFT	2	1	0
Have You Got It (multiple choice and short-response writing from *CRISS*[SM] *for Students*— see Exhibit 5)	2	1	0
Homework: Reflection on learning process	2	1	0

Total = _____
A = 11–12   B = 9–10   C = 8   D = 7   F = 6 or less

Develop a Strategic Plan.   Since I will be using the *CRISS*[SM] *for Students* materials, I will follow the 4-Step Strategic Learning Plan provided in the book. (See Exhibit 6 for an excerpt from the book.) In Exhibit 7, you will see how I have folded that plan into my own CRISS[SM] Strategic Learning Plan format, which we use at my high school.

Evaluate, Evaluate, Evaluate!   I will end this lesson with the process conference. My number one goal is for my students to become metacognitive learners.

I will ask them to think about the strategies integrated in this lesson. "What helped you learn? Did working in groups help? Did discussing and writing solidify your learning? Did two-column notes help you determine main ideas and details from the selection? Did the RAFT assignment help you think about what you had learned as you assumed the role of the octopus?"

The learning log entry also gives me evidence my objectives were reached. I will ask my students to think and write about how they can apply these learning strategies in other classes (see Exhibit 8). Hopefully, my students will realize this lesson was beneficial for developing their own toolbox of learning strategies.

◗ Summary

The CRISS^{SM} Strategic Learning Plan (CSLP) provides an instructional framework for teachers and students. This plan integrates CRISS^{SM} principles and strategies into an overall structure for learning. It also assures that students and teachers will pay attention to the *process* of learning.

This framework guides us to think about the content and purpose of our lesson and our means of assessment before we actually develop our instructional plan. As we create our lesson, we consider what strategies will be most useful to prepare our students for learning, to engage them purposefully, and to help them organize, use, and apply the newly-learned information. Finally, the CSLP guides us through an evaluation process that is self-reflective and based on input from our students.

It is our hope that you talk about the four steps of your instructional plan (prepare, be actively involved, organize, and apply) with your students. If they are to become truly independent learners, they will need to incorporate CRISS^{SM} principles and strategies into their own plans for learning.

Multiple Choice: *(Circle the letter of the correct response.)*

In this chapter, the authors say "successful readers are metacognitive." What does this mean?

A. Successful readers monitor their understanding of text and know what to do when they do not understand.
B. Successful readers never have clunks.
C. Successful readers read very carefully and slowly.
D. Successful readers never reread.

Writing Item:

According to the *Project CRISS^{SM} for Students* authors, to be a successful reader you need to do more than open a book and start reading. Using details from this chapter, explain what successful readers do to prepare for reading and to understand what they have read.

Prepare: *Write and Discuss*

▶ Up to now, the KEYS TO LEARNING have been fairly easy to understand. *Metacognition* is a word that most people (even teachers!) don't know. Here is some information which will help you get started.

> METACOGNITION is recognizing that you *understand* what you are reading, seeing, or hearing. It is also knowing when you do not understand AND knowing what to do to gain understanding
>
> METACOGNITIVE SKILLS can be learned. They are the strategies which will help you monitor your understanding and make learning easier for you. As you go through this chapter, you will probably discover you already know and are using some metacognitive skills.

▶ All readers, no matter how well or poorly they read, have some materials they can understand pretty well (a novel, a magazine, comics, baseball statistics, a picture book). They can clickity-click across the pages easily. On the other hand, most readers have some materials they have difficulty understanding, and the clickity-click turns to a CLUNK. What kinds of "clunks" do you run into with your reading? Maybe you don't have enough background knowledge or you don't know the purpose (two of our important KEYS TO LEARNING). Maybe the material is boring. List your clunks below.

▶ Share your clunks with the class. You probably have a lot of the same problems.

▶ When you are reading and come to a "clunk," what do you do? Give up? Read again? In the following space, write what you do.

▶ Share your ideas (other than "give up") with the class and start to develop a list of FIX-UP strategies.

▶ Remember to add to the list as you complete the learning plan for this chapter.

Continued on next page

Be Involved: *Identifying Clunks Using Sticky Notes*

▶ Follow along as your teacher reads through two of the rattlesnake selections on the next page and models for you what good and poor readers do. As your teacher reads, complete the following Two-Column Chart.

What poor readers do	What good readers do

▶ Now that you know what good readers do, read through the selection on the eastern diamondback rattlesnake, marking clunks, fix-up strategies, and places where you checked your understanding.

▶ Did you discover any new fix-up strategies?

Organize: *Two-Column Notes (Fix-up Strategy—Explanation or Clarification)*

▶ You have done a lot of work with clunks and fix-up strategies. Now, it is time to organize your fix-up strategies into Two-Column Notes. The notes have been started for you. Complete them by adding all of the fix-up strategies you have used so far (in the left-hand column) and an explanation or clarification (in the right-hand column). Mark this page with a sticky note for quick reference.

Fix-Up Strategy	Explanation or Clarification
1. Slow down	1. Change your reading speed for difficult material. Textbook material usually requires slower reading than a novel or short story.
2. Read on	2. Sometimes the author will explain information further into the paragraph or selection. The author might provide examples or more details as you continue to read.
3. Reread	3.

Continued on next page

▶ Now that you have your fix-up strategies ready to use, let's review the whole process which successful, metacognitive readers use.

Process for Successful Metacognitive Readers

1. Survey the reading selection to determine the topic. Look at headings, subheadings, visuals, and graphics. *(Author's Craft)*

2. Think about what you already know. *(Background Knowledge)*

3. Determine a purpose for reading. Establish some questions you want answered. *(Set a Purpose)*

4. Keep your purpose in mind as you read and monitor your understanding. *(Active Reading)*

5. If you hit a CLUNK, stop reading and plan your next move. Survey the fix-up list on the preceding page and pick a strategy. *(Metacognition)*

6. Did your fix-up strategy work? If yes, you are on your way! If no, go back to step 5 and pick another fix-up strategy. *(Metacognition)*

▶ Notice how the KEYS TO LEARNING fit into the successful reader's plan!!!

Apply: *Metacognition Journal*

Directions for Eight-Page Metacognition Journal

Note: Use 18″ × 24″ paper.

1. Fold paper left to right (24″ in half).
2. Fold top to bottom (18″ in half).
3. Fold right to left (12″ in half).
4. Open paper back up to first fold (step 1) and cut inward from center of fold side to center mark, "c."
5. Lay paper flat, unfolded with slit going lengthwise from left to right.
6. Pull cut sections straight up and let one section fold to the front and one to the back of the cut.
7. Hold on to the two ends of the paper and push toward the center, so both sides of the center slit open up.
8. Keep pushing in until the two folds, "a" and "b", meet.

Bingo, you have an eight-page booklet! Now, we need to turn your eight-page booklet into a Metacognition Journal.

1. Label the cover of your booklet "Metacognition Journal," and add your own cover design. At the bottom of the cover, put your name and period.
2. Format the next six pages so they look like the page to the right.
3. During the next week or so (your teacher will give you a due date), it will be your job to complete the six metacognitive journal entries in this booklet.
4. Bring the completed journal to class. On the back page of your booklet describe (a) how you have become a more metacognitive reader and (b) which fix-up strategies worked best for you.

CLASS:
BOOK:

CLUNK:

FIX-UP STRATEGY(IES) USED:

HOW DID IT WORK?

CRISS^{SM} Strategic Learning Plan

Topic/Selection & Standards: Metacognition, writing, discussion (district math standards—Problem Solving 1a,b, 2a, 3a,c // NCTM Standards—Problem Solving, Reasoning & Proof, Communication, and Connections)

Objective: Students will learn about metacognition and understand how to use it in math especially through writing and discussion.

Assessment (objective & performance): (1) & (2) *CRISS^{SM} for Students* objective question & writing prompt, (3) classroom observations, (4) writing entries on homework, (5) metacognition examples from other classes.

Learning Plan	Strategies & How Applied to Content	CRISS^{SM} Principles & Philosophy							
		BK	AI	D	W	O	M	M&E
BEFORE *Prepare*	***Learning log entry:*** Have students list "Clunks" they encounter while reading & their fix-up strategies. Discuss entries.	✓	✓	✓	✓		✓	
DURING *Be Involved*	***Two-Column Notes—"good" vs. "poor" readers:*** Model good & poor reader traits with next section of math text. Have students list traits in two columns. Give students a copy of the next text selection and have them do what I did, mark their clunks and fix-up strategies.		✓	✓	✓	✓	✓	✓
AFTER *Organize*	***Two-Column Main Idea—Detail Notes:*** Have students use this format to record fix-up strategies (left column) and explanations of the strategy (right column)	✓	✓	✓	✓	✓	✓	
POST *Use, Apply*	***Metacognition Journal:*** Have students keep track of clunks and fix-up strategies for a week using the 8-page booklet.	✓	✓	✓	✓	✓	✓	

Key to CRISS^{SM} P & P:

BK = Background Knowledge
AI = Active Involvement
D = Discussion

W = Writing
O = Organizing
M = Metacognition

M&E = Modeling & Explanation

Reflection

▶ Think about KEY TO LEARNING No. 5—Metacognition and how it helped you understand the information in your other classes.

▶ What could you have done to be more metacognitive and successful with your learning?

Apply This to Other Classes

▶ Think about how you can apply Metacognition to your other classes. Record your thoughts below.

▶ Remember to save samples of successful applications to share with the class and to place in your folder.

Multiple Choice: *(Circle the letter of the correct response.)*

With which of the following statements below would the author of this book MOST LIKELY AGREE?

    A. Octopuses are social creatures.
    B. Scuba divers should fear octopuses.
    C. Octopuses have strong backbones.
    D. Octopuses are smart.

Writing Item:

The author infers that the octopus is a skilled hunter. Use details from the chapter to support this inference.

Prepare: *Anticipation Guide*

The Anticipation Guide is a reading strategy in which you respond to several statements to activate your thoughts and opinions about a topic you will be studying. The next animal you are going to read about is the North Pacific giant octopus.

On the Anticipation Guide below, check (✔) whether you AGREE or DISAGREE with the six statements. After you have INDEPENDENTLY completed the Anticipation Guide, have a discussion with your partner to see if you agreed or disagreed with one another. Be prepared to share your opinions with the class.

	Agree	Disagree	Statement
1.	____	____	The octopus is a vertebrate because it has a flexible backbone.
2.	____	____	There are about 200 species of octopus.
3.	____	____	The giant octopus has over 2,000 suction cups on its six arms.
4.	____	____	The octopus has no teeth.
5.	____	____	The octopus can carry up to 12 crabs at the same time.
6.	____	____	Scuba divers have often been attacked and bitten by octopuses.

Be Involved: *Read-and-Say-Something*

Now read the *Tough Terminator #3, North Pacific Giant Octopus* selection to see if your opinions were correct. Your teacher will give you directions on how to read the selection with your partner.

Organize 1: *Anticipation Guide Revisited*

After reading the selection, complete the following guide. For each of the original Anticipation Guide statements, if you found your response was correct, check (✔) that you found SUPPORT for your answer and write the information that proves you were right in the EVIDENCE column. If you were wrong, check (✔) that you found NO SUPPORT for your answer and write the correct information to the right in the EVIDENCE column. You will end up with six true statements in the EVIDENCE column when you have finished.

Were you curious to find out if your answers were correct? This strategy arouses your interest, sets purposes for your reading, and helps to clear up any misconceptions you may have on the topic. These are all very important to your learning!

	Support	No Support	Evidence
1.	____	____	_____
2.	____	____	_____
3.	____	____	_____
4.	____	____	_____
5.	____	____	_____
6.	____	____	_____

Organize 2: *Main Idea—Detail Notes*

Complete the Two-Column Notes chart on the following page to organize the information from the selection on the octopus.

Main Idea—Detail Notes

Main Idea	Detail

Continued on next page

Apply: *RAFT*

RAFT is an acronym. Each letter represents a part of a writing assignment. R is the *R*ole of the writer or author; A is the *A*udience, the person or people to whom the writer is writing; F is the *F*ormat in which the author writes; and T is the *T*opic selected by the writer. On the following page, write the RAFT paper described below.

Role	=	Octopus
Audience	=	Scuba Diver
Format	=	Letter
Topic	=	Apologize for scaring the diver

Work with a partner. Use the Role Definition Matrix to help you plan before you write your RAFT. Be prepared to share your letter with the class.

Role Definition Matrix		
Personality: *Who am I and what are some aspects of my personality?*	**Attitude:** *What are my feelings, beliefs, ideas, concerns?*	**Information:** *What do I know that I need to share in my writing?*

RAFT Paper

CRISS℠ Strategic Learning Plan:
North Pacific Giant Octopus

Content Standards:

- Selects and uses pre-reading strategies that are appropriate to the text such as discussion, making predictions, brainstorming, generating questions, and previewing, to anticipate content, purpose and organization of a reading selection.
- Applies a variety of response strategies, including rereading, note taking, and summarizing.
- Writes fluently for a variety of occasions, audiences, and purposes, making appropriate choices regarding style, tone, level of detail and organization.

Purpose Setting:

- Students will become familiar with the strategies, Anticipation Guide, Read-and-Say-Something, Main Idea—Detail Notes, and RAFT, and be able to apply these strategies to other classes.
- Students will determine from the selection why the North Pacific giant octopus is considered to be a skilled hunter.
- Students will think about what makes them strategic learners.

Assessments:

	Very Good	Fair	Poor
Participation in completing the Anticipation Guide	2	1	0
Participation in Read-and-Say-Something	2	1	0
Main Idea—Detail Notes	2	1	0
RAFT	2	1	0
Check your Understanding (multiple choice and short response writing found in *CRISS℠ for Students*)	2	1	0
Homework: Reflection on learning process	2	1	0

Total Points = _____

Grading: **A** = 11–12   **B** = 9–10   **C** = 8   **D** = 7   **F** = 6 or less

Preparing for Understanding:

- Students begin with an Anticipation Guide which contains six statements. They are to mark whether they agree or disagree with the statements. Students will work independently, share with a partner, and then share as a whole group.
- Students will preview the chapter for important and unknown vocabulary words. Word maps will be completed for challenging words.

Integrating Strategies for Understanding:

- The teacher and students discuss the overriding purposes of this lesson.
- The students work in pairs to complete Main Idea-Detail Notes.
- The teacher introduces and models the Role Definition Matrix (Personality, Attitude, Information).
- The students work in groups of four to complete a RAFT assignment. R = Octopus A = Scuba Diver F = Letter T = Apologize for scaring the diver. Groups share their letters with the whole class.

The teacher will also write the RAFT assignment to share with the class.

Checking for Understanding:

▶ **Check your Understanding**
Students return to the Anticipation Guide to see if their original decisions (Agree-Disagree) were accurate and to correct any misinformation.

Students complete the multiple choice item and the short response writing item from *CRISS*^{SM} *for Students*.

▶ **Process Conference**—The teacher asks students the following questions to help them reflect on the learning process.

Did the Anticipation Guide make you curious about the North Pacific giant octopus? Did you want to find out if you were right and to learn more about this animal?

Did Read-and-Say-Something help you stay engaged with the text? What part did you like the best? Were there any confusing parts or unknown vocabulary words?

Did completing Main Idea—Detail Notes help you find the main ideas and supportive details from the selection?

Did the RAFT assignment make you think about the octopus and its effects on man? Did writing about it make you think more?

How might you apply the strategies you learned in this lesson to other classes?

How might you apply what you learned in this selection to your own life?

Reflection

▶ Think about how the strategies of Anticipation Guide, Read-and-Say-Something, Main Idea–Detail Notes, and RAFT helped you to understand and remember the information in the selection on the octopus.

▶ What could you have done to be more successful in your learning?

Apply This to Other Classes

▶ Think about how you can apply these learning strategies to help you study in your other classes. Record your thoughts below.

▶ Remember to save samples of successful applications to share with the class and to place in your folder.

BLACKLINE MASTERS

Name: _____   Date: _____

Content Text Assessment Rubric
for Teaching & Learning

Name of text: _____

Author(s): _____   Class: _____

Copyright: _____ Publisher: _____   Grades: _____

3 = Excellent
2 = Fair
1 = Poor

Section A

Content/Standards	Evidence/Comments	Points (1–3)
The content of this text reflects the essential concepts in your course.		
The content flows in a logical progression appropriate for this topic—from simple to complex, chronological, topical, etc.		
The content, including illustrations and examples, appropriately presents ethnic and gender diversity.		
The content addresses both local and state standards.		

Total points for section A = _____

Section B

Pre-Reading Features: *Background Knowledge*	Evidence/Comments	Points (1–3)
The chapter introduction helps students relate their own life experiences and previously learned information to the topic.		
The author builds on the students' prior knowledge within the chapter subsections.		

Subtotal _____

Pre-Reading Features: *Purpose Setting*	Evidence/Comments	Points (1–3)
The chapter begins with a list of objectives, statements, or questions indicating what students will learn.		
Section headings are specific enough that students can convert them to focus questions which direct their reading.		

Subtotal _____

Total points for Section B _____

Name: _____   Date: _____

Content Text Assessment Rubric
(continued)

Section C

Active Reading Features: *Main ideas*	Evidence/Comments	Points (1–3)
Titles of sections within the chapter indicate the main idea of each section.		
The main idea of each paragraph is clearly stated and easy to locate.		

Subtotal _____

Active Reading Features: *Support for Main Ideas*	Evidence/Comments	Points (1–3)
Main idea explanations are thorough.		
Charts, pictures, and other graphics support the main ideas and are appropriately located.		
Interesting details are included to expand on the essential information in the text and to engage students.		

Subtotal _____

Active Reading Features: *Organization of Information*	Evidence/Comments	Points (1–3)
The text is organized logically, so students can easily take notes.		
Signal words are provided to indicate how ideas in the section are related to one another.		
The presentation of main ideas and details is consistent in each chapter.		

Subtotal _____

Name: _____ Date: _____

Content Text Assessment Rubric
(continued)

Section C

Active Reading Features: *Vocabulary Development*	Evidence/Comments	Points (1–3)
Important words/concepts are highlighted in the text (bold, italics, color).		
Important words/concepts are clearly defined or explained within the reading.		
Concrete examples or analogies are included to clarify abstract ideas.		
The author provides more than just a definition (e.g., pictures, examples, analogies, counter examples)		
The number of highlighted vocabulary terms is appropriate for the concepts being explained. (Avoid too much jargon!)		

Subtotal _____

Active Reading Features *Author's Writing/Students' Engagement*	Evidence/Comments	Points (1–3)
The author's style engages students—sentence structure is varied and not overly complex, verbs are mostly in the active voice.		
The author uses imagery and concrete examples to help students visualize information.		

Subtotal _____

Total points for Section C _____

Section D

Post-Reading Features: *Megacognition*	Evidence/Comments	Points (1–3)
The author provides quality questions within and at the end of each chapter. They correlate to the chapter objectives, help students check their understanding as they read, encourage higher order thinking, and promote class or small group discussions.		
The summary accurately reflects the main ideas and key supporting information within the chapter.		

Total points for Section D _____

Name: _____   Date: _____

Content Text Assessment Rubric
(continued)

Section E

Teacher's Guide and other Resources	Evidence/Comments	Points (1–3)
The teacher's guide includes activities for helping students to organize information, to lead their own discussions, and to work in cooperative groups.		

Total points for Section E _____

Section F

Ancillary Materials* for Students	Evidence/Comments	Points
Ancillary materials expand knowledge of content by focusing on essential ideas.		
Ancillary materials meet the varying individual needs of students.		

*Workbooks, blackline masters, skill sheets, CDs, videos, DVDs, multi-level libraries, and primary resource documents

Total points for Section F _____

Total Points Section A =
Total Points Section B =
Total Points Section C =
Total Points Section D =
Total Points Section E =
Total Points Section F =

Total Points for Text
(Possible 84)

Additional Comments:

Reviewed by: _____   Date: _____

Name: _____ Date: _____

Sample Queries

Initiating Queries

What is the author trying to say here?

What is the author's message?

What is the author talking about?

What does the author expect you to know?

Follow-Up Queries

What does the author mean here?

Did the author explain this clearly?

Does this make sense with what the author told us before?

How does this connect with what the author has told us before?

Does the author tell us why?

Why do you think the author tells us this now?

Narrative Queries

How do things look for the character now?

Given what the author has already told us about this character, what is this character thinking now?

How does the author let us know that something has changed?

Name: _____   Date: _____

Discussion Web

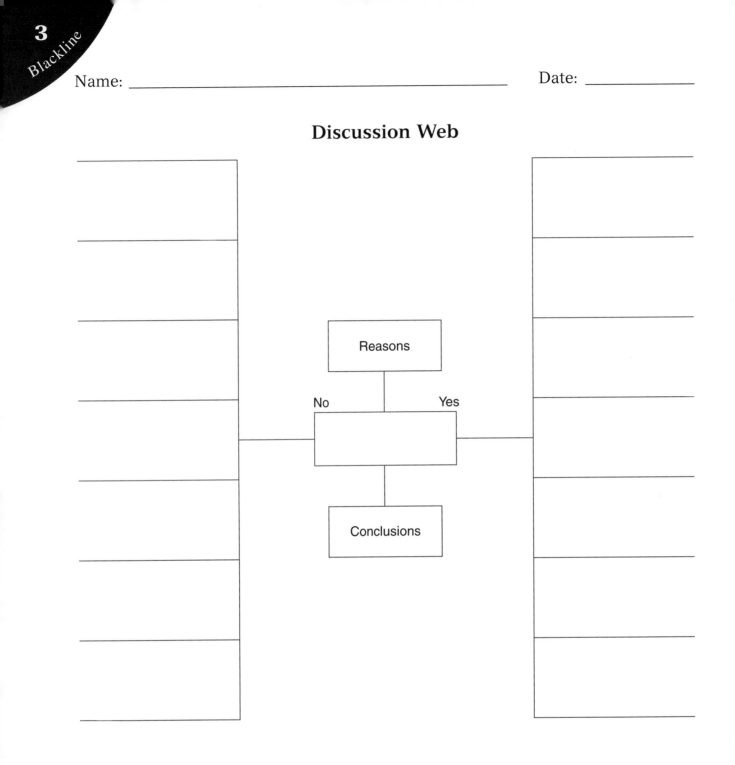

Reasons

No   Yes

Conclusions

Discussion Roles

You will meet at least twice per week in your discussion groups. Each of you will have a specific role in your group. Everyone will get a chance to work in each role at least once. If you don't start in the role you want, be patient—you will get your chance.

Roles: There are five roles for this activity (five students in a group). You will get a chance for each role at least once. The roles are numbered (1–5). Draw numbers to determine your initial roles.

1. **Discussion Director:** Lead the group in discussion of questions either assigned by the teacher or developed by the students in your group. Take notes during the meeting, and make sure that every group member participates in the discussion.

2. **Quote Finder:** Find important and memorable sections and/or quotes to read out loud to the group. Write drown the important passage and the reasons why the passage is important, or mark important passages with sticky notes along with notes about why the passage is important.

3. **Illustrator:** Provide graphic or artistic response to the text through drawings, pictures, or political cartoons. Explain the graphic to the group.

4. **Summarizer:** Prepare a brief, written summary (at least one full paragraph) of the assigned reading. Present the summary to your group for revision.

5. **Vocabulary Expert:** Find and share complicated or important words. Include at least 5 words from the reading and their definitions. Explain how words were used in the text.

The progression of role assignments for succeeding discussions will be as follows:
(1 to 2, 2 to 3, 3 to 4, 4 to 5, 5 to 1)

Grading: You will turn in the work for each role. Every assignment is worth 10 points. I will be checking mainly for completion, but I will deduct points for lack of effort.

Name: _____ Date: _____

Discussion Director

Book: _____ Assignment pp: _____

Facilitator: Your role is to develop questions to help your group get started with the discussion. Write questions that will promote thinking about the selection. Write questions for which you may not have the answers. You may want to use some of the ideas below to develop questions for your group.

Authentic questions

1.

2.

3.

4.

5.

Some ideas:

Where do you feel tension?

What were you feeling when you read?

What do you think is going to happen next?

Was there anything going on in our reading that you didn't really understand?

What have you learned about the setting?

What have you learned about the characters?

Name: _____   Date: _____

Bridge Builder

Book: _____   Assignment pp: _____

Bridge Builder: As you read, think about your family, friends, school, community, and what is happening in the world. What connections can you make between this reading and your own world? What bridges can you build?

How does this reading remind you of other books or stories that you have read? What bridges can you build between this writing and those of other authors or selections written by the same author? There are no wrong answers here.

Name: _____ Date: _____

Seed Maker

Book: _____ Assignment pp: _____

Seed Maker: Your job is to develop two or three discussion seeds. As you read, think about what is important to bring to the group. "Seeds" are your own comments and questions that come to mind as you read. Try to develop strong seeds that will help others think about the selection.

Some possibilities are:

- Comments about things that seem interesting or surprising
- Things in the story that remind you of other things that you have read or events in your life
- Places in the story where you really don't understand what is going on
- Predictions about what you think might happen next

Discussion seeds:

Present one of your seeds to the group. Ask each person in the group to comment on your seed before you talk about it.

Name: _____ Date: _____

Word Detective

Book: _____ Assignment pp: _____

Word Detective: Find two to four words that you think the rest of your group should learn. As you read, put a sticky note by these words. When it is your turn to lead the discussion, have everyone find the word in the selection; then talk about what the word might mean. After your discussion, write down what you think the word means based on its context, and then add information about the word from the dictionary.

	Word	Page	Definition from context	Additional information from dictionary
1.				
2.				
3.				
4.				

Name: _____   Date: _____

Quote Finder

Book: _____   Assignment pp: _____

Quote Finder: Find several passages to read aloud to the group. These selections might be:

- interesting
- well written
- confusing
- funny
- powerful
- surprising

Mark the selections with sticky notes. Read the selections aloud and talk about why you selected them.

Page _____   Why I selected it?

Page _____   Why I selected it?

Page _____   Why I selected it?

Page _____   Why I selected it?

Page _____   Why I selected it?

Page _____   Why I selected it?

Name: _____   Date: _____

Picture Maker

Book: _____   Assignment pp: _____

Picture Maker: After reading, make a quick picture about the reading. This could be a cartoon, a sketch, a scene, a flow chart, a stick figure or a diagram. The drawing might be about a character, setting, problem, tension, prediction, surprise, or whatever strikes you as noteworthy. You might even want to add some words to your drawing.

Show your picture to the others in your group. Ask them what they think it might mean. After everyone has had a chance to talk, tell them what you think.

Name: _____   Date: _____

QUESTION-ANSWER RELATIONSHIPS - 4 Types of Questions

In the Book QARs

Right There
The answer is in the text, usually easy to find. The words used to make up the question and words used to answer the question are *Right There* in the same sentence.

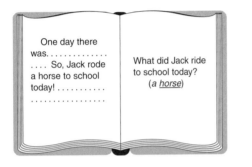

One day there was. . . . . So, Jack rode a horse to school today! . . . .

What did Jack ride to school today? (*a horse*)

In My Head QARs

Author and You
The answer it <u>not</u> in the story. You need to think about what you already know, what the author tells you in the text, and how it fits together.

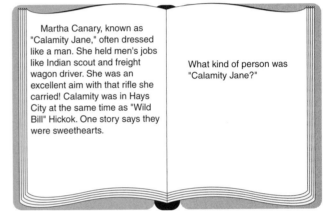

Martha Canary, known as "Calamity Jane," often dressed like a man. She held men's jobs like Indian scout and freight wagon driver. She was an excellent aim with that rifle she carried! Calamity was in Hays City at the same time as "Wild Bill" Hickok. One story says they were sweethearts.

What kind of person was "Calamity Jane?"

Think and Search (Putting It Together)
The answer is in the selection, but you need to put together different pieces of information to find it. Words for the question and words for the answer are not found in the same sentence. They come from different places in the selection.

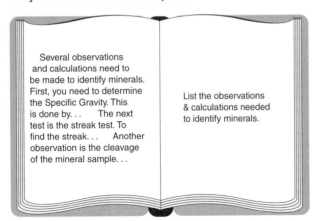

Several observations and calculations need to be made to identify minerals. First, you need to determine the Specific Gravity. This is done by. . .   The next test is the streak test. To find the streak. . .   Another observation is the cleavage of the mineral sample. . .

List the observations & calculations needed to identify minerals.

On My Own
The answer is not in the selection. You can even answer the question without reading the selection. You need to use your own experience. Use your prior knowledge.

Before a unit on Martin Luther King. . .

What are the traits of a great leader?

Question Starters & Frames for Higher-Level Questions

Recall: *who, what, list, repeat, identify, name, when, define*

What is _____ ?

Define _____ .

Identify the _____ .

Who did _____ ?

Analysis: *summarize, categorize, divide, separate*

What is the main idea of _____ ?

List the main events of _____ .

What are the parts of a _____ ?

What is the topic of _____ ?

Comparison: *differentiate, compare, contrast*

Compare _____X_____ to _____Y_____ . In what ways are they similar?

How does _____X_____ differ from _____Y_____ ?

Inference: *predict, conclude, what if, anticipate, infer*

What do you think will happen next in _____ ?

What do you conclude about _____ ?

Predict what _____ will do.

What would happen if _____ ?

Evaluation: *judge, defend, prove, assess, evaluate*

What is your opinion of _____ ?

What is the best solution to the problem of _____ ?

Evaluate the writing of _____ .

Defend your opinion about _____ .

Name: _____   Date: _____

K-W-L Chart

What I **K**now	What I **W**ant to Know	What I **L**earned

Categories of Information:

Name: _____ Date: _____

Venn Diagram

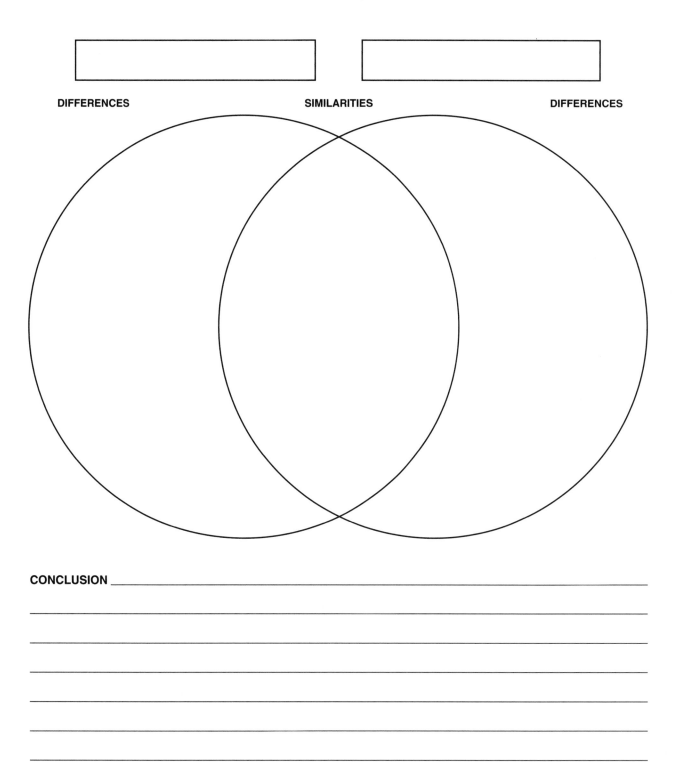

DIFFERENCES   SIMILARITIES   DIFFERENCES

CONCLUSION _____

_____

_____

_____

_____

_____

_____

Name: _____ Date: _____

Contrast & Compare Chart

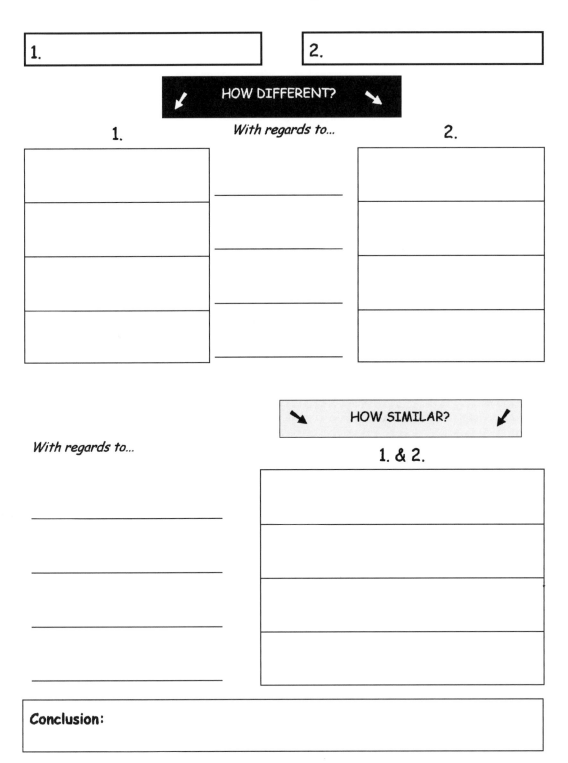

1. |

2. |

HOW DIFFERENT?

1.

With regards to...

2.

HOW SIMILAR?

With regards to...

1. & 2.

Conclusion:

Name: _____   Date: _____

Triangular Comparison Diagram

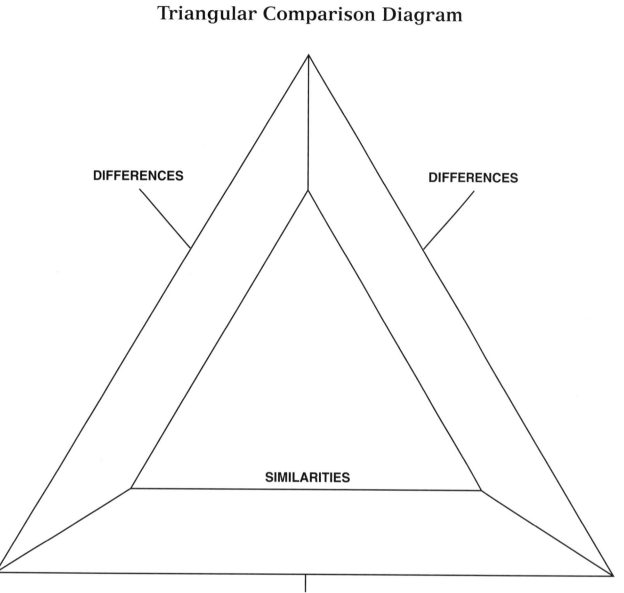

Name: _____   Date: _____

One-Sentence Summary Frames for Common Text Structures

Description   1. A _____ is a kind of _____ that . . .

Compare/
Contrast   2. _____x_____ and _____y_____ are similar
in that they both . . . , but _____x_____ . . . , while
_____y_____ . . . .

Sequence   3. _____ begins with . . . , continues with . . . , and
ends with . . .

Problem/
Solution   4. _____ wanted . . . , but . . . , so . . . .

Cause/
Effect   5. _____ happens because . . . .
_____ causes . . . .

Name: _____   Date: _____

Problem Analysis

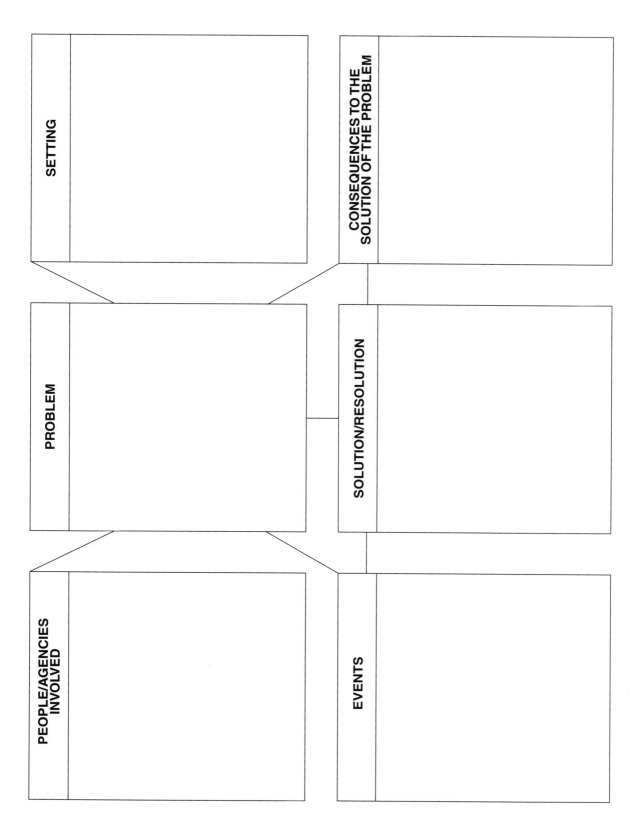

SETTING

CONSEQUENCES TO THE
SOLUTION OF THE PROBLEM

PROBLEM

SOLUTION/RESOLUTION

PEOPLE/AGENCIES
INVOLVED

EVENTS

Name: _____ Date: _____

Problem-Solution Graphic Structure

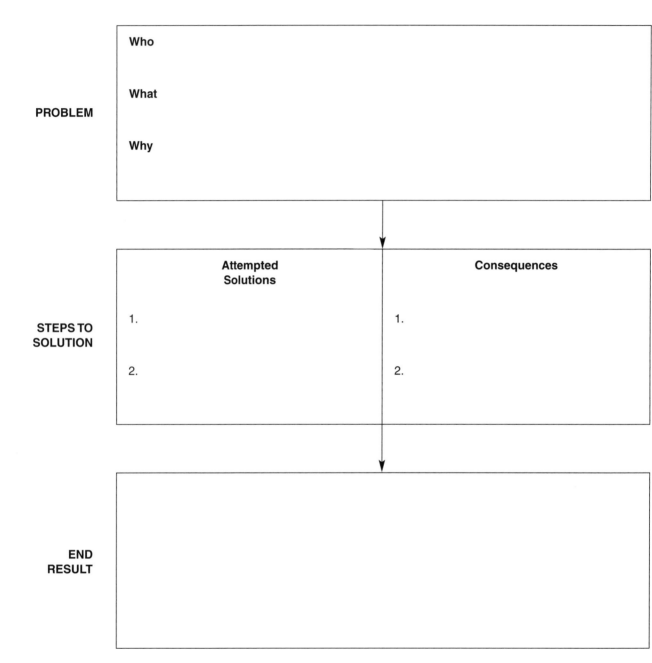

PROBLEM

Who

What

Why

STEPS TO SOLUTION

Attempted
Solutions

1.

2.

Consequences

1.

2.

END RESULT

Word Problem Process Notes

Write the question.	
List clue words and facts.	
Identify the variable(s).	
Make a drawing.	
Choose a strategy.	
Solve the problem.	
Write your answer in a complete sentence that answers the question.	

Checks:
    Credibility (Does your answer make sense?)
 	
    Mathematical	

Name: _____   Date: _____

Problem-Solving Organizer

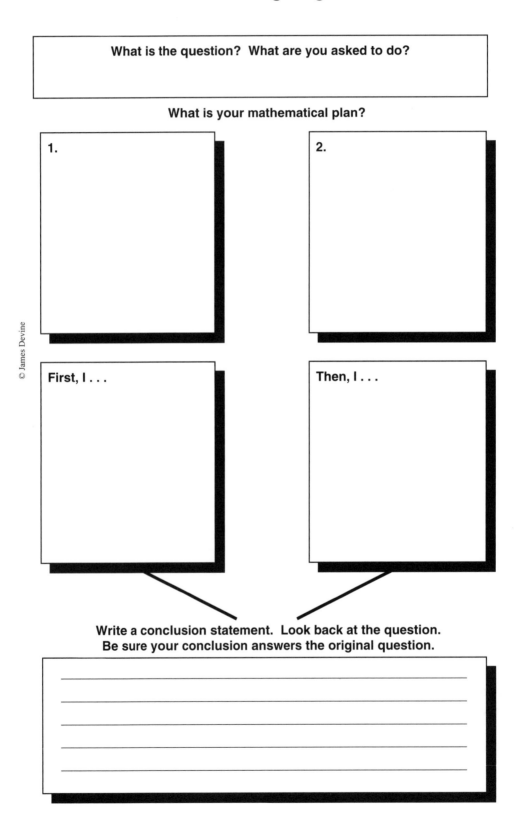

What is the question? What are you asked to do?

What is your mathematical plan?

1.

2.

First, I . . .

Then, I . . .

Write a conclusion statement. Look back at the question.
Be sure your conclusion answers the original question.

© James Devine

Advanced Problem-Solving Organizer

THINK - What is the question? What are you being asked to do? Rewrite the question.

SOLVE - What is your mathematical plan? Show your work.

Step 1	Step 2	Step 3

EXPLAIN - What was your thought process? How did you solve the problem?

First, I...	Then, I...	And finally, I...

WRITE a conclusion. Make sure your conclusion answers the original question.

_____

_____

_____

_____

_____

_____

Developed by James Devine. Adapted by Crown Region ACEE.

Name: _____ Date: _____

Story Plan

Setting

Characters

Problem

Goal

Events

Resolution

Name: _____   Date: _____

Transitions

1. Continuation signals (*Warning—there are more ideas to come.*):

and	again	a final reason	last of all
moreover	other	too	also
and finally	furthermore	likewise	next
secondly	with	another	first of all
in addition	more	one reason	similarly

2. Change-of-direction signals (*Watch out—we're doubling back.*):

although	despite	however	in spite of
the opposite	rather	while	but
different from	in contrast	nevertheless	on the contrary
still	though	conversely	even though
instead of	otherwise	on the other hand	yet

3. Sequence signals (*There is an order to these ideas.*):

first, second, third	into (far into the night)	then	since
after	later	last	for one thing
next	now	while	until
during	always	before	earlier
in the first place			

4. Illustration signals (*Here's what the principle means in reality.*):

for example	for instance	such as	in the same way as
specifically	to illustrate	much like	similar to

Name: _____   Date: _____

Transitions (continued)

5. Emphasis signals (*This is important.*):

major development	the chief outcome	the basic concern
key feature	significant factor	the principal item
central issue	major event	primary concern
especially important	distinctive quality	above all
important to note	especially relevant	most of all
most noteworthy	it all boils down to	pay particular attention to
remember that	more than anything else	the crux of the matter
the main value	should be noted	

6. Conclusion signals (*This ends the discussion and may have special importance.*):

as a result	from this we see	hence	consequently
in conclusion	last of all	finally	in summary
therefore			

7. Cause, condition, or result signals (*Condition or modification coming.*):

because	for	while	that
as	so that	yet	resulting from
if	from	then	until
whether	therefore	thus	consequently
of	so	but	since
in order that	unless	due to	

8. Comparison-contrast signals (*We will now compare Idea A with Idea B.*):

and	too	either	more than
even	much as	but	yet
opposite	though	or	best
less	same	then	like
different from	however	rather	also
most	less than	better	while
analogous to	still	although	

Categories of Leads

- **Typical:** Yesterday, Mom and I went to the pet store for rabbit food. We saw a box holding puppies. We went over to the box and I started to play with them. There was this one puppy that was so cute. I wanted her.

- **Action:** I slammed the car door and ran into the pet shop to buy rabbit food. I grabbed a box of rabbit pellets and then stopped in my tracks. I knelt down by a box of cocker spaniel puppies. The tiniest one waddled over to my hand and started to lick my fingers.

- **Dialogue:** I was sitting in my bedroom listening to the radio when I heard Mom's voice. "Laura, I'm going to the pet shop. We need rabbit food. Wanna come with me?"

  "Yes," I hollered back.

  Soon, Mom and I were in my favorite store, Noah's Bark. It was then that I saw the puppies.

  "Oh, Mom, look at these puppies. Look how this little black one is nibbling my fingers."

  "They are so cute," my mom answered as she picked up the black puppy and held it in her arms. "I suppose you want this puppy,"

  "Mom, you are kidding me, aren't you? I thought you hated dogs."

- **Reaction:** (a character thinking) I couldn't imagine where Mom and I were going. She just told me to get into the car without any explanation. Why does she have this little smile on her face? Why is Mom behaving so strangely? Why are we stopping in front of my favorite pet store, Noah's Bark?

Additional categories:

- **Setting the mood:** It was almost December, and Jonas was beginning to be frightened. No. Wrong word, Jonas thought. Frightened meant that deep, sickening feeling of something terrible about to happen. Frightened was the way he had felt a year ago when an unidentified aircraft had overflown the community twice. — Lois Lowry, *The Giver.*

- **Amazing facts:** Try to imagine a star so big that it would fill all of the solar system within the orbit of Earth, which is 93 million miles from the sun. A star so turbulent that its eruptions would spread a cloud of gases spanning four light-years, the distance from the sun to the nearest star. A star so powerful that it glows with the energy of 10 million suns, making the brightest ever observed in our galaxy, the Milky Way. — John Noble Wilford, *At the Core of the Milky Way, the Brightest Star Ever Seen.*

- **Spoken Words:** "Your father has met with an accident." Avi, *The Barn*

  It was my first morning in high school. I have seven notebooks, a skirt I hate, and stomachache. — Laurie Halse Anderson, *Speak*

- **Presenting a question.** Have you ever imagined what it would be like to play in the NBA? To glide down the court, matching strides with the greatest basketball player in the world? To hear the roar of the crowd as you throw down a dunk, or swat an opponent's shot into the bleachers? It's every kid's dream.

  And for the fortunate few who make it to the NBA, it's a dream come true.

  — Joseph Layden and James Preller, *NBC Game Day*

Name: _____ Date: _____

Spool Paper Planning Sheet

Introductory Paragraph

Lead

Thesis statement (Power 1):

List the Power 2 ideas:

2a.

2b.

2c.

Body

2a. Topic sentence

    3. Detail sentence

    3. Detail sentence

    3. Detail sentence

2b. Topic sentence

    3. Detail sentence

    3. Detail sentence

    3. Detail sentence

2c. Topic sentence

    3. Detail sentence

    3. Detail sentence

    3. Detail sentence

Concluding Paragraph

Restate the thesis using different words (Power 1):

Wind-down/conclusion

Name: _____ Date: _____

RAFT

Roles / Audiences

ad agencies	ecologists	politicians	historical figures
athletes	editors	movie stars	TV characters
cartoonist	historians	older/younger students	poets
characters in stories/novels	homesteaders	radio announcer	
	lawyers	animals	

Format

advertisement	editorial	news story	riddle
apology	epitaph	obituary	sermon
application	eulogy	pamphlet	ship's log
cartoon	graffiti	petition	slide show script
bumper sticker	interview	photo essay	slogan
commercial	invitation	poetry	telegram
complaint	joke	poster	travelogue
confession	journal or diary	radio play	TV script
conversations and dialogues	legal brief	recommendation	video
	letter to the editor	resume	wanted poster
dramatic monologue	marriage proposal	review	warning
			will

Verbs

admonish	demand	grumble	resign
accuse	deny	guide	reward
advise	disagree	harass	satirize
apologize	discourage	honor	scare
attack	emphasize	identify	sell
beg	evaluate	inquire	shock
blame	encourage	interpret	tattle
boast	entertain	justify	taunt
clarify	excite	laud	teach
complain	excuse	notify	tease
condemn	explain	pacify	testify
confide	flatter	proclaim	urge
congratulate	flaunt	pester	warn
convince	forbid	plead	welcome
dazzle	foretell	prod	woo
defend	formulate	protest	yield

Name: _____ Date: _____

Concept of Definition Map

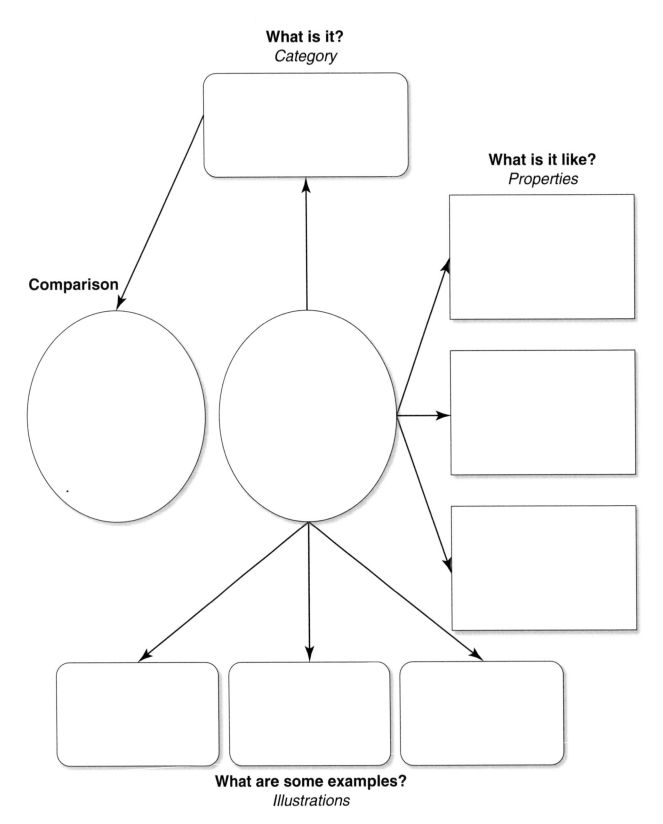

What is it?
Category

What is it like?
Properties

Comparison

What are some examples?
Illustrations

Name: _____ Date: _____

Frayer Model

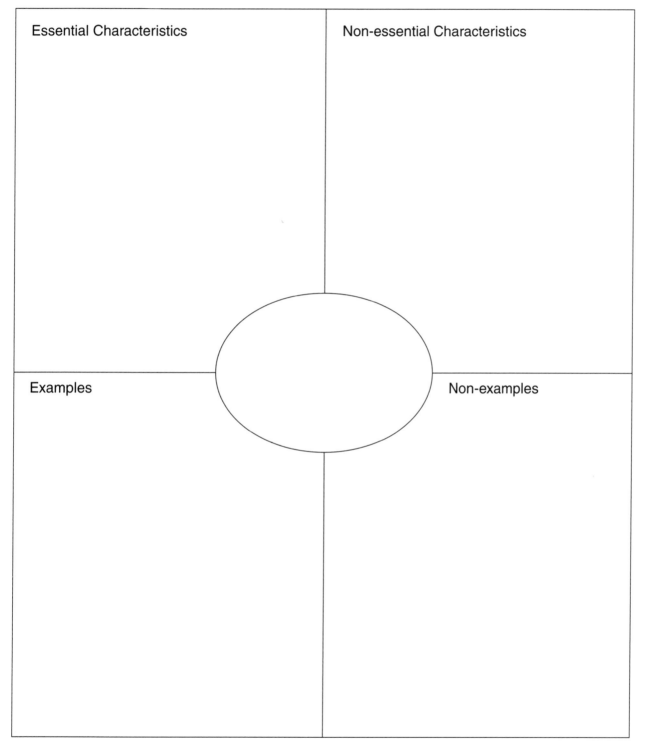

| Essential Characteristics | Non-essential Characteristics |
| Examples | Non-examples |

(Frayer, Frederick, & Klausmeier, 1969)

Classroom Strategies for Interactive Learning, 2nd Ed., by Doug Buehl (c)2001. Newark, DE: International Reading Association. May be copied for classroom use.

Name: _____ Date: _____

Semantic Feature Analysis

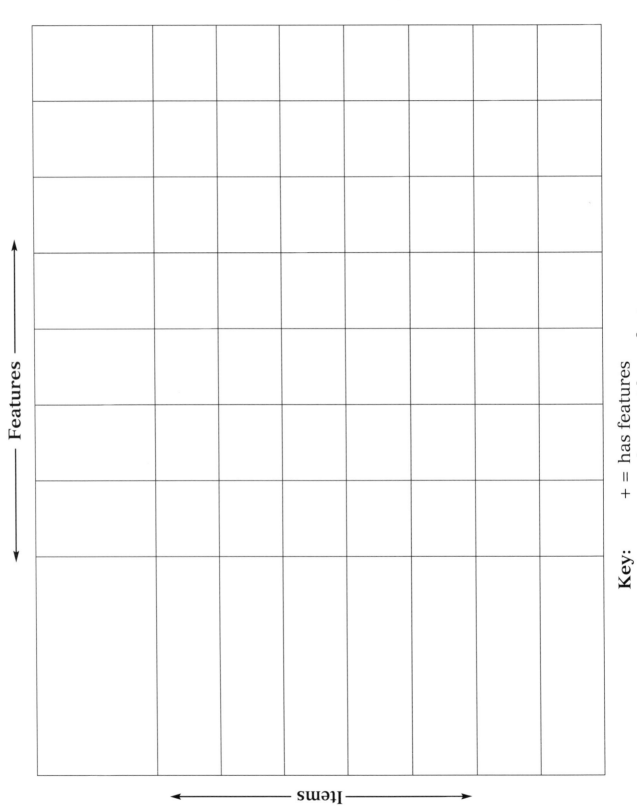

Features

Items

Key:

+ = has features
− = does not have feature
0 = no relationship, not applicable

Five Star School Evaluation Plan

Criteria for Five Star School	Where are you now?	What are your next steps?
Workshop Participation		
1. 100 percent of the teachers have participated in a CRISS^SM Level I workshop.	1.	1.
2. 100 percent of the administrators have participated in a CRISS^SM Level I workshop.	2.	2.
3. At least one staff member has participated in a CRISS^SM Level II workshop and completed the rest of the requirements to become a certified CRISS^SM trainer.	3.	3.
Follow-up		
4. The school provides regularly scheduled follow-up to all trained teachers. This follow-up should include . . . • *group support* through meetings before or after school, during planning periods, or during scheduled in-service days, etc. and • *individual support* through conferences, peer review, certified CRISS^SM trainer modeling and guidance, etc.	4.	4.

Name: _____   Date: _____

Five Star School Evaluation Plan (continued)

Criteria for Five Star School	Where are you now?	What are your next steps?
On-site Certified CRISS[SM] Trainer 5. School or district has at least one on-site certified CRISS[SM] trainer who . . . • provides Level I workshops for building/district staff as needed using a format that fits with individual and district needs. • keeps current with CRISS[SM] and learning strategies through conferences, newsletters, electronic communication, and reading professional literature. • uses CRISS[SM] daily in own classroom. Or, if the Trainer does not have a classroom, she or he has opportunities to model CRISS[SM] strategies in classrooms taught by other teachers. • encourages teacher research. • disseminates professional articles to teachers and arranges opportunities for professional discussion. • coordinates/facilitates follow-up opportunities. • facilitates parent workshops.	5.	5.

Name: _____   Date: _____

Five Star School Evaluation Plan (continued)

Criteria for Five Star School	Where are you now?	What are your next steps?
Administrator's Role 6. All school administrators have been CRISS^{SM} trained and they . . . • use CRISS^{SM} as a basis for classroom walk-throughs. • support CRISS^{SM} by providing opportunities for teachers to collaborate with each other. • look for evidence of CRISS^{SM} in lesson plans. • incorporate CRISS^{SM} into teacher-parent meetings, staff meetings, school board presentations, and other school and district communications. • promote and attend CRISS^{SM} for Parents workshops. • include CRISS^{SM} as part of the school or district professional development plan.	6.	6.
Teacher's Role 7. All teachers have been CRISS^{SM} trained and they . . . • effectively implement the CRISS^{SM} Principles, Philosophy, and strategies as evidenced by: • the teacher Pre-/Post-Training Surveys, • self-assessment through use of the Level of Use Matrix, and • observational data gathered by the administrator's classroom walk-throughs. • include CRISS^{SM} principles and strategies throughout their CRISS^{SM} Strategic Learning Plans (planning, implementation, and assessment). • use teacher research projects to guide their instruction.	7.	7.

Name: _____   Date: _____

Five Star School Evaluation Plan (continued)

Criteria for Five Star School	Where are you now?	What are your next steps?
Student's Role 8. The student has ownership of the CRISS^SM principles, philosophy, and strategies as evidenced by . . . • the inclusion of CRISS^SM as a variable in comparing student performances on state assessments. • data collected on student use of principles and strategies by the Student Pre-/Post-CRISS^SM Survey and/or other forms of qualitative research.	8.	8.
Assessment 9. The school continually assesses the appropriateness and effectiveness of the Project CRISS^SM program by . . . • correlating the CRISS^SM principles and strategies with the state curriculum frameworks. • integrating CRISS^SM principles and strategies into the school district's curriculum (content standards). • developing an overall assessment plan which includes CRISS^SM as a component.	9.	9.

Name: _____ Date: _____

Teacher *Pre-CRISS*^{SM} Survey

School: _____ Grade(s): _____

Class(es): _____

Please circle the number to the right of the statement which best describes your teaching BEFORE you took CRISS^{SM} training.

	Never	Rarely	Sometimes	Usually	Always
1. I provide students direct instruction in generating background knowledge about a topic or concept before reading or learning about it.	1	2	3	4	5
2. I help students set goals and determine a purpose before a reading or learning activity.	1	2	3	4	5
3. My students use the author's style and organizational clues (titles, introductory statements and paragraphs, bold print, italicized words, and summary statements) to help them understand a reading assignment.	1	2	3	4	5
4. I teach a variety of organizational strategies to help my students understand and remember information.	1	2	3	4	5

In the box to the right, check the strategies your students use. Below, please show or name other strategies they use:

Organizing Strategies:
a. ☐ Content Frames
b. ☐ K-W-L or K-W-L Plus
c. ☐ Mapping (power, picture, etc.)
d. ☐ Conclusion-Support Notes
e. ☐ Power Notes
f. ☐ Problem-Solution Notes
g. ☐ Selective Underlining
h. ☐ Sticky Notes
i. ☐ Story Plans
j. ☐ Two-Column Notes
k. ☐ Venn Diagram
l. ☐ Word Maps

Name: _____   Date: _____

Teacher *Pre-CRISS*^{SM} Survey (continued)

	Never	Rarely	Sometimes	Usually	Always
5. I help my students become metacognitive. They are aware when they don't understand, and they know what to do to gain understanding.	1	2	3	4	5
6. I provide opportunities for students to discuss in pairs and groups, what they are learning.	1	2	3	4	5
7. I expected my students to write in journals and/or learning logs about what and how they learn.	1	2	3	4	5
8. I teach a variety of organizational formats to help students with their formal writing assignments. *In the box to the right, check the strategies that your students use. Below, please show or name other strategies they use:*	1	2	3	4	5

> **Organizing Strategies for Writing:**
> a. ☐ Mapping (power, picture, etc.)
> b. ☐ Conclusion-Support Notes
> c. ☐ Power Notes
> d. ☐ Spool Paper organizer
> e. ☐ Story Plans
> f. ☐ Venn Diagram
> g. ☐ Word Maps

9. I teach students a variety of ways to learn vocabulary concepts (rather than memorizing definitions). *In the box to the right, check the strategies that your students use. Below, please show or name other strategies they use:*	1	2	3	4	5

> **Vocabulary Strategies**
> a. ☐ draw a picture f. ☐ list examples
> b. ☐ list synonyms g. ☐ list antonyms
> c. ☐ write the word in a sentence
> d. ☐ use the word in discussions
> e. ☐ make word maps

10. I model learning strategies until students can do them on their own.	1	2	3	4	5
11. When I return students' assignments and tests, I give them opportunities to talk and think about how they learn and how they might improve.	1	2	3	4	5
12. My students know how to read, learn, and remember the important information without my help.	1	2	3	4	5

Name: _____   Date: _____

Level of Use Matrix

Component	Ideal	Acceptable	Unacceptable
1. **Student background knowledge** **Strategies:** *Brainstorming, K-W-L, think-pair-share, writing, drawing pictures*	Before reading, students know to activate their own prior knowledge. In addition, they skim or preview classroom materials to set purposes for their learning before reading.	The teacher helps students remember their background knowledge by asking questions or by having them write or discuss what they already know. The teacher helps the students develop a purpose for reading.	The teacher does not provide opportunities for students to elicit their prior knowledge, or the teacher tells students the background knowledge they need. The teacher does not provide any purpose or focus for reading.
2. **Student knowledge of author's craft and text structure** **Strategies:** *Think alouds, selective underlining of text*	The student is aware of the author's style of writing and is able to use it to determine how information is presented, how main ideas are illustrated, and how vocabulary is defined. Students are able to use the author's craft to determine appropriate background knowledge and the focus or purpose for reading.	The teacher models how to determine the author's style by reading classroom materials and thinking out loud. The teacher talks about headings and subheadings; bold, italicized, and colored print; the location of main ideas and details in paragraphs; vocabulary and concept development; and any special features like illustrations, questions, or marginal notes. The teacher demonstrates how these features can be used to facilitate learning and note taking.	The teacher does not discuss text features or model how to use those features to facilitate learning and/or note taking.

Name: _____   Date: _____

Level of Use Matrix (continued)

Component	Ideal	Acceptable	Unacceptable
3. Active strategies for student learning **Strategies:** *K-W-L, instructional conversations, writing (formal or informal), summarizing, note taking, mapping, reciprocal teaching*	All students are actively involved, transforming content information through a variety of writing, discussing, organizing, and/or reorganizing strategies of their choice. The teacher acts as a facilitator, providing assistance in setting up an activity, then only getting involved when additional help is required by the students.	The teacher provides opportunities for students to be actively involved, but not *all* students are involved. The teacher provides transformational formats (writing, note taking, or discussing) for students to use that allow for a variety of high-level thinking responses.	The teacher stays in control of the classroom. Students only talk when called on by the teacher. Student comments are evaluated by the teacher. Writing, discussing, and notetaking formats are all provided by the teacher, and require only factual information to be filled in by students.
4. Student metacognition **Strategies:** *Process conferences, writing, discussion with elaboration of ideas, teacher and student modeling (think alouds)*	Students are familiar with the concept of metacognition. Teacher-student or student-student process conferences occur frequently after learning activities and/or strategy use. Both the teacher and students talk about their learning successes and failures. The use of multiple resources for learning (texts, literature, films, technology, field trips, speakers, labs) is emphasized along with "real world" applications of learned information and processes.	The teacher periodically holds process conferences to have students talk about their methods of learning. The teacher provides opportunities for students to become metacognitive through writing and discussing. The teacher allows students to be flexible with strategy use.	The teacher and students do not talk about the process of learning.

Name: _____   Date: _____

Level of Use Matrix (continued)

Component	Ideal	Acceptable	Unacceptable
5. Student use a variety of transformational or organizational strategies **Strategies:** *Power notes, concept or picture mapping, two-column notes (main idea-detail, conclusion-support, problem-solution, process), content frames, story plans, pattern puzzles*	Students use a variety of transformational strategies of their own choice. Students monitor their learning and use more than one strategy to gain comprehension.	The teacher guides the use of organizational strategies, yet allows students to modify the strategy or use an alternative format if that better meets their learning needs. The teacher incorporates a variety of strategies throughout the school year.	The teacher provides students with notes from text or partial notes, which students supplement with missing factual information. The teacher dictates the type of organizational format that students must use and does not allow modification.
6. Students' involvement in instructional conversations **Strategies:** *Think-pair-share, focused discussion, sticky-note discussion, read-and-say-something, seed discussions, Question Answer Relationship (QARs), etc.*	Students frequently participate in instructional conversations (IC) with the whole class or in small groups. With ICs, students discuss a teacher or student generated prompt. They respond to one another, support or refute statements with evidence, and encourage each speaker to elaborate on his or her ideas.	The teacher uses ICs more often in a discussion situation than the more traditional *teacher question/student answer/teacher evaluation* "discussion" format. The teacher encourages students to respond to each other and elaborate on or clarify their answers.	The teacher only uses the question/answer/evaluation format for discussions.

CRISS℠ Manual **317** ◀

Name: _____ Date: _____

Level of Use Matrix (continued)

Component	Ideal	Acceptable	Unacceptable
7. Writing to learn—informal and formal formats **Strategies:** *INFORMAL- learning log entries such as free writes, dialogue, pre- and post-reading response, observation, perspective, explanation* *FORMAL-writing templates, spool paper, RAFT*	Students incorporate informal writing into their regular routine for learning. The teacher provides *regular* opportunities for students to write for both graded and non-graded situations. For formal papers, the teacher makes sure students know the purpose, format options, and teacher expectations before writing. Students *plan* before doing any formal writing by using an organizational format.	The teacher provides opportunities for students to write both in graded and non-graded situations. The teacher models various types of writing and provides opportunities to use writing as part of learning.	The teacher provides few, if any, opportunities for student writing. Writing expectations are not clear, and various formats are not modeled before being assigned.
8. Student use of vocabulary strategies **Strategies:** *Vocabulary Map, semantic feature analysis, word combining, frayer model, concept of definition map, sentence and word expansion, word elaboration*	Students skim content material and pick out words/concepts they do not know. To learn the unknown terms, students use strategies that work best for them—including a combination of mapping, writing, and discussing. Students monitor their understanding and use additional strategies if comprehension is not complete.	The teacher selects vocabulary concepts that are critical to understanding the content. Those terms are presented in the context of the topic. The teacher guides students to understanding the terms by using a variety of strategies that incorporate mapping, writing, and discussing.	In order to learn vocabulary concepts, the teacher has the students learn the definitions as presented in a text, dictionary, or other resource book. The teacher is not selective in choosing vocabulary concepts to learn.

Name: _____ Date: _____

Level of Use Matrix (continued)

Component	Ideal	Acceptable	Unacceptable
9. Teacher modeling during strategy instruction **Strategies:** *Teacher think-alouds*	The teacher introduces the strategy by telling what it is and when and how it is used. Then, the teacher models the strategy using "think alouds" to explain how it is applied to classroom materials. The teacher stresses the connection between the author's craft and the selection of an appropriate strategy. The teacher encourages students to model their strategy applications as well. Eventually, the teacher releases control of the strategy selection to the students, so that they can use the process that works best for them with any given task.	The teacher introduces the strategy by telling what it is and when and how it is used. The teacher always models the strategy application using "think alouds" to explain how it is used with classroom materials. Occasionally, the teacher asks students to share their thinking.	The teacher shows the students a completed or successful strategy application and then expects them to replicate it in a new situation. The teacher actually uses the strategy, but does not think aloud or share with the students HOW the application is achieved.
10. Assessment—teacher/student research **Strategies:** *On-going performance assessment combined with instruction, portfolios*	The teacher incorporates strategy use into the assessment process. For example, students can be evaluated on the organizing strategies used to prepare for essays as well as on their final products. The teacher incorporates the completion of a note-taking format like the Venn diagram or conclusion-support notes into an evaluation tool. Students keep portfolios, which contain samples of their best strategy applications. The teacher and students become researchers, always assessing what works best with any given task and topics.	The teacher incorporates strategy use into the assessment process. Assessment is on-going, not just an end-product.	The teacher uses only objective-type assessments and evaluates only at the end of a unit of study.

CRISS℠ Manual **319**

Name: _____ Date: _____

CRISS^{SM} Learning Plan

Topic/Standard(s): _____

Objective: _____

Assessment: *(objective & performance)* _____

Strategies & How Applied to Content		CRISS^{SM} Principles & Philosophy						
		BK	AI	D	W	O	M	M&E
BEFORE *Prepare*								
DURING *Be Active*								
AFTER *Organize*								
POST *Use, Apply*								

Key to CRISS^{SM} P & P:

BK = Background Knowledge
AI = Active Involvement
D = Discussion

W = Writing
O = Organization
M = Metacognition

M&E = Modeling & Explanation

Name: _____ Date: _____

CRISS^{SM} Learning Plan (continued)
Review & Reflection Sheet

As you *develop* your Learning Plan, consider:

1. Alignment with content and performance standards (District, State, etc.).

2. Objectives which represent the "Big Picture"—ideas which have value beyond the classroom.

3. Strategies/content which will achieve the desired outcomes.

4. Strategy implementation-Where are students in terms of strategy application? Do they need an introduction, modeling, guided practice, or are they at the independent stage?

5. Student choice on strategy selection, as appropriate.

6. Multiple and on-going ways to assess students on the desired objectives (performance, objective tests, etc.).

7. A variety of individual, paired, and group activities.

8. Multiple sources of information (reading, viewing, listening).

As you *implement* your Learning Plan, use the following questions to monitor and adjust your instruction.

1. Do students need more/less modeling and guidance with strategy instruction?

2. Do students need more background knowledge to deal with the content—if so, what kind?

3. Do students understand the purpose for reading (viewing, etc.)?

4. Do students need additional opportunities to transform information through discussing, writing, and/or organizing?

After *implementing* your Learning Plan, reflect with your students.
Sample discussion questions:

1. How did you organize the information?

2. Did you assess your learning progress? What strategies worked best for you? Why?

3. Did you evaluate your understanding throughout this lesson?

4. What could you do next time to improve your understanding?

5. How can you apply what you have learned to your own life?

***After implementing* your Learning Plan, evaluate by responding to the following questions:**

1. Did my assessment adequately measure the desired objectives?

2. What could I do to improve my Learning Plan?

3. Did my Learning Plan move students toward increased independence?

Name: _____   Date: _____

CRISS^{SM} Unit/Lesson Plan

Subject: _____   Date: _____   Period(s): _____

Topic: _____   Pages: _____

Materials needed: _____

Content Standards

_____

_____

_____

Purpose Setting

Understandings: *Students will...*

_____

_____

_____

Essential questions that guide and focus teaching and learning:

_____

_____

_____

Assessment

Performance tasks:

_____

_____

_____

Other (quizzes, tests, work samples):

_____

_____

_____

Instructional Strategies
Anticipation Guide
Chapter Survey
Character Mapping
Concept Mapping
Concept of Definition
Conclusion-Support Notes
Content Frames
Contrast and Compare Guide
K-W-L
Learning Logs
One-Sentence Summary
Pattern Puzzles
Picture Mapping
Power Notes
Problem-Solution Notes
QARs
RAFT
Read-and-Say-Something
Reciprocal Teaching
Selective Underlining
Semantic Feature Analysis
Sequence Mapping
Spool Paper
Sticky Notes Discussion
Story Plans
Think-Pair-Share
Two-Column Notes
Venn Diagram
Vocabulary Map
Word Elaboration
Writing Template

Key Elements of Learning

background knowledge (BK)
defining purpose (DP)
understanding the author's craft (AC)
active involvement (AI)
discussion (D)
writing (W)
transforming, organizing information (T)
metacognition (M)

Four Instructional Steps

Introduction
Modeling
Guided Practice
Independent Application

CRISS^{SM} Unit/Lesson Plan (continued)

Instructional Activities:

- Preparing for Understanding

- Integrating Strategies for Understanding

- Checking for Understanding

Name: _____ Date: _____

CRISS^{SM} Unit/Lesson Plan (continued)

Lesson Plan Rubric

Put a check by each item accomplished in this lesson.

_____ I aligned the lesson with performance standards.

_____ I have formulated one or two clearly worded statements, the enduring understandings that represent exactly what I want my students to know.

_____ I determined how I would assess whether my students truly understood the big ideas of the unit.

_____ I introduced, modeled, and gave guided practice before students worked on their own.

_____ My students and I selected instructional strategies to understand the big ideas of the unit. These strategies helped them:

    _____ use their background knowledge.

    _____ organize information.

    _____ discuss key concepts.

    _____ write about their learning.

    _____ monitor their understanding.

_____ I ended my lesson with a process conference where students had opportunities to talk about themselves as strategic learners and what they did in the lesson to learn. Sample discussion questions:

- Did you have a clear understanding of what you would be learning in this unit of study before starting?

- What helped you learn the information?

- What learning strategies worked for you?

- What could you do next time to improve?

- How can you apply what you have learned from this unit to your own life?

CRISS^{SM} Unit/Lesson Plan (continued)

Teacher's Learning Log

Did this lesson plan lead your students to a deep understanding of the material? What evidence do you have to support your conclusion?

Which parts of the lesson were most satisfactory?

Which parts would you change?

Sources: *CReating Independence through Student-owned Strategies,* Dr. Carol Santa *Understanding by Design,* Grant Wiggins and Jay McTighe.

Name: _____ Date: _____

School: _____ Teacher: _____

Subject: _____ Grade: _____ Date: _____

Walk-through Observation Sheet

Level of Student Engagement Count number of non-engaged students	
Alignment with District/State Curriculum **(Level of Understanding)** • Determine assignment or lesson • Materials (single/multiple source/multi-leveled/authentic) • Ask students the content and the purpose of the lesson	
Strategic Use of the CRISS^{SM} Philosophy and Strategies • Key Elements of Learning • Four Instructional Steps • CRISS^{SM} Strategies/Graphic Organizers (Refer to CRISS^{SM}-at-a-Glance)	
Display of Student Work • Walk the walls	
Lesson Plans (Strategic integration of the CRISS^{SM} philosophy and strategies?)	
Nature of Assessment	
Safe Learning Environment • Emotionally Safe • Physically Safe	
Other Comments	

Four Instructional Steps
- Introduction
- Modeling
- Guided Practice
- Independent Application

Key Elements of Learning
- Background Knowledge (BK)
- Defining Purpose (DP)
- Understanding the Author's Craft (AC)
- Active Involvement (AI)
- Discussion (D)
- Writing (W)
- Reorganizing Information (RI)
- Metacognition (M)

Valdez 8/02

Name: _____   Date: _____

Student *Pre-CRISS*^{SM} Survey
Learning Strategies Inventory

Teacher: _____   Grade: _____

Class: _____

a) How long have you been a student at this *school district? (Circle the response below.)*

    less than one year / one to two years / over two years

b) How long have you been at your present *school? (Circle the response below.)*

    less than one year / one to two years / over two years

Please circle the number to the right of the numbered statement which best describes how you feel in this class.

	Never	Rarely	Sometimes	Usually	Always
1. Before reading, I think about what I already know and want to learn about a topic.	1	2	3	4	5
2. Before reading, I know what I am looking for and what I should be taking notes on.	1	2	3	4	5
3. I use organizational clues and the author's style (titles, introductory statements and paragraphs, bold print, italicized words, and summary statements) to help me understand the assignment.	1	2	3	4	5
4. I use a variety of organizational strategies to help me understand and remember information.	1	2	3	4	5

In the box to the right, check the strategies which you use. Below, please show or name other strategies you use:

Organizing Strategies:
a. ☐ Conclusion-Support Notes
b. ☐ Content Frames
c. ☐ K-W-L or K-W-L Plus
d. ☐ Mapping (power, free-form, etc.)
e. ☐ Power Notes
f. ☐ Problem-Solution Notes
g. ☐ Selective Underlining
h. ☐ Sticky Notes
i. ☐ Story Plans
j. ☐ Two-Column Notes
k. ☐ Venn Diagram
l. ☐ Word Maps

Name: _____   Date: _____

Student *Pre-CRISS*^{SM} Survey (continued)

	Never	Rarely	Sometimes	Usually	Always
5. When I don't understand, I know what to do to help me learn.	1	2	3	4	5
6. I have the opportunity to discuss, in pairs and groups, what I am learning.	1	2	3	4	5
7. I write about what and how I am learning in journals and/or learning logs.	1	2	3	4	5
8. I plan before doing any formal writing by putting information into an organizational format. *In the box to the right, check the strategies which you use. Below, please show or name other strategies you use:*	1	2	3	4	5

Organizing Strategies for Writing:
a. ☐ Conclusion-Support Notes
b. ☐ Mapping (power, free-form, etc.)
c. ☐ Power Notes
d. ☐ Spool Paper organizer
e. ☐ Story Plans
f. ☐ Venn Diagram
g. ☐ Word Maps

9. To learn new vocabulary, I do more than just copying the words and memorizing the definitions. *In the box to the right, check the strategies which you use. Below, please show or name other strategies you use:*	1	2	3	4	5

Vocabulary Strategies
a. ☐ draw a picture   f. ☐ list examples
b. ☐ list synonyms   g. ☐ list antonyms
c. ☐ write the word in a sentence
d. ☐ use the word in discussions
e. ☐ make word maps

	Never	Rarely	Sometimes	Usually	Always
10. I learn a variety of learning strategies by watching my teachers demonstrate them.	1	2	3	4	5
11. When assignments and tests are returned, I think about how I studied and how I could improve.	1	2	3	4	5
12. When given a reading assignment, I know how to read, learn, and remember the important information without my teacher's help.	1	2	3	4	5

BIBLIOGRAPHY

Almasi, J. 1995. The nature of fourth graders' sociocognitive conflicts in peer-led and teacher-led discussions of literature. *Reading Research Quarterly,* 30 (3):314–351.

Alvermann, D. 1991. The discussion web: a graphic aid for learning across the curriculum. *The Reading Teacher.* 45:92–99.

Anders, P. and C. Boss. 1986. Semantic feature analysis: an interactive strategy for vocabulary development and text comprehension. *Journal of Reading,* 29:610–616.

Anderson, R. C. and J. W. Pichert. 1978. Recall of previously unrecallable information following shift in perspective. *Journal of Verbal Learning and Verbal Behavior,* 17:1–12.

Atwell, N. 1998. *In the Middle: New Understandings about Writing, Reading, and Learning.* NH: Boynton/Cook.

Bauman, J. 1986. Effect of rewritten textbook passes on middle-grade students' comprehension of main ideas: making the inconsiderate considerate. *Journal of Reading Behavior.* 18:1–22.

Bauman, J. 1988. Direct instruction reconsidered. *Journal of Reading.* 31:712–733.

Beck, I., M. McKeown, and J. Worthy. 1995. Giving a text voice can improve students' understanding. *Reading Research Quarterly,* 30:220–238.

Blachowicz, C. and P. Fisher. Vocabulary instruction. In M. Kamil, P. Mosenthal, P. D. Pearson, R. Barr (Eds.), *Handbook of Reading Research,* Vol III. 503–523.

Blachowicz, C. and D. Ogle. 2001. *Reading comprehension: strategies for independent learners.* New York, NY: Guilford Press.

Bos. C. S. and P.L. Anders. 1990. Effects of interactive vocabulary instruction on the vocabulary learning and reading comprehension of junior-high learning disabled students. *Learning Disability Quarterly,* 13: 31–42.

Bos, C. and P.L. Anders. 1992. Using interactive teaching and learning strategies to promote text comprehension and content learning for students with learning disabilities. *International Journal of Disability, Development and Education,* 39: 225–238.

Buehl, D. 2001. *Classroom Strategies for Interactive Learning.* Newark, DE: International Reading Association.

Calkins, L. 1994. *The Art of Teaching Writing.* Portsmouth, NH: Heinemann.

Carr, E., and M. Mazur-Stewart. 1988. The effects of the vocabulary overview guide on vocabulary comprehension and retention. *Journal of Reading Behavior.* 20: 43–62.

Dole, J., C. Sloan, and W. Trathen. 1995. Teaching vocabulary within the context of literature. *Journal of Reading.* 38: 452–460.

Duke, N. and P.D. Pearson. 2002. Effective practices for developing reading comprehension. In A. Farstrup and J. Samuels. *What Research has to say about reading instruction* (pp. 205–242). Newark, DE: International Reading Association.

Duffelmeyer, F. 1980. The influence of experienced-based vocabulary instruction on learning word meanings. *Journal of Reading.* 24: 35–40.

Gambrell, L. 1996. What research reveals about discussion. In L. B. Gambrell and J. F. Almasi (Eds.) *Living discussions!: Fostering engaged reading* (pp. 25–38) Newark, DE: International Reading Association.

Gambrell, L. and P. Koskinen, P. 2002. Imagery: A strategy for enhancing comprehension. In C. Block and M. Pressley. *Comprehension Instruction: Research-based practices.* 305–318. NY: Guilford Press.

Gardner, R. and M. Gillingham, M., and J. White. 1989. Effects of "seductive details" on macroprocessing and microprocessing in adults and children. *Cognitive and Instruction.* 6:41–57.

Goldenberg, C. 1994 Instructional conversations: promoting comprehension through discussion. *Reading Teacher.* 46 (4):316–326.

Goldman S. and J. Rakestraw. 2000. Structural aspects of constructing meaning from text. In M. Kamil, P. Mosenthal, P. D. Pearson, R. Barr (Eds.), *Handbook of Reading Research,* Vol III: 311–335. NJ: Lawrence Erlbaum Associates.

Graves, D. H. 1994. *A Fresh Look at Writing.* NH: Heinemann.

Harp, S. and R. Mayer. 1997. The role of interest in learning from scientific text and illustrations: on the distinction between emotional interest and cognitive interest. *Journal of Educational Psychology.* 89:92–102.

Holliday, W. 1991. Helping students learn effectively from text. In C. Santa and D. Alvermann (Eds.), *Science Learning: Processes and Applications.* DE: International Reading Association.

Jensen, E. 1998. *Teaching with the brain in mind.* VA: Association for Supervision and Curriculum Development.

Johnson, D. and P. D. Pearson. 1984. Teaching reading vocabulary (2nd ed.). NY: Holt, Rinehart and Winston.

Kagan, S. 1989. The structural approach to cooperative learning. *Educational Leadership.* 40 (4): 12–13.

Kintsch, W. 1980. Learning from text, levels of comprehension or: Why anyone would read a story anyway? *Poetics.* 9:89–97.

Kletzien, S. and L. Baloche. 1994. The shifting muffled sound of the pick: facilitating student-to-student discussions. *Journal of Reading.* 37:540–545.

Laflamme, J. 1997. The effect of the multiple exposure vocabulary method and the target reading/writing strategies on test scores. *Journal of Adolescent and Adult Literacy.* 40:372–381.

Lorch, R. F. 1989. Text signaling devices and their effects on reading and memory processes. *Educational Psychology Review.* 1:209–234.

Marzano, R., D. Pickering, and J. Pollock. 2001. *Classroom Instruction that Works: Research-Based Strategies for Increasing Student Achievement.* VA: Association for Supervision and Curriculum Development.

Meichenbaum D. and A. Biemiller. 1998. Nurturing Independent Learners: Helping Students Take Charge of Their Own Learning. Mass: Brookline Books.

Morrow, L. and L. Gambrell. 2000. Literature-based reading instruction. In M. Kamil, P. Mosenthal, P. D. Pearson, R. Barr (Eds.). *Handbook of Reading Research,* Vol III: 563–586. NJ: Lawrence Erlbaum Associates.

Nagy, W. and J. Scott. 2000. Vocabulary pocesses. In M. Kamil, P. Mosenthal, P. D. Pearson, R. Barr (Eds.). *Handbook of Reading Research,* Vol III:269–284. NJ: Lawrence Erlbaum Associates.

Narvaez, D. 2002. Individual differences that influence reading comprehension. In C. Block and M. Pressley. *Comprehension Instruction: Research-based practices.* 158–175. NY: Guilford Press.

Nash, R. J. and D. A. Shipman. 1974. The English teacher as questioner. *English Journal,* 63: 42–45.

Nist, S. and M. Simpson. 2002. College studying. In M. Kamil, P. Mosenthal, P. D. Pearson, R. Barr (Eds.). *Handbook of Reading Research,* Vol III:645–666. NJ: Lawrence Erlbaum Associates.

Ogle. D. 1986. (K-W-L) A teaching method that develops action reading of expository text. *Reading Teacher.* 40: 564–70.

Ogle, D and C. Blachowicz. 2002. Beyond literature circles: helping students comprehend informational texts. In C. Block and M. Pressley. *Comprehension Instruction: Research-based practices.* 259–271. NY: Guilford Press.

Paris, S., B. Wasik, and J. Turner. 1991. The development of strategic readers. In M. Kamil, P. Mosenthal, P. D. Pearson, R. Barr (Eds.), *Handbook of Reading Research,* Vol II:609–640. NY: Longman.

Pearson, P. D. and L. Fielding. 1991. Comprehension instruction. In M. Kamil, P. Mosenthal, P. D. Pearson, R. Barr (Eds.). *Handbook of Reading Research,* Vol II:815–860. NY: Longman.

Pichert, J. W. and R. C. Anderson. 1977. Taking different perspectives on a story. *Journal of Educational Psychology,* 69 (4):309–315.

Pressley, M. 2000. What should comprehension instruction be the instruction of? In M. Kamil, P. Mosenthal, P. D. Pearson, R. Barr (Eds.). *Handbook of Reading Research,* Vol III: 545–561. NJ: Lawrence Erlbaum Associates.

Pressley, M. 2002. Comprehension strategy instruction: a turn-of-the-century status report. In C. Block and M. Pressley. *Comprehension Instruction: Research-based practices.* 11–27. NY: Guilford Press.

Principles and Standards for School Mathematics. 2000. VA: National Council of Teachers of Mathematics, Inc.

Raphael, T. and J. McKinney. 1983. Examinations of fifth- and eighth-grade children's question-answering behavior: an instructional study in metacognition. *Journal of Reading Behavior,* 15:67–86.

Raphael, T. and C. Wonnocott. 1985. Heightening fourth grade students' sensitivity to sources of information for answering comprehension questions. *Reading Research Quarterly.* 30:206–282.

Reif, L. 1992. *Seeking Diversity.* NH: Heinemann.

Richgels, D., L. McGee, and E. Slaton. Teaching expository text structure in children's comprehension of text: research into practice. In D. Muth (Ed.), *Children's Comprehension of Text: Research into Practice.* 167–184. DE: International Reading Association.

Romano, T. 1987. *Clearing the Way: Working with Teenage Writers.* NH: Heinemann.

——— 1995. *Writing with Passion: Life Stories, Multiple Genres.* NH: Heinemann.

Rosenbaum, C. 2001. A word map for middle school: a tool for effective vocabulary instruction. *Journal of Adolescent & Adult Literacy.* 45:44–49.

Rosenshine, B., C. Meister, and S. Chapman. 1996. Teaching students to generate questions: a review of the intervention studies. *Review of Educational Research,* 66 (2):181–221.

Rupley, W., J. Logan, and W. Nichols. 2002. Vocabulary instruction in a balanced reading program. In *Evidence-Based Reading Instruction: Putting the National Reading Panel Report into Practice.* DE: International Reading Association.

Santa, C. and D. Alvermann (Eds.) 1991. *Science learning: processes and applications.* DE: International Reading Association.

Santa, C., S. Dailey, and M. Nelson. 1985. Free-response and opinion-proof: a reading and writing strategy for middle grade and secondary teachers. *Journal of Reading.* 28: 346–352.

Schmidt, P., S. Gillen, T. Zolo, and R. Stone. 2002. Literacy learning and scientific inquiry: children respond. *The Reading Teacher.* 55 (6):534–548.

Schwartz, R. 1988. Learning to learn vocabulary in content area textbooks. *Journal of Reading,* 31:108–118.

Schwartz, R. and T. Raphael. l985. Concept of definition: a key to improving students' vocabulary. *The Reading Teacher.* 39:190–205.

Slater, W. and M. Graves. 1989. Research on expository text: implications for teachers. In D. Muth (Ed.), *Children's Comprehension of Text: Research into Practice.* 140–166. DE: International Reading Association.

Sousa, D. 2001. *How the Brain Learns* (2nd edition). CA: Corwin Press, Inc.

Spandel, V. and R. Stiggins. 1997. *Creating Writers.* NY: Longman/Addison Wesley.

Stahl, S., J. Brudge, M. Machuga, and S. Stecyk. 1992. The effects of semantic grouping on learning word meanings. *Reading Psychology,* 13:19–35.

Taylor, B. and R. Beach. 1984. The effects of text structure instruction on middle grade students comprehension and production of expository text. *Reading Research Quarterly.* 19:134–146.

Trabasso, T. and E. Bouchard. 2002. Teaching readers how to comprehend text strategically. In C. Block and M. Pressley, (Eds.). *Comprehension Instruction: Research-based practices.* 176–200. NY: Guilford Press.

Vallaume, S., T. Worden, S. Williams, L. Hopkins, and C. Rosenblatt. 1994. Five teachers in search of a discussion. *The Reading Teacher.* 47:480–487.

Wade S. and B. Adams. 1990. Effects of importance and interest on recall of biographical text. *Journal of Reading Behavior,* 22:231–353.

Wade, S., W. Buxton, and M. Kelly. 1999. Using think-alouds to examine reader-text interest. *Reading Research Quarterly,* 34 (2):194–213.

Wade, S. and E. Moje. 2000. The role of text in classroom learning. Classroom language and literacy learning. In M. Kamil, P. Mosenthal, P. D. Pearson, R. Barr (Eds.) *Handbook of Reading Research,* Vol. III:609–627. NJ: Lawrence Erlbaum Associates.

Wade, S., G. Schraw, W. Buxton, and M. Hayes. 1993. Seduction of the strategic reader: effects of interest on strategy and recall. *Reading Research Quarterly,* 28 (2):92–114.

Wiggins, G. and J. McTighe. 1998. *Understanding by Design.* VA: Association for Supervision and Curriculum Development.

Wilkinson, L. C. and E. Silliman. 2000. Classroom language and literacy learning. In M. Kamil, P. Mosenthal, P. D. Pearson, R. Barr (Eds.). *Handbook of Reading Research,* Vol III:337–360. NJ: Lawrence Erlbaum Associates.

Zinsser, W. 1988. *Writing to Learn.* NY: Harper & Row.

INDEX